CONFESSIONS
OF A
CELEBRITY PSYCHIC

**(How To Become Rich & Famous
As A Fraudulent Psychic Entertainer & Consultant)**

Jonathan Royle

COPYRIGHT NOTICE

British Library Cataloguing In Publication Data

A Record of this Publication is available
from the British Library

ISBN 1846850568
978-1-84685-056-1

Published January 2006 by

Prospect House Publishing
In Association With
Exposure Publishing, an imprint of Diggory Press,
Three Rivers, Minions, Liskeard, Cornwall, PL14 5LE, UK
WWW.DIGGORYPRESS.COM

*An Ebook Edition of this book is also available from all
good ebook retailers including www.amazon.com*

CONTENTS

DEDICATION

THIS BOOK ENTITLED:

CONFESSIONS OF A CELEBRITY PSYCHIC

And Subtitled:

**"How To Become Rich & Famous
As A Fraudulent Psychic Entertainer & Consultant"**

Written by

Dr. Jonathan Royle

IS DEDICATED TO:

MY DAD WHO TAUGHT ME THE ROPES IN SHOWBIZ,

AND

MY MUM WHO WROTE THIS POEM AND I LOVE DEARLY

ENTITLED

A BIRTHDAY WISH TO MY SON

A BIRTHDAY WISH TO MY SON

The 13th of August '75
Was the happiest day that I've had
When you came screaming into the world
The pain suddenly seemed not so bad.

The years flew by so quickly
And at 4 you started school.
That first day I was so upset
But you stayed oh, so cool.
Until it came to lunchtime
And then the tears came fast
You wanted to stay for your dinner!
Home for lunch? That day was the last.

Remember the Christmas production?
You were one of the Billy Goats Gruff.
And watching you up there I felt so proud
But for you it wasn't enough.

You wanted to go on performing
And went with your Dad as a Clown.
You stole the show from the TV chimps
When you appeared in New Brighton town

Then again to Gandey's Circus
With your Dad you once more set off.
But you played in a place where you shouldn't
And a Puma pulled your ear off.

But it didn't stop you performing
Off to hospital for treatment and pad,
An injection and sweet – then a quick change
And back in the ring with your Dad.

We moved to a house in Ainsworth
You didn't like it much there.
But at church you sang a solo
And at home showed your magical flair.

Then we moved back to Heywood
At one time we'd nearly a zoo
With rabbits (and babies) and pigeons
And then there was Smokey too.

No time and you were eleven
And off to Siddal Moor.
I was at work, so each morning
You saw me off at the door.

Then bad news we lost Granddad Nation.
I couldn't be here for you then.
He left us so many good memories
Don't you wish we could live them again?
You carried on with your magic,
Fire-eating and juggling too.
Then came the tarot and hypnotism
Is there anything you can't do?

Well your childhood has gone so quickly
We've seen all the illnesses through.
Measles and Mumps, German Measles
And a bad case of Chickenpox too.

Now today you're 18 and an adult
You've the rest of your life ahead
But I'll always remember your years as a child
When I'd watch you asleep in bed

And so, to the future you're looking.
I wish you Good Luck and Success,
Good Health, Good Friends and a long life,
I hope filled with happiness.

But I'll always be there if you need me.
You'll always have somewhere to come.
And there'll always be someone who loves you
While I'm on this earth – your Mum!!

WHAT THE EXPERTS SAY ABOUT ROYLE'S BIZARRE PSYCHIC COURSE

"Mr Royle's suggestions, advice and routines are solid, practical and seem to be grounded in experience! Someone who tried this approach would probably recoup their investment quite quickly and it's true to say that Jonathan Royle has used the techniques he reveals to garner an awful lot of Publicity"

MICHAEL CLOSE
MARKETPLACE SECTION, MAGIC MAGAZINE
JUNE 2002
www.magicmagazine.com

REVIEW OF: "THE BIZARRE PARANORMAL WORLD OF JONATHAN ROYLE" – SIMPLEX COLD READING:

If you are a Psychic Entertainer or Reader looking for something novel to add to your repertoire that will get you noticed then this is the book for you! If you'd rather not get great advice on how to gather lots of Free Media Publicity for your talents then bypass this book!

As far as readings is concerned you will learn about Belly Button Reading and Pet Paw Readings. His method of Belly Button Reading – nicely named as Navel Gazing – is a case study of how to take a standard New Age belief (such as Chakra Points) and turn them into a convincing, commercial and fun method of reading.

You may not take up Navel Gazing Yourself but you will certainly be inspired to come up with your own original reading methods. This is also the first time I've seen mention of Psychic Healing in a text for Mentalist's and his handling of it is something I find acceptable. You don't make any outrageous claims and what you do could well actually help people!

What's great in particular about this book is that it doesn't just give you some great "how tos" but also tells you **WHAT** to do with the methods. You'll find out how he has successfully used his methods of Belly Button Reading and Paw Reading for pets to regularly get on Radio, Television and to get lots of features in National Newspapers and Magazines.

As if learning how to read Belly Buttons and Dog's Paws isn't enough you also get a heap of stunts suitable for the Psychic Entertainer that are practically guaranteed to get you noticed! Whilst some of them may not be entirely original, Jonathan gives them an update and puts his own unique spin on them. Some of them are risky however and it has to be said you'd need to be pretty sure of your aims to want to carry them out.

Where else would you find valuable information on publicity gaining gems as "Hosepipe Readings" or creating designer babies by Astrology?

All in all, this is a valuable resource for anyone interested in gaining a reputation as a Psychic Wonder Worker – Royle's Cold Reading methods are amazingly simple and yet uncannily effective & Powerful!

FINDLAY HOSIE
PROFESSIONAL PSYCHIC ENTERTAINER
Member of The Mentalist's Asylum – Yahoo Newsgroup

"The methods that Jonathan explains are both practical and professional and indeed for the modern publicity and success seeking Psychic Entertainer they should prove invaluable! Royle made his name almost a household word in the UK and in his book he generously reveals his bizarre and unique methods, for the very first time! I feel that all Mentalists, Psychics and Hypnotists can learn much from his modern & pioneering approach!"

MR EDDIE BURKE
MENTALIST & HYPNOTIST
www.mreenterprises.co.uk

REVIEW OF: "THE BIZARRE PARANORMAL WORLD OF JONATHAN ROYLE" – SIMPLEX COLD READING

His knowledge emanates from the page, and enthuses the reader with new ideas, principles and concepts that would otherwise have not been apparent.
The originality of thought that he injects into each stage of the courses he has written, means that any purchaser simply has to attempt the techniques which are contained inside, to be assured of success.

He is a confident and calming tutor, you just know that whatever questions you may have will be answered within the body of his eminent texts, and that your education will be a full and thorough one.

Jonathan clearly scribes, with detail and effort, in such a manner as to inspire and to give you that 'Eureka' moment. That's the moment when, at last, you fully understand what has been eluding you and that has failed to be taught to you, in some so-called 'manuals' on the subject.

Everything is written in a language, which we all can understand, and in a manner which makes pleasant and stimulating reading. I would unreservedly recommend any Psychic and/or Hypnotic training product by Royle!

MIKE BARLOW
PORTRAYER PUBLISHERS
http://www.portrayer.co.uk

INTRODUCTION

WELCOME to what is probably the Strangest Ever Book written on the subject of becoming a Fraudulent Psychic Consultant and Entertainer.

Although much of the subject matter in this book is weird to say the least, I can assure you that everything is 100% commercial and practical as in most all cases I have tried these approaches out in the real world with much success as you will discover as you continue reading.

The Key Secret to many of the approaches in this book is "Cold Reading" and as such I would highly recommend that you also obtain a copy of Ian Rowlands excellent book "The Full Facts Book of Cold Reading" which is available from the Internet site of: *www.ianrowland.com* as armed with the knowledge in Ian's Book along with the Secrets revealed herein, you truly could become a Psychic Millionaire.

Also as one of the main themes of this book is to help you think "outside of the box" and create your own original and bizarre approaches which are easy to gain International TV, Radio, Newspaper and Magazine Publicity with, I would also recommend that you obtain a copy of "The Shiels Effect" – How to Become a Psychic Superstar by Tony "Doc" Shiels which is available from: *www.theshielseffect.com*

Regards "Psychic Techniques" other than the contents of this book which you are now reading there are just 15 items I would recommend which once studied will in my opinion give you all the knowledge you will ever need to become a Professional Psychic Consultant and/or Psychic Entertainer and these are:

ROYLES "MUST HAVE" LIST

1. I'd firstly recommend that you obtain the entire "Home Study Psychic Course as written by Joe Riding which is available from the site of: *www.joesmagic.co.uk* – It's the information in this course which had me reading Palms & Tarot Cards in just a few hours and enabled me to start earning Several Hundred Pounds a day as a Psychic Consultant at Top Psychic Events all over England from the age of 14 in 1989. You are taught everything you need to know about The Tarot, Numerology, Palm Reading and of course Cold Reading techniques, which work in the real world.

2. Next I'd recommend the Bible for all Psychic Entertainers which is 13 Steps to Mentalism by Tony Corinda which is available from all good Magic Retailers and contains enough Secrets, Routines & Material to last for a lifetime. Put an original spin and new angle on the contents and ideas in this book and you'll soon be performing a unique psychic show with no direct competition and that's how reputations are made by being Unique, Original and offering something which is truly different

3. Thirdly I'd advise you to get Psychophysiological Thought reading by Banachek which will teach you a technique called "Muscle Reading" and using this you will truly be able to convince people you are Psychic, its also a great technique to use when demonstrating your apparent powers of Dowsing and/or using a pendulum to find things by Psychic Mind Power!

4. Next you need to read "Psychological Subtleties" again by Banachek (Steve Shaw) as using the ideas in this book will enable you to "prove" you are truly psychic anytime, anyplace, anywhere.

5. Psychokinetic Time is the name of the next manual on my list and again its by Banachek. In my opinion this is by far the strongest impromptu Psychic Style Miracle that I have ever had the pleasure of performing and used correctly will help you establish a reputation as a genuine Psychic.

6. The next item on my "must have" list is a training video by Gerry & Banachek entitled "Psychokinetic Silverware" which will have you bending Metal like Uri Geller in next to no time.

7. In conjunction with item six I'd advise you to study another video entitled "Metal bending" by Patrick Kuffs as then your education in Uri Geller Style Metal Miracles will be complete.

8. Next get "Gellerism Revealed" by Ben Harris as then, in combination with studying the other titles mentioned here you will be able to duplicate every stunt that Uri Geller has ever done during his career.

9. The Shiels Effect by Tony "Doc" Shiels – mentioned earlier it is available from: *www.theshielseffect.com*

10. Again as mentioned earlier, The Full Facts Book of Cold Reading by Ian Rowland available from his personal site of: *www.ianrowland.com*

11. Flim Flam by James Randi which is subtitled: "Psychics, ESP, Unicorns & other Delusions" this is available from any bookstore such as *www.amazon.com* and I would say is truly essential reading for anyone who desires to pass themselves off as a genuine Psychic Superstar.

12. The same applies for another James Randi book entitled "The Faith Healers" which in my opinion is the best training book ever written on how to become Super Rich as a Fake Spiritualist or Psychic Healer.

13. Next I'd say you need to read "The Truth About Uri Geller" also by James Randi and also available from *www.amazon.com*

14. To add the awesome power of Hypnotism, Suggestion and NLP to your work as a Psychic you owe it to yourself to get a copy of **"Confessions Of A Hypnotist"** subtitled "Everything You Ever Wanted to Know About Hypnosis but Were Afraid to Ask" – this has 513 information packed pages and is by me Dr. Jonathan Royle. It currently retails for £19.99 ($35) on *www.amazon.com* – After reading this you'll also have another lucrative income available to you as a Stage Hypnotist and/or Hypnotherapist, whilst also learning many Secrets, Ploys & Techniques which will prove invaluable to any serious Psychic Consultant & Entertainer.

15. From a gaining Publicity for your Psychic Talents point of view you would be well advised to check out **"Secrets of Hypnotic Success"** by me Dr. Jonathan Royle which is an Eleven DVD training set with a CDROM of extra notes. I teach you Tried, Tested & proven to work Advertising, Marketing & Publicity Techniques which used correctly truly can help you to become "Rich & Famous" this set is only available direct from my site of *www.hypnotherapycourse.net*

A huge list of Magic Retailers who stock many of these items can easily be found on the sites of *www.magicweek.co.uk* and also *www.magictimes.com*

By the way at the time of releasing this book in this format (January 2006) you would be able to purchase all of the above items for a combined total cost of less than £550 UK Sterling which at todays exchange rate is approx $970 US Dollars.

Together with the price you will have paid for this book £19.99 Sterling which at time of writing is approx. $35 US Dollars, means that for **FAR LESS THAN £600** you have an entire New Career open to you as a Psychic Consultant & Entertainer with the lucrative sidelines of Hypnotherapy, NLP & Stage Hypnotism.

The Best part of all being, that if you follow my advice, study the books and DVDS I have recommended and put the Techniques you learn into action than you should recoup that entire amount of £600 from your very first Stage Hypnotism or Psychic Show or from your first day working as a Psychic Consultant.

Then you'll have a Career, Knowledge and Skills inside your head which requires no Special Equipment and can profitably be taken with you anywhere in the World where you can either speak their language or their can understand yours.

Indeed in many cases you could even work through an Interpreter if need be!

For now I wish you the Best of Luck in your Career and trust that you will find that buying this book was the best ever investment in your future success as a "Psychic"

Best Wishes
Dr. Jonathan Royle
January 2006 – England
www.hypnotherapycourse.net

CHAPTER ONE

WHY BELLY BUTTON READING?

The Key Reason that my approach of Psychic Belly Button Reading is so Successful is, I believe because it is very personal to the person you are doing the reading for, after all what could be more personal and intimate than studying an area of their own body?

Secondly the fact that Belly Buttons are strange and unusual sounding things and have a very interesting background as detailed within this chapter makes the idea of Psychic Belly Button Reading seem all that more believable.

In other words it seems so wacky and bizarre that it must be true as surely you wouldn't try and fool somebody with something as daft as this if it wasn't real would you?

That's the state of mind people will be in when you start doing Psychic Belly Button Readings for them.

Oh and of course the Human Navel can also be used as a focus of concentration as it is in Yoga and Meditation which is often referred to as ""Navel Gazing", however if you read my other book "Confessions Of A Hypnotist" available from same source as this book, then you will be able to put people into Hypnotic States by getting them to stare at their own navels!

That perhaps could become your own personal marketing gimmick as you become "The Belly Button Hypnotist" and make a fortune helping people to cure their habits, Fears, Phobias and emotional problems by Staring at their own Belly Buttons as you place them into a Trance.

Now for some History and background information on the Human Belly Button which has been collected from various Public Domain Internet Sites including, but not limited to the following sites all of which you are recommended to personally visit for even more useful information and inspiration:

http://www.harpercollins.com.au/drstephenjuan/news_navel.htm
http://www.serenapowers.com/unusual.html
http://www.abc.net.au/science/k2/lint/facts.htm

BELLY BUTTON NAMES

The belly button has many names, including the fairly technical term "navel". "Navel" comes from the Anglo-Saxon word "nafela".

The Romans called the belly button the "umbilicus".

The Greeks called it the "omphalos". So if you add the Greek word "tomê" (meaning "cutting"), you get "omphalotomy". This word means "cutting of the umbilical cord".

Omphalos also means "knob" or "hub". The Greeks erected a holy stone, or fetish stone, in the Temple of Apollo at Delphi (on the slopes of Mount Parnassus near the Gulf of Corinth). They called this rounded conical stone the Omphalos (or Navel), as they thought that it marked the exact centre of their universe.

The tallest mountain in Bali is Gunung Agung. One Balinese myth says that their deities had mountains as their thrones, and that the highest mountain of all was Gunung Agung. The Balinese call this mountain the "Navel of the World".

The original inhabitants of Easter Island called it "Rapa Nui" ("Great Rapa") or "Te Pito te Henua" ("Navel of the World").

NAVEL-GAZING

The phrase "contemplating one's own navel" has the ring of a long and honourable history behind it. The word "omphaloskepsis" (also called "omphaloscopy"), meaning "contemplating one's navel as an aid to meditation", sounds like it is thousands of years old.

"Skepsis" is a Greek word meaning "the act of looking, or inquiry". However, the Merriam-Webster web site "Word of the Day" column claims that omphaloskepsis was invented only in the 1920s.

This was not the first time people tried to find enlightenment in the navel. In the past, an "omphalopsychic" was one of a group of mystics who gazed at their own navel so as to induce a hypnotic reverie.

The Greek Christian monks of Mount Athos used a specific method of navel contemplation called Hesychasm, to maximise the divine enlightenment. This method would presumably have given them many different insights into divine glory.

But another navel divination method, "omphalomancy", gave only one specific item of information. It predicted how many children a woman would give birth to, by counting the number of knots (bumps in the fleshy plaiting) in her umbilical cord when she was born.

BELLY BUTTON SCAR

Your belly button is your very first scar. It's scar tissue left over from where the umbilical cord joined you to your mother's placenta when you were in her womb. Just like fingerprints, no two belly buttons are alike.

All the nourishment going to the baby and all the wastes coming out passed through the belly button, via the umbilical cord. Once you had been delivered, your umbilical cord was usually clamped or tied, and then cut. The stump withered and fell off after a few days, leaving behind the scar we call the belly button.

Your abdominal wall is made up of various layers, including skin, muscle and fat. They are all fused together at your belly button. You have subcutaneous (literally, "under the skin") fat that plumps up the skin all over your body. But the fat cannot lift the skin at the belly button, because the skin at that location is fused to your abdominal wall. That's why the belly button is concave.

The umbilical cord is made up of four different structures : there are two arteries (taking waste to the placenta), one vein (supplying oxygenated blood and food), the allantois (which degenerates and turns into the bladder) and the vitello-intestinal duct (which turns into the gut).

PLACENTA & UMBILICAL CORD

Until the baby is born, it relies almost entirely upon the placenta. The placenta is a strange, flattish organ that acts as a combination of liver, kidney, lungs and intestines.

The placenta supplies the baby-to-be with oxygen and all the nutrients needed for growth. At the same time, it is a barrier that separates the baby from the mother.

It grows on the inside of the uterus and lies entirely outside the baby's body. (When I was a medical student, I decided that the uterus was my favourite organ, because of its wonderful design features.)

The placenta is where the baby's blood dumps all its wastes and picks up nutrients. It looks a little like a small, flat cake ("placenta" is the Latin for "cake"). It's about 20 cm across, 3 cm thick in the centre and much thinner at the edges.

The placenta keeps the blood vessels of the mother quite separate from the blood vessels of the baby. However, the blood vessels of the mother and baby run so close to each other that chemicals drift straight through the blood vessel walls.

Nutrients travel from the mother's blood vessels to the baby's, and waste products go in the other direction.

Even though the placenta is only the size of a small cake, it has a total surface area of about 13 square metres to ensure efficient exchange of nutrients and waste products. At birth, it usually weighs roughly one-sixth of the weight of the baby - about 500 grams.

But the placenta is also a very hard-working organ. At full term, it makes about 7.5 grams of protein each day. No other organ in the human body makes that much protein.

The umbilical cord is the lifeline that runs from the baby's belly to the placenta. It's a twisted structure about 2 cm in diameter. It increases in length during the pregnancy.

On average, at birth, the umbilical cord is roughly as long as the baby, 50-60 cm, but it can vary between 12 and 152 cm. If it is too long, there is a risk that a loop of the umbilical cord could get caught around the baby's neck as it enters the outside world, strangling the baby in the process.

One umbilical cord was so long that it "looped once around the baby's body, then over the shoulder, under an armpit and twice around the neck, with a good length left over to its root in the placenta". If the cord is too short, there can be difficulty in delivering the baby.

Before you were born, the umbilical cord, with its two arteries and single vein, was your lifeline. The power supply to push the blood to and from the placenta was your tiny foetal heart.

The two umbilical arteries carried low-pressure, de-oxygenated blood, loaded with waste products, through your belly button from your body to your mother's placenta.

The single umbilical vein carried high-pressure, oxygenated blood, full of nutrients, back in through the belly button.

(This is one of the rare cases where arteries carry de-oxygenated blood. Another one occurs in the lungs. Here the pulmonary arteries carry de-oxygenated blood from the right ventricle of the heart to the lungs - and pulmonary veins carry the red oxygenated blood back into the heart's left atrium.)

The blood moves through the umbilical cord at around 6.5 kph. At full term, about 1 litre of blood flows through the umbilical cord every minute.

About one-fifth of babies come out with the umbilical cord around their neck. Modern foetal monitoring techniques can warn the obstetrician or midwife of this occurrence.

After the baby is delivered, it still has the umbilical cord connected to the placenta. The placenta cannot be left inside the uterus - like the baby, it also has to be delivered. If the umbilical cord is too short, as the baby is delivered, it might pull the whole placenta off the uterus before it is "ready" to let go, or tear it apart. The baby could then die from massive blood loss, as its blood drains out through the umbilical cord.

UMBILICAL CORD SURVIVES INTERNALLY AFTER BIRTH

The umbilical cord forms in the foetus's second month of life. It contains four main structures, all running through the belly button. They are the pair of umbilical arteries, the single umbilical vein, the allantois, and the vitello-intestinal duct.

Early on, most of the allantois disappears. Inside the baby's body it turns into the bladder.

The vitello-intestinal duct is a structure that ultimately turns into the gut. By the time the growing embryo is just six weeks old, the vitello-intestinal duct has disappeared from the umbilical cord - 98% of the time.

After the baby is delivered, the four structures of the umbilical cord shrink and close up entirely. They turn into internal tendons or cords.
The two obliterated umbilical arteries run downwards to become the lateral umbilical ligaments, which join with the arteries supplying the bladder.

The obliterated umbilical vein becomes the ligamentum teres, which runs upwards and attaches the liver to the belly button. The obliterated allantois is now a cord that runs down to the tip of the bladder.

Once you've been an air-breathing baby for a while, there should be no connection between your gut and your belly button. But the vitello-intestinal duct can occasionally remain open along its whole length, or just part of its length, up until birth. Very rarely, it remains open past the birth and into adult life.

There are three main outcomes, depending on which section remains open. Sometimes it can discharge mucus or faeces. Sometimes it can form a little cyst behind the belly button. And sometimes it can even form a band that knots around part of the gut, and causes a life-threatening obstruction of the intestine.

About 2% of the population have a Meckel's Diverticulum. It's a little tube located on the front border of your ileum (part of your small intestine). The Meckel's Diverticulum reaches towards the belly button, but doesn't quite make contact.

Bailey and Love's Short Practice of Surgery says that the "*umbilicus is a creek into which many . . . streams may open . . . an enlarged inflamed gall bladder . . . may discharge gallstones through the umbilicus. Again, an unremitting flow of pus from ... the umbilicus of a middle-aged woman led to the discovery of a length of gauze overlooked during hysterectomy five years previously*".

BELLY BUTTON SHAPES

In medicine and surgery, a "symptom" is something that the patient complains of, e.g., "I urinate a lot and I'm always thirsty." A "sign" is something that the doctor would notice, such as yellowish tissue near the eye.

Hamilton Bailey wrote a famous textbook devoted to signs, Demonstrations of Physical Signs in Clinical Surgery. He included many of the signs of the human body that he could describe and/or photograph.

He became strangely poetic when he wrote that "*every time an abdomen is examined, the eyes of the clinician, almost instinctively, rest momentarily upon the umbilicus. How innumerable are the variations of this structure!*"

ROYLE NOTICE

Dr. Gerhard Reibmann, a Berlin psychologist, sees the belly button differently from Hamilton Bailey. He believes that you can diagnose a person's life expectancy, general health and psychological state purely by looking at their belly button. He paid for the publication of his own book, which he called *Centred: Understanding Yourself Through Your Navel.*

All of my Internet Searches regarding this book have so far only found articles and comments about it from between 2001 & 2004, which is very interesting as I've been doing Belly Button Reading as a Navel Psychic for almost 15 Years (since 1990) and have been extensively featured in International Media doing so since 1996.

And perhaps most interesting is the fact that the information on Belly Button Reading inside this book was written by me and has been on sale as a CDROM since the year 2000.

Now I may be wrong but this seems to indicate that my creation and information on the subject has inspired other people, I say this because on various Internet Sites there is an extract from his book which seems to have been released (after my secrets went on sale) and the examples given are practically identical to those I give in the first chapter of this book – perhaps co-incidence – perhaps not?

And even if its not down to my book, much of this information was published from 1996 onwards in international media publications who did feature articles about me, so it would be logical that these article's could easily have been the source of Dr. Gerhard Reibmann practically identical to my approach information.

Either way it gives an apparently more believable background from which to gain Media Exposure as a Belly Button Psychic.

Read this Extract From: *Centred: Understanding Yourself Through Your Navel* and then read Chapter One of this my book and tell me if you notice any similarities..

In it, he reckons that there are six different types of navel. He claims that each one has a specific personality type and a specific life expectancy associated with it.

It's easy to be sceptical of something this "easy", although it may turn out to be as inaccurate as phrenology (diagnosing character type by feeling the lumps and bumps on a person's skull).

Gerhard Reibmann, a Berlin psychologist, claims that if you have a horizontal navel (spreading sideways across your tummy), you're likely to be highly emotional, live for only 68 years.

But if you have a vertical navel that runs up and down your belly, you'll magically be generous, self-confident and emotionally stable. Somehow, this means that your life expectancy will be around 75 years.

A person with an outie, or protruding belly button, is claimed to be optimistic and enthusiastic and will live for 72 years.

However, a person who has a concave, bowl-shaped navel will be gentle, loving, cautious, delicate, sensitive and rather prone to worrying. Presumably, this worry will take a toll on their health, so they'll have the shortest life expectancy of all - only 65 years.

A person with a navel that's off-centre is supposed to be fun-loving and to have wide emotional swings. They're expected to live for only 70 years.

The final (and luckiest) type of navel is the evenly shaped and circular navel. This person is modest and even tempered and has a quiet, retiring personality - and as a result will live for 81 years.

Now, as we all know, anything to do with the human body always turns out to be more complicated than you first thought. How long will you live if your navel fits more than one of the six categories?

Easy, according to Gerhard Reibmann - just add the number of years together and divide by the total number of categories to work out your personal life expectancy.

The average life expectancy in Australia is 83.2 years for women and 77.2 for men. I guess that a lot of Australian women must have navels that are rounder than round.

LITERATURE & BELLY BUTTON LINT

The blue colour of Belly Button Lint is specifically mentioned in The Troublesome Offspring of Cardinal Guzman, by Louis de Bernières.

A town is being held under siege by bloodthirsty and cruel religious crusaders. Elders from the town go and ask a mad Englishman, Don Emmanuel, for his advice on how to annoy the crusaders as a form of guerrilla warfare. In his reply, Don Emmanuel speaks of BBL as "dingleberries". Strangely, he admits that he does not perform his own BBL removal, but has Felicidad do it for him . . .

"*Don Emmanuel grinned, scratched his rufous beard and then his pubic region, and said, 'I will give you all the advice in the world if only you can tell me why it is that the dingleberries excavated from my navel by Felicidad are always composed of blue Lint, when I possess no clothes of that colour.'*"

Extract from The Troublesome Offspring of Cardinal Guzman by Louis de Bernières, published by Secker & Warburg. Used by permission of The Random House Group Limited.

CANCER & THE BELLY BUTTON

Very rarely, a secondary cancer can be found in the belly button. It's called a Sister Joseph's Nodule, or Sister Mary Joseph Nodule, in honour of Sister Joseph of the Mayo Clinic.

Sister Joseph had an observant clinical eye for patients and their lumps. She had honed it very finely indeed, over a period of very many years. In particular, on a few occasions, Sister Joseph had noticed that a certain type of lump in the belly button would later be associated with a cancer.

This cancer would usually be in its late stages. She told this to Dr William Mayo, who agreed with her. Her "sign" now has a permanent place in surgical history.

ADAM & THE BELLY BUTTON

In the Christian Bible and the Jewish Torah, Adam is the first man and Eve is the first woman.

The existence of Eve is explained in Genesis 2:7 and 21-22, which says: "7 *And the Lord God formed man of the dust of the ground . . . 21 And the Lord God caused a deep sleep to fall upon Adam, and he slept: and he took one of his ribs, and closed up the flesh instead thereof; 22 And the rib, which the Lord God had taken from man, made he a woman, and brought her unto the man.*"

Things get even more complicated with the creation of Adam. His belly button gave rise to many philosophical problems.

Some theologians have argued that because he was the first man he had no human parents. Therefore he did not come from a mother, did not have an umbilical cord and did not have a belly button.

And surely, they claimed, God would not give us the false impression that Adam (and Eve) came from a mother. But other theologians disagree. So what was a painter of 500 years ago to do?

Some painters took the easy way out, and covered the belly button area with a strategically placed fig leaf, tree or forearm. But braver painters such as Raphael and Michelangelo gave Adam a navel.

In fact when Michelangelo painted Adam on the roof of the Sistine Chapel in the Vatican he gave him a navel - where any worshippers, including the Pope, could easily see it.

One of today's radio preachers has condemned Michelangelo as "*immoral and unworthy of painting outhouses and certainly not worthy of painting ceilings*".

Half a millennium later, in 1944, Adam's navel was a problem to a subcommittee of the US House Military Committee (chaired by Congressman Durham of North Carolina).

His subcommittee refused authorisation of a 30-page booklet, *Races of Man*, that was to be handed out to American soldiers fighting in World War II. The original booklet had an illustration that showed Adam and Eve each with a navel.

The subcommittee ruled that showing Adam's and Eve's navels would be "*misleading to gullible American soldiers*". It makes you wonder how the soldiers dealt with the horrors of war.

BELLY TO BREAST

Plastic surgeons are now able to insert breast implants via the belly button. The advantage of this is that it leaves no obvious scar.

The surgeons cut in through the belly button, and insert an endoscope tube under the skin. They work their way over the ribcage until they get to each breast, and then make an opening between the breast and the ribcage. They then insert a rolled-up breast implant into each breast. Once it's in place they fill it with salt water.

INNIE vs OUTIES

Your normal belly button is concave, with an attractive upper hood. The base of the belly button usually joins onto the muscle wall of the abdomen. Around the belly button there is subcutaneous fat. In the "outie", there is a protuberant mass of subcutaneous scar tissue between the bottom of the belly button and the muscle wall of the abdomen. This scar turns the concave "innie" into a convex "outie".

DRIER LINT IS A CANARY

In the old days, coal miners would take a canary down the mine. Canaries were exquisitely sensitive to some of the dangerous gases. If the canary keeled over, they'd leave the mine.

The lint from your laundry dryer could be a modern-day canary, according to Peter G. Mahaffy from the King's University College in Edmonton, Alberta, and his colleagues.

Back in 1994, the Edmonton Board of Health became concerned about high lead levels in the child of a radiator mechanic. Many of today's car radiators are made of various synthetic plastics. But back then they were made of copper pipes, and fins were soldered onto the pipes using a lead solder. (As the air went over these fins, it took the heat away.) So a radiator mechanic's regular work involved contact with a lot of lead.

Dr Mahaffy realised that lead particles could make their way onto the radiator mechanic's overalls, and then via the family washing machine into the rest of the family's clothes - and into their bodies.

The group tested the clothes dryer lint from radiator-shop employees, and compared it with the lint of people who had no known exposure to lead. The radiator-shop workers had dryer lint with lead levels up to 80 times higher than non-radiator-shop workers.

This is a rather neat screening test for lead. In general, the lead test involves drawing blood, which many children don't enjoy. Screening for lead by examining dryer lint is far cheaper and less invasive.

UMBILICAL CORD & BARBERS POLE

The umbilical cord has bright red veins spiralling through its white Wharton's Jelly. We see it every day symbolised in the barber's pole.

HAIR TRACK DIRECTS JOEY'S

Marsupials give birth to their young outside their pouch. The joey (the baby kangaroo) has to find its way to the pouch, by following a "track" in the fur of the mother kangaroo. Inside the pouch lies the source of life, the nipple. Is nature giving us a clue about the origin of BBL? The joey follows the hairs; does BBL take the same path?

BELLY BUTTON CLEANERS

A few different people sent in Belly Button Dusters. I didn't know that these devices existed before our survey. They have one job only - to remove BBL from your belly button.

One person sent in a small article from the *South China Morning Post* (10 September 2000) which tells of a different style of belly button cleaner.

This Stick-on Belly Button Cleaner is a Japanese invention. It's an adhesive pad which you apply *"over and into the offending area, and then remove it after 10 minutes (making sure you dispose of the evidence discreetly)"*.

They're available from the Lung Shing Dispensary Company in Hong Kong at a cost of HK$48 for six adhesive strips. I reckon it'd be cheaper just to yank the lint out manually - or you could use a friend's or relative's electric toothbrush . . .

GREEN BELLY BUTTON LINT – (BBL)

Zev Ben-Avi was in the military for 27 years, and is currently an advocate for the Vietnam Veterans Motorcycle Club of Queensland. He wrote to me telling me that *"in all my time, I never saw 'blue' Belly Button Lint, only green - jungle green, as in issue-type singlets"*.

However, he is not convinced that the lint comes from the clothing alone. *"To ease the situation with the troops, I found that intellectual activities in the form of apparently inane questions often occupied hours of funny but pointless debate.*

Obtain three army issue, brand new, jungle green athletic singlets. Weigh them very carefully on a precise machine that will register small but accurate increments. Record these weights on paper and then log the wash, wear and store cycles as they are rotated daily.

Every morning and evening, collect and carefully store the Belly Button Lint that has accumulated.

After about 12 months, again weigh the accumulated Belly Button Lint (which is GREEN, not blue) and again weigh the three singlets. The singlets will not have depreciated in weight and the accumulated Belly Button Lint will approximate the weight of one singlet.

The question then remains as to where the 'green' Belly Button Lint comes from. The questions to be asked are:

1. *If the Belly Button Lint is not from the singlet, then where did it come from?*
2. *If the Belly Button Lint comes from the singlets, then why do the singlets not decrease in weight?*
3. *If the Belly Button Lint does not come from the singlets, then why is it green???"*

I agree with him that BBL still grips tightly onto a few mysteries.

ANIMALS & BELLY BUTTONS

All mammals have belly buttons. However, in some dogs and cats, they're a little hard to see because they've healed well and they are covered with hair.

BELLY BUTTON REFERRED PLEASURE & PAIN

Leanne rang in to my Science Talkback show. She wanted to know why up until a year earlier, whenever she touched her belly button she had felt a pleasurable sensation in her clitoris. Unfortunately, after she had a laparoscopy (which went in via her belly button) she stopped feeling pleasure in her clitoris. In fact, she wondered if she would ever get it back again - because it felt pretty dang good.

The email response was huge. Both Katie and Sharon had had experiences similar to Leanne's. Luckily, their laparoscopies left them with some (but reduced) pleasurable sensation.

KF said that she also got pleasurable clitoral sensations when she scratched the lower half of her belly button really deeply. However, KS said touching her belly button made her go to the toilet. J said that the sensation was more painful than pleasurable. L said that scratching her belly button gave her a sensation in her right forearm (but only after she had broken her right elbow).

Greg said that touching his belly button made him nauseous - but only after sex. Jason got a sharp pain in the end of his penis when he scratched his belly button. Rick experienced an unpleasant sensation in his penis while being tattooed around, and partly inside, his belly button.

In reading all the emails, it seemed that most women enjoyed the belly button stimulation, while most men did not.

This seems to be a case of referred sensation. Imagine that both the navel and the genitals send sensation signals to one certain part of the brain. If you stimulate the navel, that certain part of the brain gets the same sensations as if you had stimulated the genitals.

However, I have not yet been able to find any references to the nerves of sensation from the navel and genitals being linked in this way. We can only hope that we will become further enlightened in this area.

MORE NAVEL HISTORY

According to Chinese lore, the best belly button is a concave one, rather than a protruding one, and the deeper the belly button the more children you will have. In these days of reliable contraception, the prediction relates more to the ability to have many children, rather than the inevitability.

Dreaming of your own belly button is traditionally associated with starting up a new venture with possible long-term benefits, and dreaming of someone else's navel denotes a new love affair.

According to Indian Tantric lore, the belly button is also used to diagnose health problems. Following this system, the navel is where energy is received and processed coming in from the universe.

The belly button represents fertility and it is also a reminder of the connection between the generations, in other words it connects you to your past and future. It is also seen being the "centre" of human beings.

The second form of omphalomancy is based on the umbilical cord. A Jamaican old wife's tale holds that the number of knots in the umbilical cord of a newborn baby shows how many more brothers or sisters are yet to come. It is interesting that this one has been verified and it seems to be accurate.

Apparently "Omphalomancy" is the Scientific Sounding Mumbo Jumbo name for Belly Button Reading and Navel-Gazing.

SUMMING -UP

So as this chapter illustrates there is far more to the Human Belly Button than many people realise and its this "genuine" information which we can use as a basis and strong foundation for the fabricated information we will create and release in further Chapters.

That incidentally is one of the Key Secrets of any good Marketing or Media Scam, the Scam itself (in this case Belly Button Reading) must have its roots in something which is provable and genuine so that the scam itself is instantly credited as genuine & believable.

For example I once came up with the idea of Psychic Bottom Reading, and by way of my then "personal reporter & journalist" Alan Breeze, we together found a Yorkshire Based Lady who was prepared to play the part of the Psychic Bottom Reader.

The Serious Sounding background to this being that Psychic Bottom Reading is based on The Age Old Divination Art of Phrenology within which the reader examines and interprets the bumps on the clients head.

With Psychic Bottom Reading our female Psychic was doing the same only she was feeling, touching and examining peoples Bottoms and interpreting the bumps, dents and such like that she found on them.

Incidentally this was a quite successful scam and her "talents" were featured on various TV & Radio Shows and also in National & International Media Publications.

On this occasion a pretty female touching up men's bottoms was the Naughty but Nice Sensationalist angle that the Media love, had it been a man touching up women's bottoms then I don't feel it would have been as successful as then the media may have taken a more "Sexual Assault" attacking angle on the stunt.

So read on and within the pages of this book you will find the True Secrets of How to Become Rich & Famous as a Bizarre Modern Day Psychic Superstar!

Good Luck & Enjoy

Dr. Jonathan Royle – BSc
www.hypnotherapycourse.net

CHAPTER TWO

NAVEL-GAZING

(The Bizarre Paranormal Arts of Psychic Belly Button Reading/Healing & Mind Reading Revealed!)

My Unique & Bizarre Paranormal talents of Psychic Belly Button Reading, Healing and Mind Reading have enabled me to meet some of the worlds leading celebrities whilst earning a fortune into the bargain.

Becoming a regular face on National & International TV & Radio shows, whilst regularly being featured in Newspapers and Magazines making predictions for some of the worlds leading household names has just been an added bonus, and after reading this manual you too will be able to achieve all these things!

Navel-Gazing is the name I have given to my bizarre talent of examining a person's Belly Button to reveal their Past, Present and Future.

Navel-Healing is the name I gave to my demonstrations of how "Psychic Healing" can be achieved through the use of a Quartz Crystal placed into the subjects Belly Button.

And Navel-Mind Reading is the name for my experiments in Mind Control and Thought Reading which apparently are all achieved by studying the persons Belly Button which you tell them is one of the most powerful Psychic areas of their body!

NAVEL-GAZING

Navel-Gazing which is the technical name for Psychic Belly Button Reading is a way of examining a human beings Navel in order to reveal their Past, Present and Future!!

Navel-Gazing is based on beliefs and experiences, which are hundreds of years old, including those of The Native American Indians.

The Native American Indians have a Religion called Shamanism and amongst their many beliefs is the fact that we all have Seven main Psychic Energy Points in our body called "Chakras".

31

The Chakra most commonly used by Psychic Readers and most often talked about by the public is the Chakra located in the centre of our foreheads which is often referred to by many as "The Psychic Third Eye!"

However my studies showed me that there is a Chakra almost perfectly in line with the Human Navel, and this Chakra which is called "The Base Chakra" is the Chakra (Psychic Energy Point) used by me for Belly Button Reading.

Interestingly enough it is also the Base Chakra, which is almost in line with the Navel that is spoke about in The Karma Sutra and in many publications on Tantric Sex.

Apparently if both the male and female imagine the energy from their Base Chakras being transmitted from their Navels and joining together with the energy stream being sent out of their partners Navel, then the sexual experience will be out of this World as will any Orgasms achieved.

As my studies revealed, most all forms of Psychic Divination have the reader tap into some form of Psychic Energy Source in order to gain their inspiration and information for the readings and indeed much the same thing is done in Navel Gazing.

I decided that whilst you could tap into the other Chakras and Energy points within the Human Body I would use the Base Chakra located almost perfectly in line with the Navel as this is the point to which you can get closest by physically sticking your finger into the Volunteers Navel.

When in a relaxed state I discovered that the moment I placed my finger into a persons navel that it was rather like sticking a plug into its socket and energy would flow from the Chakra through the Navel and then up through my finger and into my body.

At this point images would appear rapidly on the Blank TV Screen which I had been imagining in my minds eye and it is these images and the meaning of them that I would then relate to the Volunteer with often stunning accuracy.

These Images would enable me to tell the Volunteer about Past, Present and Future Events in their life and then as a further convincer that this was a serious method of divination I would reveal their TRUE Personality to them and the audience.

In other words the person they really are inside and not the person they pretend to be and this makes for dramatic viewing.

I would reveal their True Personality thanks to the Unique and Individual Physical appearance and traits of each human beings Belly Button.

These Traits I have discovered through many years trial and error can be read rather like the lines and markings on the hand are read during Palmistry.

Indeed in much the same manner as the Human hand the Navel has dents, lines, bumps and other characteristics all of its own.

For example I have found that in general:

1. The more a Persons Navel sticks outwards, the more extroverted and confident they tend to be.

2. The more a Persons Navel sticks inwardly, the more introverted and shy they tend to be.

3. People with Navels that neither seem to stick outwards or inwards and instead seem to be level with their chest tend to have Split Personalities and are very unpredictable and often emotionally unbalanced indeed.

4. People with a Horizontal line/dent across their Navel tend to be very down to earth, they call a spade a spade and are very realistic and relaxed about life.

5. People with a Vertical line/dent across their Navel tend to be very headstrong (as line points to their head). They can be very stubborn indeed, they have one hell of a temper and when they lose it boy do people know about it. Once their minds are made up they won't listen to reason even if it means shooting themselves in the foot in the long-term.

6. People with lots of dots/dents in their Navel tend to be very stressed/worried individuals who then worry about the fact they are worrying. Also this could mean they are very analytical thinkers and spend far too much time analysing things before coming to a decision.

Many people have said to me in the past that these theories are all well and good and my results often amazing but then they say "Doesn't the Navel just end up the way it is because of the manner in which the Umbilical Cord was cut off at birth?"

Well say I to these doubting Thomas's, this may be correct but my belief is that everything that happens to us from the moment of our conception through to our birth and right back to the death of this physical body are all predestined and set out as a matter of Fate/Destiny.

Therefore Fate/Destiny orchestrated the action of your Umbilical Cord being removed in a certain manner in order that your Navel would fit you like a Fingerprint and like a good picture would speak a thousand words about you – and its these "words" which are observed in Psychic Belly Button Reading.

The creator's of Navel-Gazing were two British Psychic's called David Williams & Alex Alexander (both being past stage names of mine – yes both people are me Jonathan Royle!) and Navel Gazing although developed in the late Eighties, first made its appearance in the UK National Media during 1996.

Since then Navel-Gazing has been featured in British National Newspapers such as: The Sun, The Star, The Mirror, The Sport, Sunday People and The Stage & Television Today amongst numerous others.

Of Navel Gazing past UK Media comments have included:

THE SUNDAY PEOPLE said in August 1996 that "It Proved to be Uncannily Accurate".

THE DAILY STAR said in January 1997 that "Navel Gazing has been used to make many successful predictions for top Celebrities!"

Navel-Gazing has also been featured in many glossy magazines such as Chat, Looks, Eva, Uri Gellers Encounters and The National Enquirer amongst others.

And that's not to mention the countless times Navel Gazing has been featured to date on British, Irish & German National TV shows, along with Major Radio shows World-wide including Comedy World Radio of USA, Radio on the Cello of Spain, BBC Radio Ulster (Ireland) and most all National Radio stations within the British Isles.

On British TV shows such as C4's "Big Breakfast", BBC One's "False or True", ITV's "Taxi", UK Livings "Live at Three", Granada Breezes "Psychic Livetime", Sky's "Zest Health & Beauty Show", Anglia TV's "The Warehouse", Ulster TV's "The Kelly Show" and BBC's "Body Parts" show amongst over 90 (yes over 90) other Feature TV slots about Navel Gazing on British & European Stations between August 1996 and January 2001.

Notable achievements of Navel-Gazing include when its creator David Williams was featured in The Daily Star during January 1997 and it is documented in print that by examining The Spice Girls Belly Buttons he predicted that Geri Halliwell (Ginger Spice) would be the first to leave the group to follow her own solo career and further predicted that her solo career would not be totally successful until she became Britain's answer to Madonna.

Well she did become the first to leave the group and she didn't get a UK Number one until she appeared very scantily clad in one of her videos rather like Madonna did in her earlier career!

Secondly this Daily Star article of January 1997 Predicted that Victoria Adams (Posh Spice) would become married to a footballer and have a baby boy. Well once again these two things have become fact with her marrying David Beckham the Manchester United Footballer and having a baby boy which she has named Brooklyn.

Also an Essex Evening Standard article of late 1996 detailed how Psychic Navel Gazer David Williams had cancelled a press conference in Essex with Girl Band

"Intrigue" because having looked at photos of their Navels he had predicted the IRA's Bomb Threats to London which brought the City to a standstill on the day in question.

Celebrities who have in person (face to face with me on TV) received the Navel Reading Treatment include: The Spice Girls, Frank Bruno (British Boxer), Miss Ireland 1996, Cleo Rocus, Cynthia & Brittany (The Sweet Valley High USA Twins!), Sharon Davis (Olympic Swimmer), Rory Bremner (Top TV Impressionist), Craig Charles of Red Dwarf fame, Julia Carling, Lowry Turner, Sean Meo, Bella Emburg (Blunder-Woman), Zoe Ball, Keith Chegwin, Lily Savage and numerous others.

Whilst Celebrities for whom I have been commissioned to read the Navels of for features in major media publications include: Madonna, Tom Jones, Cher, Claudia Schiffer, Sean Connery, Jeremy Beadle, Prince Charles and numerous others.

For Television, Radio and Live Stage Performances the Navel is examined in person assuming the celebrity is there in person, and indeed for some Media articles you may get to meet the Celebrity in person for the purpose of doing the reading and more importantly from the publications point of view, to get photos of you peering into that persons Navel as it both makes a great story for them whilst also being great publicity for you!

For TV/Radio shows where the celebrities cannot be present and for many media articles it will be easier if you are given good clear close-up photographs of the persons Navel to do the reading from.

Now obviously these taken from Photos readings will not be quite as accurate as if the person were with you in person, but they are possible both by looking at the visual characteristics of the Navel through a magnifying glass and also because of another belief which is strongly held by Native American Indians and followers of the religion Shamanism.

This other belief states that each time your picture is painted or your photograph taken that part of your soul, life-force or Spiritual Energy (call it what you will) is taken from you also and enters the pictorial representation of yourself.

This means that a small tiny fraction of The Base Chakras Energy is within the photo and as such you can still tap into this for inspiration during the reading, which in this case is very akin to the Psychic art of Psychometry in which you hold peoples personal objects to reveal things about them – well how more personal can you get than a photograph of themselves?

It is very easy to get TV/Radio, Newspaper and Magazine coverage for your talents of Navel-Gazing, both because it sounds so unusual & bizarre and also because when looked at more closely by Journalists to whom you feed the story/facts which you have just read within these pages it then sounds most believable indeed!

NAVEL-GAZING GAGS!

Both on TV/Radio shows and Live on stage you will find these Belly Button and Navel-Gazing related jokes well worth using. OK so they may not be hilarious but then again you're a Psychic not a Comedian so a little humour is better than none isn't it?

- ❖ I've recently been given honouree membership to The Army because of my special talents. They've made me a member of The Navel Core.

- ❖ I learnt Navel-Gazing off my Great Grandfather who worked as a Belly Button Reader for the Army during World War One!
- ❖ He was the Head of NAVEL COMMAND!

- ❖ Yes this strange talent runs in the family, my Uncle wanted to do the same as my Great Grandfather had done for the Army during the War – but they wouldn't let him because he has two Belly Buttons instead of one!! They said he'd have to join THE NAVEL RESERVE instead!!

- ❖ Belly Buttons were originally called "done-it's". In fact they were called "done-its" for thousands of years ever since Jesus started to Christen people in the Bible! Oh yes its true, he'd dip them under the water, say his Holy blessing and then he'd tap them in the stomach like this (make visual movement of pointing your finger into someone's stomach around the area of the navel) and then he'd say "done-it!"

- ❖ It's quite easy to learn Navel-Gazing, for example two obvious things to look for when examining someone's Navel are Body Jewellery and fluff! The presence of Body Jewellery tends to indicate they are not soft people who'd start crying if they got a paper cut, whereas Fluff inside their Belly Button tends to indicate they don't have a bath very often!

- ❖ I taught Navel-Gazing to a Circus Contortionist called Sarah last year, a few months later she died – her family told me they weren't surprised about it though as SHE HAD SEEN HER OWN END!

CHAPTER THREE

NAVEL-GAZING COLD READING

Well, Fellow entertainer, as you've probably guessed already the main secret of Navel-Gazing is Cold-Reading!

However a few things are very much in your favour with Navel-Gazing which are not with other forms of Psychic Readings and these are as follows:

01) Navel-Gazing is used by me only Live on TV/Radio shows and on Stage or for use in Newspaper, Magazine or Internet articles about my talents. Therefore never do you need to talk more than five minutes maximum to any one individual and usually less than that is sufficient.

02) In other words you use Navel-Gazing to easily obtain FREE PUBLICITY for your more conventional Psychic talents and needless to say the clients these articles attract are then given only a brief Navel-Reading before going onto a more normal Tarot or Palmistry session.

03) In the case of all Navel-Readings done I always casually find out what that persons Star Sign is and then its quite easy with a basic knowledge of Astrology to waffle on convincingly and with often quite accurate results for a few minutes.

04) On most all occasions you are asked onto TV/Radio shows you will end up reading the Navels of Famous Celebrities and these are the easiest readings you'll ever have to do. Firstly you will either already have a lot of knowledge about that Celebrity or a few quick phonecalls to friends before going on air will reveal a lot of background information of much use. Most Celebrities have very similar lives and so once again a little observation of the news and gossip columns will stand you in good stead. And also best of all is the fact that I've found that on TV/Radio shows Celebrities very rarely disagree with anything you say thus making you sound correct as they know the name of the game is entertainment and they too have learned to play this game properly.

05) When reading a complete strangers Navel for TV/Radio shows you will often be sent to the "Green Room" (Hospitality) area together before going on air. In fact you can demand that this happens by saying that it takes a

good five minutes of silent meditation to tune into the subjects "Base Chakra" energy point, they will then ensure you have time to do this before going on air so as not to bore viewers. This of course is bullshit and the truth is you have now got at least five minutes to have a casual chat with the volunteers and find things out about them which of course are then fed back to them in different words than those used by them once on air. This combined with knowing their star sign should give more than enough patter to fill the airtime.

06) Make much of your patter about Predictions for the FUTURE, as these cannot be disproved at the time of the reading. Whereas you give very sketchy details of past events you can see via their navels – here for future predictions be very detailed, very precise and very enthusiastic about what you are saying – also use a little common sense. By this I mean that although future events cannot be proved or disproved until a later time, with a little common-sense you can get well over 50% of your future predictions correct as most people experience similar things in their life at one time or another.

07) Once again Celebrities are by far the easiest to do readings for whether they are with you in person for TV/Radio shows or indeed even if it is from photos for use in a Newspaper of Magazine article. Not only do most celebrities have very similar lifestyles but also some things can be predicted with almost 100% confidence for celebrities and to illustrate how common-sense is used I will give a few examples of how I have very successfully predicted things in the past – which needless to say once they have become reality I have then made all the Media aware of my predictions which were documented in print or over the airwaves some months earlier now having come true, whereas any errors are conveniently forgot!

❖ I predicted in "The Daily Star" of January 1997 that Geri Halliwell (Ginger Spice) would be the first to leave the Spice Girls. I did this because Observation and Common-sense told me that she seemed to be the one who always did the most talking at press conferences and I felt that amongst a group of then Five young girls this would not be tolerated for long by them and indeed when sparks did start flying I felt Geri would not hang around long – AND I WAS 100% CORRECT.

❖ I predicted in this same Daily Star article of January 1997 that when Geri left she would be the first to pursue her own solo career and that success would elude her until she became Britain's answer to Madonna. I said this because working on the premise she'd be first to leave The Spice Girls, I figured she would still want to go on performing hence the solo career prediction. I knew the press would give her a hard time and that Spice Girls fans would not be happy she had left – this combined with fact it was public knowledge Geri had once been a glamour model led me to make the success will elude her until she becomes Britain's answer to Madonna prediction! Here again I was 100% correct because it was not until the MI Chico Latino video in which she was scantily clad that she got a Solo UK Number One.

❖ I predicted in that same Daily Star article of January 1997 that Victoria Adams (Posh Spice) would end up involved with a footballer and that she'd have a baby boy. Well I worked on the premise that Celeb's tend to date other Celeb's and that being a very young women at the time she would like other young women I know fancy a Sportsman or two! Logic went further and told me she'd have more chance being a Celeb of meeting the person she fancied and hence the prediction was made. Babies wise I figured she like other young women would get pregnant quite early on and as for saying a boy that was a 50-50% chance. However luck was on my side AND ALL THESE THINGS BECAME 100% TRUE!

❖ I once predicted that Comedian Lee Evans would become a famous Comedy Actor which indeed he has in films such as "Mouse – Hunt" and "There's Something About Mary!" I made this prediction because quite simply throughout the history of TV and Cinema some of the best Comedians have turned their hand to acting with great success and as this seems to be a tradition in showbiz I figured the law of averages was on my side which indeed they were and it became 100% CORRECT!

❖ To clear up the IRA Bombing of London prediction allow me to say this was a sheer fluke – but like any coincidence which can be used to your advantage you should milk it whilst you can like I did to get maximum TV/Radio and Media Coverage – as the more you become a household name, the more your services will become in demand and ultimately the more you will be able to get for your services. The truth is the girl group "Intrigue" had rung me the afternoon before the press conference and said they wouldn't be able to make it because of other commitments. I sat down and decided that rather than losing face with The Essex Evening Standard I'd wait until their offices had shut that evening and then leave a strange message on their answerphone explaining that I would not be there tomorrow as planned. This I did saying something along the lines of my absence would be because I predicted that travel through London would be almost impossible tomorrow. Then coincidence of coincidences I turned the news on the next morning and London had come to a stand still due to IRA Bombing threats and needless to say the moment the Essex Newspapers team got to work and heard the message from me which their answerphone had timed and dated as being left the previous evening they took my words as a prediction of this Bomb and so a huge article validating my predictions was run in the paper. This taught me to always be very ambiguous when leaving answer messages for the media – as if they have many possible meanings as indeed mine did they can be manipulated to help your cause in many situations!

Hopefully these few explanations of past successful predictions made by myself in the British Media will have helped make it clearer to you what I mean about how easy it is to make good accurate predictions for celebrity clients.

Don't forget also that before appearing on TV/Radio shows or Live Shows with guest Celebrities or indeed before meeting these people for other Media interviews you would have been told who your subjects were going to be.

It is then a simple job to get onto the internet and visit some of that Celebrities fan club sites which quite often contain lots of little known information about the person, their past, their present and their future plans!

On many occasions I've acquired information on Celebrities which I am to meet the following day from Internet gossip sites and fan sites and then have fed this information to them by way of my Belly Button reading predictions.

More often than not the detailed nature of what I have then been revealing has stunned the celebrities in question and on one memorable occasion I told a famous female American pop star what the name of her next album would be (I'd seen lots of rumours on fan/gossip sites) and she was so amazed that she admitted that although it was not public knowledge (she must not have seen the websites) that she would admit this was correct. So don't underestimate the power of the Internet for obtaining information on clients for use in your Psychic Readings!

08) Magazines & Newspapers will occasionally require you to do readings from good clear photographs of the celebrities Navels. And here's your chance to really look good in the media as I did with National Newspapers such as "The Sunday People." Find out what fee they are prepared to pay you for doing the readings and whatever the amount say your fee is usually much dearer! However as you like their newspaper or magazine you will do it for this price if they meet you half way. You then basically get them to send you the photos of the Celeb's for each of which you write a short few lines prediction and then these are returned to them on condition that when the article appears they print you predictions within an article that says "We the Sunday People sent Navel Psychic Jonathan Royle some decapitated photographs of Celebrities!" Then it should clearly state "Despite not knowing who the celebrities were as we'd cut their heads off the photo's he

made these stunningly accurate revelations and predictions!" Yes this may sound cheeky but sooner than lose an excellent feature story you can often get reporters to bend over backwards to help you and needless to say a story which appears like this leads to even more TV/Radio work and lucrative clients.

09) For those who decide to become Navel Gazer's it would be wise to keep a scrapbook of any Celebrity photographs you see appear in Newspapers or Magazines where the persons Navel is actually visible. The logic here being you can then really do a test conditions reading instead of faking it as detailed in point 8 above. You see Newspapers and Magazines when asking me to do articles for them have I've noticed always asked me to read the Navels of Celebrities whom are currently "Hot News!" Also as Celebrities very rarely appear in photographs where their Navels are visible, if you keep copies of those which appear showing Navels and build up your scrapbook – success will be yours! You can then get the publications to Genuinely send you decapitated photo's – but as there will only be so many Photo's for them to choose from and they all tend to use the same Photo Libraries the odds are that by comparing the headless photos with those in your scrapbooks that a match will be found as you recognise the clothing matches! Then having discovered whom the Celebrity is an accurate reading is easy to do and both readers and publication alike will be amazed as you have done it under apparently impossible test conditions!

10) Remember to say very little – but appear to say a lot. This is easy to do by using lots of long and detailed words, phrases and descriptions to describe something, which is actually very simple, and either applies to everybody or to most people at some time in their lifes.

> ❖ For example I use phrases like "You've lost a little bit of your sparkle recently haven't you love?" If she says Yes I would continue "Yes I know you have, you've been feeling down haven't you?" – well here she's bound to say Yes as your only saying the same thing in a different way again!

> ❖ Then Continue "Yes you've been worrying a lot – then worrying about worrying it's become a viscous circle but its about to end and life will be like a bed of roses again in the very near future – you will keep positive won't you love?" – again she'll say Yes so you sound to be getting things 100% Correct!

> ❖ But look at what I said again and you'll see one of my favourite Cold reading techniques in action which is to say something which is detailed but then end it with a positive closed question which can only really be answered YES by the subject as to answer YES is in their own interest!

❖ Answering yes to this closed question has nothing to do with whether the predictions and information contained within the rest of that sentence were correct or not – however the audience watching or listening will perceive the subjects answers of YES as validation that your statements and predictions are correct!

❖ Obviously if she answered No to the very first question you'd shoot off in the opposite direction and say something like "Well I know you don't feel like you've lost any of your sparkle but others have noticed your working too hard – you will take a little more time for yourself from now on won't you love?"

❖ Here once again the closed question technique is used and once again it's in her interest to answer Yes – don't underestimate this cold reading technique its very useful indeed.

11) Furthermore, the more often you can get your subjects to say YES to you – the far less likely they are to either say you are wrong or indeed to even let the thought that you may be or are wrong enter their head – it is in effect mild brainwashing.

I always start readings by making it quite clear that "Whenever I ask you a question I want you to answer Loud and clear!" (Pause) "Just say YES nice and loud! – OK?"

This is perceived by them and the audience as telling them to answer clearly to questions – but at a subconscious level in their mind prompts them to answer YES to everything.

This may sound like fairytale stuff – but I've been using techniques like this for the past 15+ Years since I started doing Stage Clairvoyance shows like Doris Stokes and other famous mediums in 1990 aged 15 years old and these methods have always worked for me!

12) Next we'll discuss the use of Closed questions just a little bit more before explaining how I use the power of Open Ended Statements and Questions for Cold Reading Success.

Closed Questions are those which can easily be answered by just saying Yes or No, and as in the aforementioned examples these can be phrased so that it is in the interest of the subject to answer Yes.

To repeat what I've already said only moments ago, for which I make no apologies as this is one of the strongest ploys you can have as a Professional cold reader – closed questions can be used to make your readings seem super accurate.

This technique is especially useful to Psychics doing Live demonstrations on TV & Radio shows and also to Stage Clairvoyants who perform before a large audience.

To re-iterate what I've said already, deliver a long list of detailed sounding (yet quite general) predictions and apparently factual pieces of information to the subject and then end your rather long winded sentence with a closed question to which it is in their interest to answer Yes.

Then as everyone hears them reply YES, they perceive this as being the subject validating all the things you have said as correct when in truth they are merely answering the question which you ended your statement with.

Another example of a closed question being used in this way is as follows "With my finger in your navel I'm being shown a picture of a Valley made up of lots of hills and this is symbolic of your life to date!"

"The hills are in various sizes and I believe this is showing me the ups and downs you've had throughout your life – You're a survivor aren't you?" (It's in their interests to say Yes as its good for their ego/pride to do so)

"Now I'm being shown a picture of a brick wall and I feel this is symbolic of the wall you put around you in new encounters with people – You've been hurt in the past when you've least expected it haven't you?" (This will be answered Yes as we all have been at one time or another – yet it sounds to all listening like this is a truly detailed revelation you're making!)

"Now I'm being shown you caught between the devil and the deep blue sea so to speak – I'm being shown an image of you stuck between two people"

"Now both these people are friends, they may be in a relationship together, but what is clear to me is that you have become piggy in the middle to them because you don't want to upset anyone. Would I be right in saying you don't like upsetting people especially your friends?" (who is going to say anything else other than Yes you are right?)

"Yes I can see it clearly, there are two people around you, it may be family but I'm more inclined to say its on a friendship level. And both of these two people have been asking for your advice – yes that's it you don't want to take sides with either of them as you value the friendship of them both. You do value your close friendships don't you?" (Again Yes will be the answer)

"I can see good things for you in the future, I'm being shown prosperous times ahead for you. In fact I'd go so far too say that your going to come into some money soon. Those things you have been dreaming of aren't so far away now you'll be getting them sooner than you think – You've had your mind set on something very special to you for several years haven't you? (we all have dreams/ambitions so the answer will be Yes)

I could go on for pages and pages, in fact for days and days with examples of how closed questions can be used at the end of statements of apparent fact and can be phrased so as to guarantee a positive Yes response but I would hope that the examples I have given will set you on the right track and get you devising ones of your own.

13) Next let's turn our attention to the use of Open ended statements and questions and how these can be used by the Psychic to obtain far more information from the client about their life and problems than even they realise they are giving you!

Then later on in the reading this information which they have freely given you without even realising how much they have said can be fed back to them in a different context and/or phrased differently and will be accepted by them as amazing insights from you into their life/problems!

Quite simply an Open ended Statement is a statement, which could mean almost anything and cannot really ever be pinned down as meaning just one thing – hence its meaning is OPEN!

And Open ended questions are quite simply questions which are phrased in such a manner that they cannot be answered by just a Yes or No response and will instead provoke the subject to give you a detailed answer and therefore far more information than you actually really asked for or they realise giving you.

An example of an open ended statement would be: "I feel that at times you get very stressed and yet in other situations you are a very calm, relaxed and peaceful person."

This is neither right nor wrong for anybody! It will always be seen as being right as both possible scenarios and options are contained within the same statement of apparent fact!

Therefore the fact the statement cannot be seen as either right or wrong makes it OPEN and so it will fit everyone in some way at some time and so people will always respond as though it is CORRECT!

In other words Open statements are ones where you tell the subject they are one thing and then tell them they are at times the direct opposite as well!

Or you tell them they feel an emotion in certain situations and then tell them the direct opposite of this situation/emotion within the same statement.

I hope you get the hang of it as Open statements are a very easy way of devising Cold Reading patter which will fit every person on this planet or as it is known in the Cold reading trade "Boiler-Plate".

Open ended questions are those which cannot be answered with just a Yes or a No such as these few examples which follow:

"Why do I keep being shown images of a property matter in my minds eye?"

(They cannot possibly answer with just a simple Yes or No to a question such as this and instead will have to give a more detailed answer. If they are involved with some kind of property matter then they will tell you exactly what it is and later on in the reading you can feed this information back to them in a different context – perhaps with reassuring words that all things regarding this matter will prove successful! However if they state that they have no knowledge of a property matter you would very easily steer off on another course as follows)

"To be honest it doesn't surprise me that as yet you are not aware of this property matter (this implies there will be one soon) however I can see this image so clearly that I can very confidently predict that within the next six months period property matters will become an important focus in your life. I'm being told to warn you to consider all the options when this occurs and not rush in like a bull in a China shop! You will be careful when this happens won't you?"

Well that's one example of how to phrase an open ended question which as with all open ended questions will make one of two things happen, either:

❖ They will have something going on in their life which relates to the subject matter to which you are asking the question (asking for more information) and this they will then freely explain to you in great detail as they feel you are already aware of it – or why else would you have asked the question? Then later in this same reading this information is fed back to them in different words.

❖ Or they will have no knowledge of such matters raised – but will instead usually make you aware of other matters in their life of concern to them as part of their answer and this itself gives you information which you can return to later in the reading. You then turn this into a prediction for the future and as such either way it will only ever seem like an accurate statement/prediction on your part!

14) Also don't forget the physical traits of the Human Navel which are detailed earlier in this manual, as I genuinely have found for some uncanny reason

that these things do seem to have applied to 99.9% of all the people I've done Navel Readings for to date. And on the very rare occasion that you get something wrong it is easily covered up by saying that in this persons case that physical element must be there to serve as a reminder of areas of their ego/personality/attitude that they would benefit from working on in the future.

15) The way that people react to being asked to show their Belly Button to everyone and also the way in which they react when you stick your finger into their navel speaks volumes about their personality. After all don't forget how close to intimate sexual areas of the body our Navels are, and the fact that for many people they are Erogenous Zones (sexual turn on points)! Is it any surprise then that some people are very shy about showing their Navels in much the same way, as they may be sexually very straight-laced? And in much the same way those eager to show their navels are often outrageous flirts with broad-minded interests and opinions on all things sexual. Common Sense will work wonders here, just bear in mind what I've said and you'll see exactly what I mean when you put it into practice.

16) Another ploy to make the reading more accurate is to half way through your predictions and comments ask the subject if they have any specific questions they would like you to try and answer? Just say to them "Well I'm seeing so much in your Navel and we have so little time together today so to speed things up for you, are there any specific questions or areas of your life you'd like me to look into?" This makes it sound innocent enough, you don't seem like your probing for help and needless to say their answers give you all the information you need to carry on the reading in a very specific and accurate manner.

17) Two last points on Navel Cold Reading and these are that

   ❖ Whether you are a believer in genuine intuition and Psychic powers or not – please do trust your intuition. The method of seeing a blank TV screen in your mind and allowing images to pop onto it as mentioned earlier in this manual is not only a good piece of explanatory patter – BUT IT ALSO WORKS! OK so you might think I'm bonkers, but if I had a pound for every time I've been on TV and suddenly said the first thing that came into my head of a very detailed and specific nature with 100% CORRECT & SUCCESSFUL RESULTS – then I'd be rich!!!

   ❖ Secondly don't forget that other options are also open to you in order to make a really good impression on very important TV shows such as the use of a Mentalists Impression Clipboard before the show goes on air! You could get the people who are to have their Navels read to write down on a slip of paper three things: 1) The most important memory they have from their past. 2) The most important thing going on in their life at present. 3) Their biggest dream/ambition for the future.

They are told this is being done, as it will help make things clearer in THEIR MINDS and EASIER FOR THEM when you get on air! In other-words it is portrayed that you've had them do this FOR THEIR BENEFIT!

You then tell them to fold up the slips which you make clear you have not seen (you can see what the clipboard says later!) and to hide them in one of their pockets as you WILL NOT be using these on air – no they have just been written out by the subjects to get things CLEAR IN THEIR MINDS.

The subjects will not think anything strange of this especially as you will make the main part of their readings up from Cold Reading methods, but along the way for each subject you can reveal thanks to the clipboard one very definite and very detailed item about their Past, Present & Future.

You end up looking amazing, the viewers or live show audience are never any the wiser about the use of the clipboard before the show, and best of all Belly Button Reading and your talents in the use of it look super accurate and so even more FREE TV/Radio, Newspaper & Magazine publicity can easily be obtained.

With reference to the use of a Mentalists clipboard to obtain information for your reading please refer to the psychology behind how I use one for Pawology in a later chapter of this manual!

The Questionnaire which you get them to fill in on the Mentalists clipboard could also contain the disclaimer for "Navel-Healing" which will be mentioned shortly whilst also asking for their contact details for use in further media features.

CHAPTER FOUR

NAVEL-HEALING

Next we shall turn our attention to Navel Healing or as it is also called Belly Button Psychic Healing.

Again this is based on The Native American Indians beliefs and religion of Shamanism, along with the seven energy points in our body called Chakras.

Once again the Base Chakra which is in line with the Human Navel is used, except this time it is used for the purposes of powerful Spiritual Healing.

To help heal someone's complaints once they have first been to see a conventional Doctor (as we neither diagnose nor prescribe) we use a small pointed Quartz Crystal, which is placed into their Belly Button in order to promote natural healing!

One end of the Quartz Crystal is placed into their Navel and the other end held by the fingertips of your left hand and then your positive psychic healing energy is directed through your body, into the crystal and then into the Base Chakra energy point in order to promote rapid healing.

The reason this works so successfully is akin to the beliefs of many other complementary medicines such as Acupuncture, within which the Chinese practitioners believe that all illnesses, diseases and mind/body defects are caused by energy imbalances within the person's body.

Therefore logic states that if we feed positive healing energy into the patients most powerful psychic energy point (The Base Chakra) that this will help correct those imbalances and as such lead to successful recovery in rapid time!

The use of the pointed Quartz crystal as a way to get some of your positive healing energy into the patient is for two reasons.

Firstly the Quartz Crystal itself is used extensively in other forms of New Age Medicine such as Crystal Healing and indeed it is openly known by the majority of the public how powerful Quartz Crystal's actually are and the power they do in reality contain. This is a genuine tangible power which they contain and is the reason why small pieces of Quartz Crystal are placed into the mechanics of most all watches, as it is proven that the 100% NATURAL ENERGY within them helps the watch run better.

Also in much the same way THE NATURAL ENERGY of the Quartz Crystal helps the Human Body to run better, hence many people wear jewellery containing Quartz Crystal as a preventative health measure.

Here in Navel-Reading the Quartz crystal is used to help accelerate THE NATURAL HEALING process!

The reason why one end is stuck into the patients Navel whilst you hold the other end with the fingertips of your left hand is twofold.

Firstly The Crystal helps to amplify the power and intensity of the healing energy which is sent from our body into the patients and Secondly by holding the Crystal with the left hand things are amplified even more as it is the left side of the brain which deals with all things Spiritual and Psychic.

Once the Crystal is in position in the patients Navel you have them close their eyes and imagine a feeling of warmth starting to enter their body which is symbolised by the colour orange in their minds eye.

You explain that just so long as they concentrate on this feeling of warmth and keep seeing the colour Orange brightly in their minds eye that healing will prove successful for them.

(This also puts the blame onto them if successful results do not occur as planned – you just blame it on their lack of concentration)

The Logic of getting them to focus on a warm feeling is quite simply that people do naturally feel better within themselves when they are warm.

And the reason you get them to see the colour Orange brightly in their minds eye is both because seeing it brightly is as proven in NLP a positive thing and positive thoughts lead to positive results, but also is because the colour Orange is a powerful combination of the colours Red & Yellow mixed together and as such is the most powerful colour of the spectrum.

Then you the Healer concentrate on a blue beam of light energy flowing from all the seven energy points (Chakras) in your body, down through your left arm/hand and into the Crystal before finally entering the patients body via their Base Chakra energy point.

You concentrate on Blue energy/light as this is the curative healing energy – Just think of The Blue Cross emergency service for animals and you'll remember this easily.

Results will often be instantaneous, although they are always told this IS NOT an alternative to conventional medicine and rather is COMPLEMENTARY medicine, which just helps to dramatically speed up the healing process.

(This statement covers you both legally and morally and ensures that they seek conventional medical treatment and/or continue with any prescribed medication until a conventional Doctor says otherwise)

However results will often be dramatic and instant or within a very short space of time (which can still be used for follow up media coverage by keeping a mailing list of all participants in your show that receive Navel Healing).

The reason success so often occurs so rapidly is because of the proven fact that 90% of all reported illness is psychosomatic (all in their mind with no physical cause) and it is probable that 100% of unreported illness is also psychosomatic.

In these cases of Psycho-Somatic illness, as the illness is being caused by the patients mind – so the cure lies in their mind also, hence it is true to say that if they believe this will work for them THEN IT WILL.

Those that believe will naturally set their mind to a different way of thinking and so the end result can be one of an often apparently miraculous Cure.

Combine this with the PLACEBO EFFECT, which again all comes down to the patient BELIEVING that the treatment will work and you can now see why Psychic Belly Button Healing can be so successful.

This success combined with the perceptively bizarre method of treatment is what will attract all the TV/Radio, Newspaper and Magazine interest as it has done extensively for me in the past.

To understand both how Navel-Gazing & Navel-Healing can be and are so successful may I strongly urge you to buy or rent the excellent film "Leap of Faith" starring Steve Martin as this film is almost a course in itself of how Psychic Readings and Healing are achieved with successful results and as Steve Martins Character says in the film:

"To answer your question of if I'm genuine or fake I say this, what's it matter how I do things – Just so long as the job gets done!"

This is a sentiment I agree with entirely and just so long as you get a signed declaration from any patients you treat with Navel Healing which states:

> ❖ They agree (if they haven't already) to get a conventional Medical Doctors diagnosis and prescription as soon as possible.

51

❖ They agree to continue seeing their conventional Medical Doctor and/or continue taking any medication which they may have been prescribed.

❖ They agree to allow you to touch their Belly Button for the purposes of Healing. (This covers you from any potential assault charges!)

You are then covered both legally and morally as you will never be placing a patient into any danger and instead have their best interests at heart always.

This signed disclaimer also asks for their contact details and acts as your mailing list for people to contact for inclusion in future media features on Navel-Healing.

Their recovery will most times prove to be considerably faster after Navel Healing than if they had just had conventional treatment alone and again this is because of their BELIEF that it will help them which in itself can REVERSE many problems which were Psycho-Somatic (Psychologically induced).

One of the Key phrases I use is "Those of you with health problems who volunteer tonight will only receive truly successful healing IF YOU WANT IT TO WORK (in other-words if you believe) and if you use your powers of Intelligence, imagination and Concentration effectively!"

This Psychologically ensures that only those who BELIEVE that rapid healing will result will volunteer and indeed as such these in my experience usually tend to be the ones for whom it will work.

This Phrase also covers you for failure as if instant healing does not occur, which often cannot be proved one way or the other until the patient revisits their doctor, then the way it is phrased puts the blame for failure onto the patient.

You see the audience will just see it as failure on the patient's part for not using their powers of intelligence, imagination and concentration effectively as they were told to do!

It is in effect A FORM OF HYPNOSIS, except with Navel healing the patient HYPNOTISES THEMSELVES due to their own belief system telling them that this form of treatment will work for them!

IF THEY BELIEVE IT WILL BE SO – THEN SO IT WILL BE

Well that basically is all there is to Navel-Healing as the rest is just down to presentation on your part. Present Navel-Healing with NO DOUBTS in your mind that it will work and then this positive attitude will be sensed by your volunteers.

When your volunteers sense this confident attitude within you that Navel-Healing will be beneficial to them then they will start to be even more positive about it working and so the magic of Positive Thinking comes into play.

And need I remind you of the countless books published and medical studies done on Positive thinking which have proved beyond doubt that positive thinking can often lead to CURES in and of itself.

So with the combination of Positive Thinking, Self-Belief of the patient, The placebo Effect, Self-Hypnosis and Psychic Mumbo Jumbo all combined into one treatment method, Navel-Healing is very powerful indeed.

Usually Navel-Healing would be done with the person there in person next to you, however for TV/Radio phone ins and media articles (or mail order sales) this can be got around by using a good clear photograph of the persons Navel.

The theory as to why this will still work regards the photo is the same as with Navel-Reading, however here you also speak to them in person over the phone and step by step explain what you are doing at your end.

It is also explained to the patient what they must do at their end as you concentrate the healing energy through the crystal into the photo of their Navel and due to some of the energy of their Base Chakra being caught in the Photo, then into their body for the same healing results.

This is known as "distance healing" and just so long as the patient believes it will work, then it will prove to be just as successful as if the person was next to you in person.

I will now explain a few visual demonstrations which can be used on TV and Live stage shows to demonstrate instantly how successful the technique of Navel-Healing is, and may I point out that if these demonstrations are carried out BEFORE any actual personal one to one healing is done then results will be INCREASED!

The reason quite simply being that once the patients to be have seen these visual demonstrations of how Navel-Healing works, then their BELIEF & FAITH in it working for them will be total.

WEAK ARM – STRONG ARM TEST

This is a visual demonstration which I have used along with the other tests which will be explained with great success in the past on TV shows including "Psychic Livetime" (Granada Breeze), "Live at Three" (UK Living) and Children's "Nickelodeon" TV Station amongst many others.

I have also used it extensively as a live demonstration piece both on Stage & in Cabaret and also whilst giving lectures at many of the Psychic Fairs which in the past I have attended and exhibited at!

EFFECT

Volunteer one clenches their right fist and then with their fist in this closed position places their right arm outstretched straight in front of them.

They are told to close their eyes and imagine clearly a time in their life when they felt very weak unloved & unwanted.

They are told to now notice how weak, how drained and how NEGATIVE this makes them feel.

"Feeling weak, drained and negative from the tips of your toes to the tips of your fingers!"

You tell them to TRY to keep their arm straight out in front of them as they allow these NEGATIVE emotions and feelings to flood their entire body from tip to toe.

Then you count to three: - 1,2, and on 3 you cue a 2nd volunteer upon the stage to push down the first persons right arm which they find they are able to do with the greatest of ease.

It is explained to the audience that under normal circumstances the 1st volunteer would have been able to keep his arm much stiffer, much straighter and out in front of him for much longer despite volunteer number two pushing down on his arm.

It is explained that this demonstrates how Negative emotions in our minds can lead to Negative effects in our bodies and as a consequence often lead to unnecessary illnesses and disease.

The good news however, is that by using a form of treatment such as Navel Healing we can remove all negative emotions from our bodies and therefore end up with a far more healthy life.

To demonstrate this you have Volunteer number 1 close their eyes once again, you place the Quartz Crystal into their Belly Button and have them imagine the warmth represented by the colour Orange that is now flooding into their body.

They are told that just so long as they see the colour Orange clearly that in a few moments time something which was just a few moments ago so difficult will now become so ridiculously easy to achieve.

They are told to notice the inner strength they now feel which is making each and every muscle group in their body from the tips of their toes to the tips of their fingers STRONGER than they have ever been before.

(You of course during this time also appear to do your bit of directing energy into their Base Chakra energy point whilst thinking of the Blue Healing energy!)

Volunteer number one is then told to resume the same position as before with their right fist clenched and their right arm held outstretched straight in front of them.

Volunteer number two is then told "OK on the count of three just TRY to push his arm down and notice how difficult it is for you and how much STRONGER he has become, 1, 2, 3, That's it just TRY to push down his arm.

Volunteer number two is allowed to continue TRYING for a few seconds or so and then is told to relax. Then volunteer one is told to relax also and take their new-found strength with them.

When asked volunteer one WILL SAY how weak he felt the first time and indeed how much stronger he felt the second time around.

Volunteer two when asked will genuinely comment how much more difficult she found it to get his arm to budge the second time around.

EXPLANATION

Everything is done and carried out 100% exactly as I have just explained, with only a few points being of particular relevance as follows:

The first time around volunteer one has to hold their arm out in front of them from the very start of the demonstration and so it is little wonder that their arm is tired by the time volunteer two comes to push it down.

Also the first time around the psychological effect of thinking of negative things will genuinely make volunteer one feel weaker – its quite simply a simple form of SELF-HYPNOSIS which makes this work without fail with any willing & co-operative subject.

The suggestion of "TRY to keep your arm out straight in front of you!" suggests by that single word TRY that they will be unable to do so!

This is a technique known in Hypnosis as "The Law of Reversed Effort" which states that the harder they TRY to do something the less success they will have!

And finally with reference to the first time round where volunteer one is made to feel weak, because you cue volunteer two to push their arm down on the count of three without person one hearing you it will then come as a shock when it happens!

Because volunteer one does not know when his arm will be pushed down or indeed expect it to happen at all, it will be a complete surprise to him when this happens, he will be caught off-guard and will not have chance to tense up his by now already very tired arm.

The moment this first demonstration is done both volunteers are told to relax as normal. This gives volunteer one time to rest his arm ready for the second time!

This time volunteer one stands with his arms by his side and eyes closed as you tell him to think of the positive times in his life when he felt STRONG, confident and on top of the world.

He is told to notice that as he clearly sees these things in his minds eye so at the same time he starts to feel STRONGER in each and every muscle group from the tips of his toes to the tips of his fingers.

You then start to explain to the audience that its time to make volunteer one much stronger and healthier by the power of Navel Healing and go into the usual Psychic Mumbo Jumbo at this point!

The moment volunteer one has started to visualise the colour Orange clearly in their mind, then and only then you get them to resume their original position of having their right arm straight out in front of themselves with the fist clenched.

Volunteer one is told "Notice how much stronger you feel, notice how much stronger you are and how much stronger you have become!"

Volunteer two is then told "On the count of three I want you to TRY and push his arm down as you did before, except this time notice how much harder it becomes for you to achieve this."

Then you count 1,2, and on 3 – Just TRY to push down his hand, that's it Just TRY, TRY (continue like this for a few seconds and then say) And now everyone just relax once again.

This time volunteer one has been warned when the pushing will begin and has time to tense their arm, also this second time around it is upon volunteer two that the Law of Reversed effort is used by suggesting to her to TRY and push down his hand.

SUMMING-UP

Do exactly what I have just explained in exactly the way I have said to do it and this demonstration will work EVERY time. Yes the levels of success will vary, but in general 9 times out of ten the visual difference will be VERY DRAMATIC!

And in the other 10% of cases it will still be visual enough to show that Navel-Healing has indeed made the man stronger the second time around.

This works due to a combination of The Law of Reversed Effort (TRY), the verbal suggestions given to them and the things they think of (self-hypnosis), and the fact that second time around the man (volunteer one) has prior warning of when the woman (volunteer two) will TRY to push down his arm.

He has of course also had a minute or two to rest his arm between tests and this time only places his arm outstretched in front of him at the last second, thus not giving it time to get tired as in the first instance.

This may not sound very impressive when described like this on paper, but visually its very dramatic and makes for a good TV or Stage Show demonstration which both the audience and those whom participate in the experiment will find AMAZING!

BUCKET OF ICE TEST

This is a routine, which I originally saw demonstrated by a so-called Conventional Psychic Healer called Mathew Manning on Uri Geller's ITV Special "Beyond Belief".

EFFECT

It is explained to a volunteer seated on stage, that in a few moments time their right arm will be placed into the fish tank next to them which is full of Cold Water and Ice.

They are told to remove their hand from the Iced Water the very second that they feel it is too cold or painful to keep their hand in it any longer.

They are told to close their eyes and you then lift up their arm and place it into the tank of Iced Water without warning.

From the second their hand enters the Water until the very second they remove their hand is timed by a stopwatch which is held and operated by a 2nd Volunteer from the audience.

The time is noted and Volunteer one is told how long they managed to keep their arm under water before the Navel-Healing begins.

Volunteer One is told to close their eyes and relax as you place the Quartz Crystal into their Navel and start the Psychic Mumbo Jumbo.

You suggest to them that "In a few moments time when and only when I count to 3, then and only then I will place your right arm into the water tank beside you."

"This time you will notice that from the very second your hand enters the water you WILL FEEL calm, relaxed and confident in every way!"

"You will notice that something you once thought would be so difficult now becomes so ridiculously easy and you will feel NO DISCOMFORT whatsoever!"

Then you go into the think of the colour Orange Blurb and feel the warmth Patter mentioning to the volunteer that:

"Just so long as you keep seeing the Colour Orange brightly in your minds eye whilst feeling that warmth flooding your entire body YOU WILL FEEL NO DISCOMFORT whatsoever and will be able to keep your hand in the tank for much longer with the greatest of EASE!"

1- Relaxed, Calm & confident.
2- Feeling warm & strong inside and on
3- Just notice how, unlike last time you feel no discomfort whatsoever. (As you count three you place their hand back into the water)

At this point Volunteer number two starts the stopwatch and prepares to stop it the very second that volunteer number one removes their hand from the water again.

The times are compared and it is noticed with much amazement from both those involved and the audience that She was able to keep her hand under water for CONSIDERABLY longer the 2nd time around!

She is given a towel to dry her arm and returned to the audience to thunderous applause.

EXPLANATION

Basically if you do exactly what I have explained in the way I have explained it, and say what I have said in the way that I said it then this WILL WORK with great success for you.

The volunteer hypnotises themselves through their belief that Navel-Healing will work, as don't forget you asked only for volunteers who were willing & co-operate whilst having very good powers of Intelligence, Imagination and Concentration.

Your suggestions to them as detailed in the "effect" section are worded such as to Hypnotise them further into the belief that this will work.

The fact they have had their hand under the cold water once means that the second time around it is not so much a shock to their system and this alone will allow them to keep their arm under for longer than before.

Also second time around the idea of pain is NEVER allowed to enter their head. You see first time around they are told "Remove your hand from the water the very second it becomes too PAINFUL to keep it there!"

This suggests to them it will be painful and with this in their mind it won't be many seconds before they remove their hand from the water.

However second time around the word pain is NEVER ever mentioned and instead they are told to notice HOW LITTLE DISCOMFORT they will feel and how much easier it will be this time.

Lastly the fact they know how many seconds they kept their hand under first time around will usually make them determined to beat this second time around and in a focused state of mind such as this – SUCCESS WILL BE ACHIEVED.

For this experiment I find it works better if the volunteer with the stopwatch is a male whilst a female is used to place her hand into the water tank!

The tank by the way is nothing more than a reasonable sized fish tank, which is filled with 50% cold water, and 50% Ice cubes!

Incidentally it's a proven scientific/medical fact that women have a higher pain threshold than men and that's another reason why I use a woman for this "Bucket of Ice" test.

PSYCHIC STRONGMAN TEST

As a demonstration of Navel-Healing this experiment has been used by me on countless Television shows, and indeed this test is so good that it has been used by top psychic performer Uri Geller on many of his world-wide TV shows to date, although obviously Uri didn't present it as Navel-Healing as we will do!

EFFECT

A large volunteer is seated on a stool/chair and four other volunteers are asked onto the stage to participate.

The man on the chair is told to sit upright with his hands on his lap, whilst the four other volunteers are told to interlock the fingers of both hands so that the fingers of the left hand are against the back of their right hand and vice versa.

With their hands interlocked in this position they are then instructed to place their two Forefingers so that they point outwards with their fingertips away from their interlocked hands.

With their hands like this two people are told to place their outstretched forefingers underneath the seated volunteers armpits (one under his left armpit and one under his right).

And the other two volunteers are told to place their outstretched forefingers under the seated mans kneecap area, again one under the left side and one under the right.

On the count of 3 they are all told to TRY and lift the seated man as high as they can noticing as they do how difficult this is to achieve. 1,2,3 – OK just TRY.

They attempt to do this either with no or very little success, which demonstrates how hard the following test, will be to achieve.

The four volunteers who are stood up all overlap their hands in the air so they go, right, right, right, right, left, left, left, left in order so all four people now have their right hands on top of each other in the pile and then their left hands above these!

At this point you place the Quartz Crystal into each person's Navel and get them to concentrate on the Orange Colour and the warm feeling for a few seconds.

As you do this it is suggested to them all that "In a few moments time we are going to lift this man again and this time something you once thought would be so difficult WILL become so ridiculously easy!"

"Just so long as you think of the colour Orange at all times you will find that he becomes as light as a feather and that you become as strong as an Ox!"

"On the count of three I want you to all remove your hands from the pile and put your hands back together as they were before so that your fingers are interlocked onto the backs of your hands with only your Forefingers pointing outwards away from you.

Then immediately resume your positions as before, so your fingertips are under the mans armpits and kneecaps as you had them before and then the very second I shout NOW – that very second YOU WILL LIFT HIM UP with the greatest of ease.

1   Confident, Calm & relaxed,
2   Strong as an Ox and on
3   Resume your positions this very second.

(Allow them all to do so and then say)

NOW – Lift him up – higher and higher and higher!

This happens and yes the man is almost thrown through the roof the second time to everyone's amazement, before being returned to his chair.

EXPLANATION

Don't even ask me to explain why this works – but believe me it does! I can honestly say that I've been using this test both on TV and Live Stage shows for a number of years now and it has NEVER gone wrong.

Admittedly the patter I use is worded following the rules of NLP and as such actually does have a positive psychological effect on the volunteers.

However even if you carry out this test without using the patter I've suggested then, as you will find for yourself, this test will still work!

The most bizarre thing about this test is that at the end the seated person will swear that they actually felt themselves get lighter, whilst the four other volunteers will swear they felt themselves get much stronger.

Don't underestimate the visual & psychological impact this test has on an audience as I have always found it to be an excellent applause puller, which is long remembered by the crowd!

CHAPTER FIVE

NAVEL MIND READING

I've taught you Navel-Reading and Navel-Healing, so now its time to reveal my secrets of Navel Mind Reading or as it is also called Belly Button Mind Reading!

Essentially this is just a way of presenting standard Mentalism effects in a manner which gives the audience the impression that you are reading the subjects mind by way of looking at their Navel for information.

You can present the routines of your choice as demonstrations of Navel-Healing in one of two distinct ways as follows:

❖ You can look at the volunteers Navel whilst explaining that the Physical characteristics of their Belly Button combined with the vibes you get from the Base Chakra energy point will reveal the thing they are thinking of to you.

❖ Or you can tell the volunteer that as they think of their randomly chosen word (or whatever the routine entails) that they are to hold up their shirt revealing their Navel. They are then told to imagine a Neon Light Beam projecting from their Base Chakra energy point, out from their Navel and out into the distance before them like a bright neon sign which displays upon it the information which you are about to reveal by Psychic means! You then reveal the correct answers as if you are able to see this psychically projected neon sign!

I'm sure you can already think of numerous routines, which could be presented as demonstrations of Navel Mind Reading, but for the sake of completeness I'll explain two of my favourites.

THE PSYCHIC PROVERB TEST

EFFECT

Five volunteers are each given a pen, a blank visiting card and a small brown wage envelope before being instructed to write down a well-known proverb or saying onto the visiting card.

The five volunteers are then told to seal their visiting card into the brown wage envelope, which they have also been given, and then to place all of them into a pile on the table.

Once placed upon the table another independent volunteer mixes up the five envelopes so that neither you, the audience nor the on stage volunteers have any idea what order they are in.

You then explain that by studying their Navels, which will reveal their true personalities, you will attempt to give back the correct visiting card to the person who actually wrote it.

They are all told to keep quiet and not say or do anything which would indicate if your choice is right or wrong until you have given all five of them a card and tell them to indicate if you are correct or not.

For the first time you get to touch the envelopes and one by one you open them and by studying each person's Navel in turn give back one card to each person.

At the very last minute you change your mind about two of your choices and swap around two of the cards between two of the volunteers.

Now its make or break time and you say "I'm going to count to three and on the count of three if and only if I've given you the correct card – namely the one which you yourself wrote, then and only then I want you to wave the card in the air and shout out as loud as you can – Jonathan Royle is the world's greatest psychic Hallelujah!"

1, 2, 3 (At this point all five wave their cards high in the air and shout out that you're the worlds greatest psychic which always leads to spontaneous applause from the audience)

EXPLANATION

Despite its simplicity this routine has served me well on TV shows such as ITV's "Funky Bunker", UK Living's "Live at Three", ATV's "The Warehouse" and on Children's "Nickelodeon" station amongst numerous others.

I've also used this routine for many years on my live stage shows and on several occasions have even tailored it for product launches.

For example I was doing a Corporate Product Launch for a new string of Indian Restaurants at the Telford Moat House Hotel during 1996 and instead of proverbs I got each person to write their favourite Indian food dish onto the cards from the choice available on my clients menu!

The effect was still presented as Navel Mind Reading, but in this way also helped to promote my client's product range and variety of different dishes.

As for how its done I'm sure you are way ahead of me, the envelopes are all marked enabling you to easily tell which card in each envelope was written by which person.

On Live Stage shows things are seen by the audience exactly as described under the "effect" section and so its vital you do things in the right way!

Have the five volunteers positioned in a straight line and from left to right hand them each an envelope, pen and blank visiting card.

Needless to say that the first person (person on left) gets the envelope marked number one, 2nd person gets envelope marked number two and so on until person number five (on right) gets the last one marked number five.

The dirty work is over now, you can turn your back and they can now write down their proverbs before sealing their cards into the envelopes, which they are holding.

They tell you when this is done, but instead of turning round straight away you have them place their envelopes onto the table and get another independent volunteer to mix up the envelopes so nobody could possibly know what order they are in or which one belongs to who!

At this point you turn round and now its all down to your presentation, as quite simply each time you pick up an envelope the marking upon it reveals to whom it belongs.

For example the envelope marked as being envelope number three would be given to the person third from the left in the line up of volunteers.

As for how do I mark the envelopes? Well I snip a small V (small triangular shape) into the seal down end section of the envelopes flap.

The V cut nearest to the left hand side with the sealed down flap side of the envelope held towards you denotes person one, whilst the V cut nearest to the right denotes person number five.

The V Cut dead centre denotes person number three and I'm sure you can work the rest out for yourself.

The advantage of using the V cuts rather than pencil dots or other marks is that as you pick each envelope up you just need to run your thumb across the edge of the sealed flap and you will feel where the V cut is on that flap.

This means that just by feeling the sealed down flap you can discover which person the contents of that envelope belong to and as such the need for looking suspiciously at the envelope is eliminated.

It's a good idea to give two of the cards back to the wrong people as psychologically it looks more impressive to realise your mistake at the last second and change them to their correct owners before discovering the impressive outcome.

For TV shows the preparation is all done before going on air, which means that you can make things seem even more like they are under test conditions.

Before the show goes on air you get the person who will be presenting your section of the show and the five volunteers to join you in the green room.

Here you hand each of the five volunteers a card, a pen and a wage envelope before explaining what they should do.

You then tell the presenter that once the five people have written down their things s/he should then and ONLY then mix up the five envelopes before placing them into their pocket for safe keeping until its time for their use on air!

You then leave the room and allow all this to be done without you even being present at the time, then on air you can stress how all this was done, you never went near the envelopes, don't know who wrote what etc.

Just so long as you are clear and forceful with your instructions to the volunteers before leaving the room then THEY WILL DO EXACTLY as you've ordered!

When performing this routine I tend to combine some cold reading into it, this means that as I examine each persons Navel to ascertain to whom I should give each card I also give them a brief Belly Button Reading of their past – present and future using the methods explained earlier.

THE BASE CHAKRA PROJECTS THE ANSWER

The routine, which follows, is one, which I originally devised in 1990 for use in my stage Clairvoyance shows, and then I called it "The Psychic Third Eye Projects the Answers!"

The routine and secret of operation were exactly the same with the only difference being that I got the volunteers to demonstrate their Psychic powers by projecting the correct answer to me through the Chakra energy point in the centre of their forehead known as the Third Eye!

Incidentally it was routines like this one, which gained me much exposure in International publication "Psychic News" and which saw them dub me "The New Uri Geller and Doris Stokes rolled into one!"

EFFECT

The venue manager is beckoned onto the stage and brings with them a plastic carrier bag, which is found to contain five newly purchased decks of playing cards & the receipt for their purchase.

The venue manager leaves the stage and a large foam ball is thrown into the audience over your shoulder to randomly pick another volunteer.

The person who catches the ball is told to come up to the stage and becomes the independent adjudicator on behalf of the rest of the audience.

They confirm that the bag contains five brand new decks of playing cards and are then asked to FREELY select any one of the decks from the bag.

The bag is now discarded and the on stage volunteer is asked to open the deck of cards, this they do by first removing the cellophane from around the box and then removing the cellophane from around the cards which are inside the box.

They are asked to remove the jokers from the deck which they now do and then are told to cut the cards as many times as they want so that nobody could know what order the cards are in.

You then instruct the volunteer to hand the deck face down to someone in the front row of the audience and this person is asked to thoroughly shuffle the deck of cards again in order to ensure they are randomly mixed.

The cards are then returned to the original volunteer who now proceeds to give one card to each of ten people in the front row of the audience whilst your back is turned.

At this point the volunteer can return to their seat and you can turn around to start this amazing experiment.

You tell each person holding a card to remember Just the number or letter which is on their card and to for now forget about the suit.

They are then told to lift up their shirts/jumpers etc in order that their Belly Buttons are uncovered enough that they can project energy from their Base Chakra Energy point.

You tell them to think of the number or letter which appears on the card they ended up with and to imagine this being projected from their Base Chakra energy point in a beam of psychic light rather like a bright blue neon sign lighting up the theatre.

You comment that lights are starting to come on everywhere and that the audience tonight are very psychic indeed and then you proceed to tell each person what number or letter of card they are holding.

As an encore you ask five of the people to stand up and this time they should try to project the suit of the card they are holding also.

You then amaze everyone by revealing the suits of the cards these five people are holding also, before telling them to keep the cards as souvenirs of their first psychic experience.

PREPARATION

On the day of your show go to a large store in the general area of the performance venue and purchase Five decks of playing cards with a mixture of different coloured backs and if possible back designs as well.

Ensure that you ask them for a carrier bag, which bears the stores name, and make sure you keep the receipt, which will also bear their name.

Return home and very carefully undo the flaps or slice open (using a razorblade) the cellophane flaps at the bottom end of the deck.

You will then be able to carefully remove the cellophane cover keeping it intact for replacement later.

The sticker, which seals the deck closed, is sliced through with a razor blade enabling you to open the box and the cards are removed from within.

You carefully undo one end of the cellophane and remove the cards from it, again keeping the cellophane until later.

The Jokers are placed to one side and the deck is now set up into the famous 8 Kings deck set up, which for those few who don't know goes as follows:

8C-KH-3S-10D-2C-7H-9S-5D-QC-4H-AS-6D-JC

8H-KS-3D-10C-2H-7S-9D-5C-QH-4S-AD-6C-JH

8S-KD-3C-10H-2S-7D-9C-5H-QS-4D-AC-6H-JS

8D-KC-3H-10S-2D-7C-9H-5S-QD-4C-AH-6S-JD

The order of the cards letters or numbers as referred to in the routine is easily remembered by use of the simple Mnemonic of:

Eight – Kings – Three – Tenned – Two – Save (7) – Ninety (9) - Five (5) – Ladies (Q) – For (4) – One (A) – Sick (6) – Knave (J)

And the order of the suits is easily remembered by the Mnemonic CHaSeD. Each of the capital letters in this word referring to one of the suits e.g. the order is Clubs, Hearts, Spades and then Diamonds.

At this point place the two Jokers and the extra Joker randomly into the deck and them carefully replace the deck into its cover before sticking the cellophane back together at the bottom using clear superglue.

The sealed deck is now replaced into the box and the boxes flap is carefully shut so that it is not noticeable that the self-adhesive seal has ever been sliced.

The cellophane cover is then carefully replaced over the box and the bottom flaps of the cellophane stuck back in place using clear superglue.

The other four decks of cards are also prepared in this way and then they are placed inside the plastic bag along with the receipt and you are ready for your arrival at the performance venue.

Incidentally although this sounds very complicated It doesn't take long at all and as only one deck is used for each show, the truth is you need only prepare ONE NEW DECK for each show.

However you will still need to buy Five new decks per show if you want a receipt dated that day for the purchase of five decks of cards which is placed into the carrier bag along with the cards.

EXPLANATION

Quite obviously you know the number or letter on each persons card due to the deck set up which means that you need only glimpse the bottom card left on the deck after the cards have been handed out and you can then reveal them as desired.

The deck set up is also how you reveal the suits on five of the cards at the end of the test and the rest is presentation to make it look like an experiment in Belly Button (Navel) Mind Reading!

There are loads of psychological ploys and subtleties, which I use in this routine which if used and presented correctly will amaze even the most experienced magical performers.

Starting from the top, the first thing is that the moment you arrive at the venue you give the venue manager the plastic bag containing the five prepared decks of cards and ask him to bring them up to you on stage when requested to during the show.

When he is requested to bring them to the stage you ask him to answer a few questions loudly and clearly with a simple yes or no answer.

"You got this bag and the playing cards I need for this experiment before today's show started didn't you?" (He will answer YES)

"And you've been guarding the bag and its contents safely for me from the moment you got them until you walked onto this stage a few moments ago haven't' you?" (Again this is true so answer will be YES)

"Have you kept the receipt for the purchase of these cards for me as well?" (You told him to keep it safe in the bag so again his answer will be YES)

"And finally I've been unable to get near these cards whilst they have been in your possession haven't I?" (You haven't been able so he will answer YES)

"Now before you return to the audience could you just place the bag containing the cards onto that chair there so its nowhere near me and I can't touch them!"

"And finally I've not bribed you, set anything up with you or done anything strange which might affect this experiment have I?" (Again He'll answer no as you've asked for simple Yes/No answers)

The venue manager can then leave the stage and thanks to the way he will have had to answer these carefully worded questions the audience will now be convinced that he the venue manager bought the cards for you and brought them to the venue with him. This means the audience is convinced that you have never been near or touched the cards either during the routine or before the show!

Next you pick up the large foam ball, stand with your back to the audience and toss the ball over your shoulder into them.

The audience are told this was a random method of selecting someone to be their representative on stage and the person who caught the ball or is nearest to it is asked to come onto the stage.

They confirm that you have NEVER met them before and nothing has been set up, then they are told to remove the receipt from the bag and place it in their pocket so it does not get in the way.

They are then asked to remove all five decks from the bag so that the audience can see there really are five different decks before replacing them into the carrier bag.

You tell them to hold the bag by just one of its handles in one hand, to shake up the cards so as to mix up the boxes and then to close their eyes, reach into the bag and remove one deck which will be used for the next experiment.

They are then told to remove the deck from its box and the audience witnesses them tearing off the cellophane from the box, removing the cards from within and them removing the cellophane from the cards.

This further concrete's into the audiences mind that you have in no way ever been near and/or tampered with these cards which they perceive were purchased by the venue manager and never set eyes upon by you until this time!

You then tell the volunteer to face the deck towards themselves and to remove the Jokers and Extra jokers from the deck.

They are told to face the cards towards themselves so that the audience does not get to glimpse that the deck is set up as they are removing the Jokers.

As for the on stage volunteer they will be so nervous on stage and so busy doing as you say that they won't even notice anything strange about the order in which the deck is in.

However the mere fact the on stage volunteer has removed the Jokers from the deck and once again you have gone no where near the pack acts as an even bigger convincer for the audience.

The on stage volunteer can now cut the deck of cards to mix them up as much as they want. As we magicians already know cutting a deck of cards does NOT ALTER the deck set up which will still be in order.

However once again the audience's perception, which will be that the cards have been mixed, makes things seem even more like test conditions.

The on stage volunteer is then asked to give the cards they are holding to any member of the front row of the audience of their choice.

The fact they have a GENUINE free choice makes things seem even more random and unprepared as indeed they would be were it a genuine case of Psychic Powers at work!

As the cards are handed to the person in the front row you say "Could the person who has just been handed the cards please cut the cards and complete the cuts as many times as you want and then give them back to the person who gave you them!"

The original spectator is now told to start on the left hand side of the audience and working from left to right whilst your back is turned give from the top of the deck a card to each of ten different people.

They are told to return to the stage when this has been done and the people about to receive cards are told to look at their cards and just think of the number or letter on them as to think of the suit as well would be far too difficult and time consuming under these test conditions.

A statement such as this concrete's further into the audiences mind the idea that this is test conditions and also the idea that this is a very difficult experiment and that just revealing the letter or number will be impressive enough.

This means that the reaction you will get when you later reveal suits of cards as well will be way out of proportion with what you have actually done!

You now take the remainder of the cards from the onstage person and place them casually into your pocket as you glimpse the bottom card (face card) of the deck remembering what it is.

The on stage volunteer is now returned to the audience to a round of applause and you briefly recap on what has just happened before the revelations begin.

Here the technique of saying what they, the audience perceived (thought happened) back to them instead of what actually did happen is used. Because they think what you recap and remind them of actually happened they will believe it to be fact and this concrete's incorrect information into their minds as 100% truth.

You say something such as "Before I arrived here today the theatre manager went shopping and purchased five new decks of cards." (This is a lie)

"Tonight for the first time on this stage the theatre manager brought the cards to me and confirmed that I had at no time been anywhere near them since he bought them!" (Another lie)

"A volunteer was chosen at random by a ball thrown over my shoulder and they have acted as your eyes and ears at close quarters to me on this stage."

"Your group representative freely choose one of the five decks which have NEVER been touched by me at any point before or during this experiment and then removed them from their wrappings and box before removing the Jokers!" (Some more lies mixed with truth)

"The cards were then shuffled (this is a lie) and thoroughly mixed up by both the on stage volunteer and another person that I have never met from the audience." (Another lie)

"Ten people whom I have never met or prearranged anything with were then each freely given a card from anywhere in the deck and now its time to try the impossible thanks to the power of Navel Mind Reading"

You do your Navel Mind Reading patter and get the people with cards to reveal their Belly Buttons before starting to project the letter/number of their card to you through their base Chakra point by way of a Blue neon beam of light!

From now on its all Patter and presentation which makes this routine so impressive, as the cards were handed out from left to right you know that the stacked deck order will be correct from left to right.

You've already remembered what the bottom (face) card of the deck was when you were given it back and this tells you instantly what the first persons card and each card thereafter will be.

For example if the face card was the Ten of Clubs then the next card in the stack which is the card the first person will have will be the Two of Hearts.

(Refer to the two Mnemonics you learnt earlier and you'll see how easy this information is to work out in just a second or two!)

You can now have all ten people stand up and for visual impact have each person sit down as you correctly reveal the letters or numbers on their cards!

Personally I like to get the 3rd Persons card wrong so that they have to stay stood up and also I then get card number nine wrong as well so that they have to stay stood up as well.

For some strange reason it seems more like a genuine Psychic test if you get something wrong as only a magician would get everything right all the time is the way an audience will think.

At this point you have got eight cards right and two cards numbers or letters wrong and so you still have two people stood up.

You ask the people with a card directly either side of person A to stand up also (that will be the people with the 2nd and fourth cards respectively) and then ask the person stood to the left of person B to stand up (this will be person with card number eight).

You now tell the three people who have just stood up to think of the suit of their card and project it to you as they did before through their Naval for the letter/number.

You tell the two people who's numbers/letters you got wrong before to transmit their whole card both the number or letter and the suit to you.

You then reveal the three suits on the cards of the three people who you previously had already revealed the letter/numbers for, and as you get each one right you ask them to sit down to a round of applause from the audience for projecting the image so well to you.

The routine ends with you revealing the correct identity of the final two cards, e.g. both the Suit and letter/number. This is milked at this point as being the most difficult thing of all to get both images at once especially as you got them both wrong before!

This ensures you thunderous applause when you get them both correct and so ends an amazing yet incredibly easy to do routine.

Re-read what I've said and the way this routine is done and you'll realise just how impressive this does appear to lay people.

Many of the ploys and psychological methods used to make this routine so strong and effective can easily be adapted and used to make other routines you may perform much stronger then they are now – so get thinking!

THE RECEIPT TEST

This is the perfect follow up to "The Base Chakra Projects the Answer" routine and indeed once that routine has finished this one is already set up and its all just down to presentation.

As you may recall the volunteer who came on stage to assist early on in that routine was told to remove the receipt for the cards which were purchased that day by the theatre manager from the bag and put it into his pocket out of the way.

This means that this person now has that receipt in their pocket and you have already done all preparation necessary for this routine.

Before the show get a large sketch pad and using a pencil prepare each page of it as follows using the information which is usually printed onto receipts from large stores:

01) Onto page one put the stores name.

02) On this page put the store managers name.

03) On this page put a three line sum, the top line is the amount apparently handed over by the theatre manager to buy the cards, the second line is the amount the cards cost and the final line which is the answer is what change they got.

04) On this page put the stores VAT/SALES TAX registration number.

The pencil notes made lightly on the pad will not be visible to the audience and act as your cue of what to write down when it comes to performance time!

EFFECT

A spectator is asked if they have any shop receipts on them and then holds one in front of them whilst revealing their Navel ready for projecting thoughts to you on the stage!

Firstly you ask them to think of the store name, you write something down on a pad with a marker pen and then ask the volunteer what name they were projecting, the pad is turned around and your prediction seen to be correct.

Secondly you ask them to project the store manager's name and once again you have written it down correctly onto the pad before they say it out loud.

Thirdly they project the amount spent on that transaction, the amount tendered and the amount given in change and sure enough you have all three pieces of information correct on your pad before they have said them out loud!

Then as a stunning climax you get them to project the VAT or SALES TAX registration number and you also get this 100% correct on the pad before they shout it out loud which WILL lead to thunderous applause.

EXPLANATION

The secret is simply that as the receipt was yours before the show started you have already had access to all the information printed upon it, and indeed have already made pencil notes of this on the pad prior to the show.

Its just down to presentation then to have them project each piece of information as you write it down in clear black marker pen in big letters on the large art pad, before revealing that your reception of the things they are projecting is 100% Correct.

The reason this is so impressive is quite simply because the audience BELIEVE that you have NEVER seen the receipt that is being used.

Those few people perceptive enough to realise that you use the same person for this routine as the one you got up to assist in the last experiment will still believe that you have never seen the receipt.

This is simply because of the belief they have now that the theatre manager bought the playing cards for you and you never made contact with them prior to the show!

However as I have found the MAJORITY of people will not even realise it is the same person, especially as you allow him to stay seated in the audience whilst this experiment is conducted and just get him to shout out information as necessary.

Obviously the longer the delay is between the end of the "Base Chakra Projects the Answer" routine and this one being done, the more likely it is that the audience will not even realise that the same person is being used.

And if they don't realise it's the same person they won't ever think about where the receipt came from, which matters little anyway as those who do make the connection will still be very impressed as their memories tell them you have NEVER seen the receipt!

Just ensure that before the person is asked to project information to you these few questions are asked of them:

01) "Like many of us I always leave lots of rubbish in my jacket, do you have any shop receipts in your pocket?" (They will say YES because they put it their whilst on stage earlier!)

02) "Now we have not prearranged anything before or during this evenings show have we?" (They will say NO)

03) "And to the best of your knowledge & beliefs I have NEVER seen the receipt which you now hold in your hand or the information on it have I?" (They will answer NO as they believe it belonged to the theatre manager and that you never did see it!)

Not only will the audience be amazed as you get each piece of information almost 100% correct but also the person who is transmitting the information to you will be amazed also.

The reason I say almost correct is because to get everything right would seem like a trick, but to get some of the numbers slightly wrong or spelling a name incorrectly but meaning the same thing adds a level of realism and enchantment to it all!

I love this routine because like everything I do its simple and allows me to concentrate on the presentation, which with Mental Magic and all things of a Psychic nature is what turns a simple little experiment into a life changing MIRACLE from an audiences perspective!

This is a true REPUTATION MAKER and in my personal experience draws an audience reaction far greater than many so called finger flinging complicated miracles receive.

CHAPTER SIX

FURTHER MENTAL MIRACLES & NAVELS

Don't forget that at the conclusion of "The Base Chakra Projects the Answer" there is a plastic bag on stage which is on top of a chair and contains four perceptively brand new unprepared decks of cards which were purchased by the theatre manager.

All the Psychological conditioning has already been carried out and the entire audience will now believe that not only have you never been near the cards before the show but also as these cards inside the plastic bag have been in view throughout the show you have still NEVER touched them!!!!

This means that later in your performance you may get another volunteer from the audience and get them to randomly pick another brand new deck from the theatre managers plastic bag for use in the next experiment.

This allows you to capitalise on the very real fact that whilst on stage you have NEVER touched the cards and as such this makes your next experiment even more impressive than it would be normally.

At this point you can do any Psychic/Mental routine which requires a deck set up such as the effect called PLETHORA from DERREN BROWNS excellent book "Pure Effect".

Admittedly DERRENS routine will have to be done slightly differently in these circumstances (each deck would have to be set up with a short card in it for starters) but buy his book and consider what I've already said here and you'll be using the routine in the same way as I now do in no time at all!

In fact you can go one further and in the third section of your show go through this all again with another brand new deck being taken from the bag by yet another spectator for use in yet another experiment.

One of the routines in which I've done this before is my version of the one ahead routine, which although I am not going to go into great detail about here I will explain a few brief points:

ONE AHEAD OUTDONE!

On the first piece of paper I pretend to write down with a ball point pen the name of a holiday resort, but in fact I leave the paper blank and fold it up before dropping it into a large Brandy glass on the table.

I then ask the first spectator to tell me the name of the Holiday resort, which they have merely been thinking of and this is written on a large pad for reference later!

Onto the second piece of paper I write the name of this Holiday resort, fold it into quarters and then drop it into the Brandy glass also.

I then ask the second spectator to tell me the name of the Casino they went to that night which they had merely been thinking of and again a note of this is made on the large pad for later.

Onto the third and final square of paper I would write down the name of the Casino just given by the spectator, then fold it into quarters like the others and drop it into the wineglass.

I then Ask the Third and final spectator to tell me the name of the playing card they were dealt last during their losing game of Five Card Stud Poker in the Casino and a note of this is made on the pad.

At this point your ink thumb writer which is available from most all good American Magic supply companies is used to write the name of the card this spectator said onto another slip of paper which is on the top of the small square pad in your hand.

This is done whilst the audience is watching spectator three carry out your next instruction which is to choose a deck of cards and remove them from their wrapping and box.

You explain that as it was five-card stud they lost at they must have already had four cards in their hand before they drew the losing card.

They are asked to cut the cards as many times as they want to mix them up and then to remove the top four cards from the deck and hold them closely against their chest, before handing the remainder of the deck to you.

This gives you ample cover to fold the thumb written square of paper up just as the others were and to get it into a comfortable palm position in your hand.

As you take the remainder of the deck from them you just casually glimpse the bottom (face) card of the deck and then you know which the next four cards in the stack will be, namely the four cards held against the volunteer's chest.

The deck, pad and pen are now in your pocket or case and as the saying goes *OUT OF SIGHT IS OUT OF MIND!*

You recap on the free choices made by the spectators who MERELY thought of things and then apparently reach into the large Brandy glass to pick out a slip before changing your mind and allowing the spectator to do so instead.

In actual fact in this innocent looking moment you switch the slip in your hand for the blank slip in the Brandy glass which is easy to do as the square of paper used for the blank slip has some markings on it for easy location and sighting by you as required.

Done correctly it will just look like (and will certainly be by the audience remembered as) you just reaching towards the glass and quickly changing your mind as you say:

"Actually so I don't get accused of cheating I'd better let you wonderful volunteers remove my predictions from the glass!"

This is reverse Psychology as they will never believe you would have just done something dodgy and then draw attention to the possibility of this by making a comment such as this.

Needless to say now the switch has been made all three of your Brandy Glass predictions will match 100% CORRECTLY with the things merely thought of by the volunteers and noted upon the sketch pad for future reference.

When the applause dies down (which by now has left a suitable time gap for the audience to forget what has actually happened) you turn to the third volunteer and say:

"Whoops I almost forgot, I managed to predict the final card of your losing Five card stud hand but what about the other four cards?"

"I never touched the cards (this we know is a little lie but as it was after he'd picked his four cards the audience will have forgotten this!) And you had a free selection from the deck didn't you?" (S/he will answer YES)

"You immediately placed the cards freely chosen by yourself from the freely chosen deck against your chest and haven't even looked at them yourself yet have you?'"

"So in other-words no-one in this building tonight including both you or me could possibly know what those four other cards which made up your Five card Stud hand are could they?"

You then are able to AMAZINGLY reveal the identity (number or letter) and suit of each card held in his hand against his chest bringing this impressive routine to a close.

If you are going to do the routine in this way ensure that when the decks are set up pre show that the Jokers are inserted after a sequence of 13 cards in order that the stack is not affected.

This means that is you glimpse the face card and it's a Joker you need to just glimpse the card behind it to learn what that card is and then you know what the next four cards in sequence are.

If the face card glimpsed is not a Joker and leaves at least 4 more cards in that run of the sequence you have your answer.

If the face card is not a joker but leaves less than 4 cards in that run of sequence you know what the next three cards in the sequence would be and must state that the fourth card held in their hand will be the Joker.

This is because the Jokers were not removed and the reason for this was so that things looked different in procedure than last time one of the decks from the carrier bag was used for a routine.

Please re-read the routines explained in this manual many times not just to learn them for use in your shows but also just as if not more importantly BECAUSE the routines as I present them contains lots of Psychology and ploys which you can adapt for use in routines of your own.

Another thought is to gimmick the plastic carrier bag so that it becomes a two-way forcing bag! This is a simple DIY job, which requires two identical store carrier bags and some double-sided tape.

One bag is placed inside the other and then using the double-sided tape one exterior side (outside) of the inner carrier bag is stuck to one interior (inside) of the outer carrier bag.

Your force carrier bag is now made and once again due to the psychological ploy that the Theatre Manager purchased the contents of the bag for you it will NEVER be suspected.

The item to be forced, for example a postcard from an exotic holiday destination would be in one section of the bag right from the start of the performance.

Then when it came to the relevant routine you could show a dozen different postcards from very different holiday resorts and drop them into the plastic carrier bag, before shaking the bag to apparently mix up the cards!

The spectator then seems to have a free choice of postcard, but instead is allowed only to place their hand into the section of the bag where the dozen duplicate FORCE postcards have been hidden from the start of the show!

I'm sure you will think of many ways to use this idea, I like it lots because nobody ever suspects that a famous high street stores carrier bag would be in any way gimmicked!

Incidentally as will be discussed in later sections of this book the plastic bag could contain other items such as magazines, newspapers and drawing pads, all of which could be gimmicked as necessary.

Once again the psychological ploy of the theatre manager or other perceptively trustworthy person having apparently been the one to purchase the bag and its contents will add a powerful and often devastating edge to many of your effects!

Cbviously the bag should only contain items which it is commonly known are available from the store which has its name upon the carrier bag!

FINAL THOUGHTS ON NAVELS

The Human Navel, which prior to birth is connected to the umbilical cord inside the mother's womb, provides us with our life force before our eventual appearance into this world.

This fact combined with the very believable sounding patter contained within this manual makes the whole concept of Navel reading very credible indeed.

Navel Reading wise I honestly believe that there is more than enough information in this manual to enable you to start giving readings right away.

What's more use the Cold Reading techniques I've detailed within these pages correctly and you can instantly do Palmistry, Tarot and ALL OTHER FORMS of Psychic divination as when all is said and done the common secret is COLD READING!

Should you wish to push the idea of Navel Healing right to the edge then may I suggest that you read the book "Faith Healers" by James Randi which although intended by James to be an expose also happens to be the best "how to" manual on Psychic healing that I've ever read.

Navel Mind Reading wise, with a little imagination almost any Mentalism routine can be used as a demonstration of Navel Mind Reading.

My only suggestion would be that as few props as possible are used as after all you're meant to be a genuine Psychic. Should any props be used they should have a logical reason for being used.

For example with the "Psychic Proverb" test things are logically written down so that there is a tangible object to try and match up with its owner by way of the Navel.

And in the "Base Chakra Projects the Answer" test the cards are merely used as random ways of generating numbers and letters and then later suit symbols for the audience members to project to you by way of their Base Chakra energy point.

These secrets have been earning me a good living, an excellent reputation and extensive regular feature publicity on National TV & Radio shows along with numerous Newspaper and Magazine features – do things right and they will for you to!

CHAPTER SEVEN

PAWOLOGY

(Palm Reading For Dogs
or How To Be A Canine Clairvoyant Revealed & Explained!)

In order to keep appearing on a regular basis in National Newspapers and Magazines, along with regular spots on TV & Radio shows you need to keep on coming up with something new and different and that's why I developed Pawology.

Pawology is the name I have given to my ability of being able to do Psychic readings for dogs in much the same way as many Psychics do Palm Readings (Palmistry) for human beings.

Look at a dog's paw and you will notice that they have five pads on the underside of their paw. Four of these are in a row at the top with a fifth and final pad below them in the centre.

I have through trial and error named these pads as follows:

From left to right (whilst facing the dog) on the top level where the four pads are together are the: LIFE PAD, HEAD PAD, LOVE PAD & LUCK PAD.

And the final of the five pads, which is on its own, located in the bottom middle area of the paw is the HEALTH PAD.

I have discovered that when the front end of any pad is raised more than the rear (sticks up more at that end) that this is a positive indication in that area of the dog's life.

However where the rear end is raised more than the front (sticks up more at that end) then this is a negative indication in that area of the dog's life.

For presentation purposes I say that we look at the dogs right hand paw (left as we face it) to discover things about its Past.
And that we look at the dogs left hand paw (right as we face it) to discover things relating to its Present & Future life.

Also I have become something of a modern day Dr. Dolittle by communicating with the dog's at a spiritual and psychic level.

83

When I am holding onto a dog's paw I very often am able to communicate with them in a non verbal manner whereby they say things in their mind and I receive them (or hear it) in my mind!

I have also discovered through trial and error that the way each of a dog's paws feels also tells us a lot about their past – present and future.

For example in general the smoother that pad is the easier that area of the dogs life has been to date or will be in the future.

And the rougher it feels the more difficulties there will have been in that area of the dogs life up till now or will be in the future.

Palmistry has been found over many hundreds of years to be extremely accurate and indeed since 1995 I have found the art of Pawology to be very accurate also!

As we are all a nation of animal lovers and many of us have our own pet dogs it is little wonder that Pawology is of interest to the media.

Indeed to date numerous National press articles have appeared about my Paw Reading talents including a half page feature in The News of The World which as you may know is Britain's highest readership Sunday Tabloid!

Radio shows have included BBC Radio Belfast, GMR Radio, Talk Radio UK, 210 FM, BRMB Radio, Derby FM, Comedy World Radio (USA) & BBC Radio One amongst numerous others.

Television wise Pawology has been featured successfully on countless shows including C4's "Big Breakfast", twice on C5's "Fives Company", BBC 1's "False or True" and numerous times for productions made by RDF, RTL and Pro Sieben (7) TV for the European markets!

Pawology is also ideal as a form of live entertainment for events such as dog shows & animal society Christmas parties.

THE FIVE PADS ON THE PAW

LIFE PAD

The Life Pad is the pad we would pretend to be studying when talking about things which are going to happen or have already happened in the dogs life which do not easily or logically relate to any of the other four pads.

HEAD PAD

The Head Pad would be the pad referred to when dealing with all things of a psychological nature. For example when telling the dogs owner that his four legged friend is depressed and they are fed up with taking the same route every day for their walks.

LOVE PAD

The Love Pad would be the pad referred to when dealing with affairs of the heart. For example when telling a dogs owner that their canine friend is sexually frustrated and needs to be in the company of female dogs a little more often.

LUCK PAD

The Luck Pad would be referred to when telling a dogs owner such things as "I see great luck in the future for your dog, you will be given the chance for him to earn lots of money in the areas of animal modelling and acting!"

HEALTH PAD

The Health Pad would be referred to when dealing with past medical problems the dog may have encountered and any health issues, which the owner should be aware of for the future.

PAWOLOGY – COLD READING

Once again the secret of Pawology is little more than the use of effective cold reading techniques, the main obvious advantage here being that dogs cannot talk back and as such will never be able to say you are wrong.

This means that when you apparently discover things from the dog's paw and/or from mental communication with it and tell its owner they will have no choice but to accept it as fact.

For example telling the owner that their pooch is fed up of the routes they are being taken on for their walks is something that the owner cannot possibly argue with as they are unable to talk directly to their dog and as such have to take your word for it.

The Cold Reading methods used are IDENTICAL to those explained in the Navel Reading section of this manual and are used on the dog's owner.

You of course are apparently looking at the various areas of the dog's paw as you use these methods to gain information about the dog's life and to make apparently accurate revelations and predictions about it.

On all occasions I have found that spending a few minutes with the dogs and their owners before going on air or on stage will enable me to obtain much information about the dogs life to date just by showing a genuine sincere interest in that person and their dog which they love so much.

Remember that flattery will get you everywhere, so praise the owner's ego, tell them how lovely their dog is and before you know it they will be telling you the dogs life story before you even get on air or on stage!

You then of course feed this information back to them in your own words and with lots of predictions for the future which of course at this time cannot be proved right or wrong either way.

I also on many occasions make use of a Mentalists clipboard in order to obtain much information about the dog without the owner ever realising how I managed to find it out, in other words they end up believing that I discovered it through reading their dogs paws!

PAWOLOGY & THE CLIPBOARD

Whenever I am to see the dogs in person to read their paws I always ensure that I get to see them and their owners before the TV/Radio show goes on air or the Stage show begins.

I usually have three owners present with three very different breeds of dog as this visually looks better and I have found that three dogs gives you long enough for your interlude of dogs paw reading. (Pawology)

Before the show I meet the owners and their dogs in person, I use this opportunity to introduce myself to the dogs and their owners.

The important things here is to remember which owner is with which dog, what breed that owner's dog is and also what the dogs name is.

You then explain that to get things clear IN THEIR MINDS before going on air/stage you want them to fill in a short questionnaire about their dog.

They are told this is FOR THEIR BENEFIT and will help to make things much CLEARER IN THEIR MINDS when it comes to ShowTime.

You tell them to fill in the questionnaire as this will help burn relevant information INTO THEIR MINDS, which may or may not be referred to later in the show.

All three of them are then given a clipboard attached to that is the doggie questionnaire and a pen with which to write down their answer's.

You explain that as you don't want to be accused of cheating (this is reverse psychology as anyone cheating wouldn't draw attention to the possibility would they?) that you will leave the room for ten minutes whilst they complete their answers.

They are told to answer the questions as fully as possible within the next ten minutes and before you return to remove the paper from the clipboard, fold it up and hide it in one of their pockets so that you CANNOT POSSIBLY SEE IT as you want your demonstration of Pawology to be under test conditions!

You now leave the room and return briefly ten minutes later apparently to thank them for their time and to wish them luck before you go on air, whilst in the room however you casually pick up the three clipboards and say "As we have finished with these I'll return them to the main office!"

This comment implies that they do not even belong to you and so any thoughts about the clipboards will now be completely distant from their minds.

You can now return to your dressing room and discover what details they wrote down about each of their dogs and of course it is this information which is then used on air and fed back to them in different words.

Because of the way it was handled the dogs owners think the questionnaires were FOR THEIR BENEFIT and don't even think the clipboards belonged to you and so they will be amazed by your revelations.

And of course the viewers or live audience will be just as, if not even more amazed as they have absolutely NO KNOWLEDGE of the clipboard ever being used or the questionnaires being filled in!

So what questions should you ask on the questionnaire? Well I suggest the ones which follow as the answers given to these will give you more than enough information for your on air readings.

Incidentally you know which questionnaire relates to which dog as you have already met the dogs and their owners and know all their names & breed which can then be easily cross referenced with the completed questionnaires.

PAWOLOGY QUESTIONNAIRE

We understand that appearing on TV/Radio or Live on stage can be very nerve racking and therefore in order to make things crystal **CLEAR IN YOUR MINDS** it would be appreciated if you could answer the following questions.

Once you have answered all the questions please **REMOVE THIS SHEET,** fold it up and **HIDE IT** in your pocket, as **I DO NOT** want to see it **UNTIL AFTER THE SHOW!**

OWNERS NAME:_____   DOGS NAME:_____
DOGS AGE: _____   DOGS BREED:_____
DOGS FAVOURITE TOY/S:_____

DOGS STARSIGN (IF KNOWN):_____

01) What is the happiest thing that has ever happened in your dog's life?
02) What is the saddest thing that has ever happened in your dog's life?
03) Does your dog have any special/hidden talents?
04) Has your dog had any operations and/or Health problems in the past or at present?
05) Does your dog have a mate and if not have they ever had one in the past?
06) Does your dog have any strange habits?
07) What would you like to have happen to your dog in the future?
08) Has your dog won any prizes and/or awards in the past?
09) Is there anything else of importance you think I should know about your dog for future reference?

Thank you for completing this form to get things **CLEAR IN YOUR MIND** before ShowTime, now please just complete your contact details below as **AFTER THE SHOW** I will ask for this form and its contents may be used for future media interviews.

PRINT NAME: _____
ADDRESS: _____
TEL & MOBILE: _____
E-Mail: _____

I agree to participate in today's Pawology demonstration and to be contacted for media interviews with my dog in the future.

SIGNED: _____ **DATED:** _____

EXTRA COMMENTS_____

Notice the way in which the questionnaire is worded and you will see that not only does it serve as a way for you to gain information before going on air/stage, but also helps you build up a database of dogs & their owners for use in your future media promotion.

Also the fact it says you will want to get the completed sheet off them AFTER the show gives a totally logical reason as to why they are being asked to fill it in at all!

It seems that you don't want to see it before going on air as then you could be accused of cheating, however as time will be short after the show you want them to complete it now and will get the completed sheets off them later as you need this information on your files so they can be contacted for potential use in future media articles!

Not only is this a great psychological ploy but it also helps you build up a contact list of people who will talk to the TV/Radio, newspapers and Magazines about you, your talents of Pawology and their experience of consulting you with their dogs!

Incidentally don't forget that when they tell you what the dog's star sign is this alone will give you more than enough patter for your reading.

You simply need a little knowledge about Astrology for humans and then much of this can easily be adapted for use with dogs and indeed other animals!

MAIL ORDER READINGS

When the dog is unable to be there in person with you such as in the instance of Television or Radio phone interviews or for some printed media interviews and of course for mail order sales of your dogs paw readings a different approach must be taken.

In all these cases you must ask for a good clear close-up photo of the underside of each of the dogs two front paws clearly marked as to which is which and a normal snapshot of the dog itself.

They should also send you a clear paw print (get them to press the dogs paw onto an inkpad and then onto a sheet of paper to make this) of both the dogs front paws again clearly marking which paw is which.

And they should supply you with the dogs date of birth (for Astrology purposes) and any specific questions they want answering or areas of the dogs life which they want you to look into.

The truth is that only the questions they ask and areas of the dogs life they mention along with its star sign will give you anything from which to glean information for your reading.

We must get them to send us the other stuff for two reasons though, firstly as it makes the whole thing seem more credible and believable to them and secondly because these paw prints and photos will become useful props for use in future media interviews and on stage!

Incidentally it is quite often the case that when newspapers and magazines ask you to read dogs paws for them and supply photo's of dogs for you that they will usually be celebrity doggies.

By this I mean the dog itself will either be a celebrity as in an animal actor from Films/TV or it will be a dog belonging to a celebrity as this makes the feature more "newsworthy" for their publication.

So just as I told you to build up a scrapbook of celebrity Navels I would advise you also build up a scrapbook of celebrity dogs for exactly the same reasons and for use in exactly the same way.

For mail order readings, media interviews and other occasions when you can find out the breed of the dogs you will be doing the Pawology for it is then useful to visit your local library or to look on the internet for information.

This is because once you know what breed you are dealing with you can find out loads of useful stuff such as what illnesses and health complaints that breed is most likely to suffer from, what their personalities are usually like and loads, loads more.

This information is freely available from books in your local library and/or on numerous Internet web sites about that dogs particular breed.

SUMMING UP

Use your Imagination, Common sense and Initiative and I'm sure that like me you will find that Pawology serves you well!

For example when on TV shows you can demand that they get three dogs there on the day all of whom have had near death experiences in the past.

Needless to say this information will be revealed to you in detail on the Pawology Questionnaire given to the owners before the show and can then be revealed on air to much amazement.

If you can't remember the logic behind this then you'd better go back and read the Navel's section of this manual again hadn't you?

CHAPTER EIGHT

HYPNOTISING ANIMALS

There is actually no such thing as genuinely Hypnotising an Animal, what actually occurs is a sort of muscular paralysis which has no ill effects on the animal subjects used.

You can find much information about these techniques on the Internet by using the Search Terms "Animal Hypnosis" – "Hypnotising Animals" and also "Tonic Immobility"

HEN = It is a well known fact that if a hen is placed so that its beak is touching the ground and a chalk line is drawn from the beak, the Hen will not Move, being under the impression that it is tied with this mark!

The eyes of the Hen are focussed upon the mark and the line of vision converges practically at the end of its beak.

HEN = Holding the Hen in One Hand, you can produce a similar effect by gazing intently into its eyes and receiving the return gaze directed into your eyes, bringing the Hen closer to your eyes as you do this!

This Produces an eye-strain which also converges the line of vision as the Hen is brought nearer your face and has the same effect as the chalk line.

ROOSTER = Take a Rooster and place it on a table or on a small stand with its legs folded beneath it.

Then hold its head and beak resting on the table, it will stay there and appear to be in a Trance for a short time.

CHICKEN = A Chicken can be placed into a Sleep Like State by rhythmically swinging it back and forwards.

RABBIT = The Rabbit is held with both hands, the back of the Rabbit being towards yourself.

Now you gently swing the Rabbit up and down, and its struggling will soon cease and the Rabbit will appear to be asleep.

RABBIT = Another easy way is to place the Rabbit on a table, near the edge, on its side, with its head dangling over the side of the table.

You then hold the Rabbit still until any struggling stops and the rabbit appears to be either dead or asleep!

However a gentle touch on its ears will instantly bring the Rabbit out of this state.

GUINEA PIG = These can easily be placed into a Trance Like State by rolling them over and over several times and then placing them on their backs.

Their eyes remain open, it appears to be in a dazed condition and will remain there for a short time.

However any movement in front of its eyes, or a noise will restore this animal to its normal condition.

DUCK = It is possible to hold a Duck in the palm of one hand with its feet uppermost. A gentle swaying movement will appear to place the Duck under Hypnosis, then the Ducks beak can be drawn down onto its stomach and left there for a moment.

DOVES – PIGEONS – VARIOUS BIRDS = Doves, Pigeons and Various other Birds are easy to apparently Hypnotise. You simply hold the Bird in one hand so that the Birds Back is on the Palm of your hand, then you push its head downwards towards the floor and when struggling stops you may open out the fingers of the hand which the Bird is resting on and it will look as though the Bird is "Asleep".

SNAKES – ALLIGATORS – CROCIDILES = All of these are placed into a Sleep Like State when Placed flat on their backs. Hold them in this position for a minute or two and then you can let go and they will stay there as if in Trance.

FROGS – TOADS – CHAMELEONS – LIZARDS ETC = These Can also apparently be placed into a Trance Like State by similarly placing it on its back and holding them in place for a moment or two until their struggling ceases.

However with Lizards and such like, prevent the Jaws from closing and hold its head at the same time.

SHELLFISH = Lobster & Crayfish are both easy Hypnotic Subjects. They may be stood on their heads, using the two forefeet and the head to act as a tripod.

Gently stroke their back towards their head, once the trance like state is visibly noticeable they will remain in most any position until the state wears off.

LIONS – TIGERS – MONKEYS ETC = Most any larger animal can apparently be Hypnotised using a somewhat bizarre method as follows which like all techniques in this manuscript and in this entire book you use entirely at your own risk as all things in life (especially trying to do this on Lions & Tigers etc) carry Risks!

A solution of one half Rose Water, and one half Chloroform is placed into a tightly capped bottle, a tube is led from the top of this bottle to a position on the wrist band around your wrist of one arm.

Another tube from the left hand has a rubber bulb (perfume spray bulb) which when deflated forces air into the bottle, as this is also going into the top of the bottle and as such will drive the odour of the Gas through the second hole in the bottles cap, through the other tube and therefore ejecting the Chloroform Gas out of the tube at wrist level.

The Strong projection of this gas into the Nostrils of any Beast or Animal will create a bewildering effect, passes in front of the animals eyes, together with more Gas ejected, will produce a state of stupification and of course could be carried on until the beast is in a mental daze and apparently in Trance!

Performers in the past have used this method to apparently place Lions, Tigers and other large beast into a Hypnotic State.

You should be careful not to stand in the direction of oncoming wind, otherwise as you spray the Gas out it may be blown back into your face and make you rather than the animal pass out, which could obviously potentially prove fatal with and animal like a Lion or Tiger!

This technique was used for many years, however I feel it must constitute cruelty to animals and as such would be against the Law to use and as such is presented here for information purposes only.

ZOO ANIMALS & DOMESTIC ANIMALS = There are now companies who train animals for TV Commercials and Films and if you were to contact such a company they would be able to train most any Domestic or Zoo Style Animal to react as if asleep and under Hypnosis in response to a simple visual or audio signal.

They could then teach you this signal and you'd apparently be able to place the animal into an Instant Trance, as it would react when it received the signal as if it had gone to sleep.

This piece of information could prove very useful indeed for the Publicity minded Hypnotist.

FLY'S & OTHER INSECTS = You need to catch a fly and freeze it. This puts it in a temporary coma. This can be done by swatting the fly hard enough to immobilise it and then placing it in a small container in the freezer. When it comes to performance time, the fly then needs to be quickly taken to a suitable windscreen IN THE SHADE and placed there. It is important that the car is in the shade to prevent the fly from defrosting too quickly. Then go and find a spectator and take them back to the car, which should appear to be randomly picked. The heat of your hand will revive the fly, which should soon start to move. A lot of this trick is in the actions of you reviving the fly. It may be necessary to practice how long it takes for the fly to revive itself. Freezing the fly with dry ice or even one of these aerosol canned air products for cleaning computers is a better way of freezing the fly as it is quicker and causes less damage to the fly. You of course can start of by showing the Frozen non moving fly and explaining its in a Deep Hypnotic Trance and then as you warm it up and its eventually Flies off you can pretend to awaken it from its Sleep like state! This will also work with some other small insects so try it out with some!

I've included this bizarre chapter both for completeness and also because those of you who are Publicity and Success minded will see what a great Marketing Ploy becoming an Animal Hypnotist could be!

I bet Millions of Dollars could be made selling self-help Hypnotherapy tapes to Animal owners to treat their pets – just an idea!

CHAPTER NINE

PSYCHIC TREE SLAPPING

Psychic Tree Slapping was developed in order to help trees and plants growing in unnatural environments to grow with more natural results!

It can also be used on trees & plants growing in their natural environment as a way to accelerate their growth and speed of development.

Some people think that when trees move they create the wind, however the reality is, that it is the wind, which makes the trees move.

Trees/Plants growing in natural environments are used to and indeed grow better when subjected to all the NATURAL weather changes, which of course also includes wind & rain.

Some Trees/Plants however are unfortunate in the fact that they are growing in UN-NATURAL environments and therefore will not be subjected to natural weather climates, which means that they will not grow with NATURAL results.

Using a combination of Metal Fish Spatula's, Plastic Fly Swatter's, water spray, snoring music and Psychic healing powers a new therapy for Trees/Plants has been devised, tested and perfected which I have called "Tree Slapping".

Scientists at London's Kew Gardens have discovered that Trees or Plants growing in unnatural environments such as indoors can be made to grow more naturally by sending vibrations through the soil they are planted in.

This in effect stimulates them in the same way, as the wind hitting their stems/trunks would have done in a more natural setting.

In Tree Slapping I first make mental communication with the Tree/Plant to be treated and then I use the items as follows:

01) The Metal fish Spatula is slapped against the stem/trunk to simulate the effect fast or hard wind would have on it in a more natural environment.

02) The Plastic Fly Swatter is used in the same way to simulate the softer or slower wind types.

03) The hand held water spray is used to simulate light rain fall (when sprayed slowly) and heavy rainfall (when sprayed rapidly).

04) A half-hour tape recording of me SNORING is also used.

Initially the Spatula is in one hand and the Swatter in the other whilst I randomly SLAP the stem/trunk at various different points, the combination of the soft & hard SLAPS making it like a natural environment where there would be slow/fast & hard/soft wind!

After a few seconds of this the tree starts to "TALK" to me by mental communication and rather like a human having a massage who tells the masseur to rub further down their back, so the Tree tells me by Telepathy where on its Trunk it wants to be SLAPPED!

Five minutes of this mixed slapping sensation is then followed up by Five minutes of concentrated hard slapping which is done with a Metal Fish Spatula in each hand SLAPPED randomly over the Trees trunk.

Next its time for five minutes of soft slapping whereby a plastic Fly swatter is used in each hand to randomly slap the tree.

We then randomly spray water over the trunk in both fast and slow bursts in order to simulate the effects of hard & soft rainfall!

Finally its back to a few minutes of combined soft/hard tree slapping use one instrument in each hand and this time slapping only where the tree tells us by telepathy that it feels it needs a little more attention.

The therapy session is now over, however an important thing, which should not be forgotten, is the music, which is played during the session.

This music is a half-hour tape, which was recorded one night of me snoring in my sleep.

I went to bed that night and focused on having dreams of trees & plants growing more naturally & rapidly and the snores recorded onto this tape were the result of these dreams.

This "Sound Therapy" also seems to help the trees grow, again it could be something to do with the vibrations that sound make helping to stimulate the plant as in the research done by Kew gardens in London.

This treatment is carried out twice a week until the desired results are achieved, however those wishing their Trees/Plants to experience a happy and natural lifespan would continue the treatment at least once a week indefinitely in order that it continues to believe and react as if it were growing in a natural environment.

Tree Slapping can easily be taught to anybody and that's why it appeals to TV & Radio Gardening shows and Specialist magazines, along with the national press alike!

Those unable to devote the time to the therapy for their trees and plants or indeed those with very small plants which could not at this time stand the therapy are encouraged to buy my audio tape "Sleep & Grow" with Jonathan Royle!

It has been found by many that playing this half-hour tape of my snoring, recorded whilst transmitting my Psychic Healing energy through my dreams in the vicinity of the patient (trees and plants) often leads to amazing growth results.

Indeed UK Livings "Live at Three" show discovered that 2 out of 3 plants treated by me with just a few minutes of "Tree Slapping" grew better than all 3 comparable plants in similar conditions which were not!

TREE HUGGING

A perfect follow up to "Tree Slapping" is to discuss and demonstrate "Tree Hugging".

Tree Hugging is tapping into a Trees natural healing energy to help us humans achieve inner peace, calmness and relaxation, it is also rumoured that it can help heal many health complaints.

In truth all that happens with Tree Hugging is that people quite literally Hug trees by sitting on the floor in the countryside and wrapping their arms and legs around the trunk.

They then sit there with their eyes closed, breathing deeply and regularly for around half an hour at a time or for longer if desired.

By doing this they absorb the healing energy of NATURE from the tree, and obviously its best to do this with a totally healthy tree which has been treated itself with Tree Slapping.

TREE SLAPPING & HUGGING SECRETS

As you may have guessed there is no real secret to "Tree Slapping" other than there isn't a secret!

What I have just described is the basis behind the idea and the correct patter to use explaining the concept and how it works to the media.

Don't ask me how 2 out of 3 plants I treated grew better than those I didn't on UK Livings "Live at Three" because I really haven't got a clue!

To be honest I don't think there was any difference, but to make good television the presenters will often say things have occurred even when they haven't!

If nothing had occurred (or the presenter had said this) then I would have covered myself by saying that a usual session of "Tree Slapping" therapy lasts for around half an hour as opposed to the few short minutes they gave me!

Although it sounds balmy, because of the Kew Gardens link which is TRUE it actually becomes believable to many people!

And best of all this one has merchandising built in as you can sell the complete "Tree Slapping" kit by mail order and via your Internet website!

This Kit would contain 2 Metal Fish Spatulas, 2 Plastic Fly Swatters, A hand held water spray container, the audio tape of you snoring (which contains your psychic healing energy) and an instruction manual.

The instruction manual would basically tell the reader the same spiel as I've just given you here by way of their instructions of how to carry out the therapy!

The only addition being some mumbo jumbo about how to get telepathic communication with the Tree! This would tell them to relax and hit the first area of the trunk which came into their head as this their intuition would have picked up the trees request!

As for Tree hugging there is no secret other than it gets some people out into the NATURAL open air and the countryside which in and of itself is healthy, also as the Trees Trunk becomes a focus of attention it is slightly Hypnotic which could account for the Stress relief many say Tree Hugging gives them.

Incidentally some of Britain's biggest Blue chip companies have been known to send their executives on Tree Hugging weekends, this basically means they have paid hundreds of pounds to stop at a country hotel and spend lots of time each day hugging the trees!

I know it seems hard to believe but many of these stressed executives swear by Tree Hugging as a form of relaxation and group bonding.

Relaxation being achieved apparently by hugging the tree and bonding apparently by chatting to their work colleagues who are also hugging a near by tree!

Yes I know what you are thinking strange but true, but like all the other ideas I've given you in this manual it has the potential to make you MILLIONS!

You may think I've totally lost the plot, but selling DIY Tree Slapping & Hugging kits by mail order and the internet which of course would be plugged by all your media appearances WILL MAKE SOMEONE A MILLIONAIRE of this I'm sure – will it be you?

I know there is lots of scope in this one as not only have I managed to obtain TV/Radio and Newspaper coverage for this Zany Talent, but also a colleague of mine Andy Ford a stand up Comedian from England took with my permission the snoring idea and during 1996 had a field day with it!

He just used the snoring makes plants grow story line and as a result he gained a large feature in THE SUN (the highest read British daily paper), features in several glossy magazines and also TV appearances on shows including C5's "Fives Company" and ITV's "GMTV" amongst numerous others.

Best of all I believe he sold loads of his snoring tapes as a result of his media appearances, consider this and then tell me if you still think I'm crazy?

TREE SLAPPING – TV DEMO

A good way to demonstrate the effectiveness of Tree Slapping for TV shows and on stage is to use Uri Geller's famed effect of getting a seed to germinate whilst held inside someone's hand!

The secret of how to do this is quite simply to switch the seed which has been examined for one which you have allowed to sprout before the show (by conventional growing methods) so that the sprouted seed goes into the volunteers hand as they close their hand around it.

Much hilarity can now be had slapping the spectators hand and spraying them with water as your demonstration of Tree Slapping whilst you explain how this would be carried out on Trees or Plants.

Then low and behold after a minute or two of this the spectator opens their hand to discover that the seed has sprouted which as it happened (like all the best close up magic) in their own hand will amaze both them and the audience!

You then end the routine by saying something such as "If we can get that seed to germinate in a matter of two minutes just imagine what a proper half hour session of tree slapping can do for trees growing in unnatural environments!"

Suddenly it doesn't seem such a bizarre idea after all does it?

DARE TO BE DIFFERENT!

DARE TO BE A SUCCESS!

CHAPTER TEN

OTHER BIZARRE PSYCHIC TALENTS

Within this section of the manual I shall only be giving you the "Bare Bones" information necessary to put these other bizarre Psychic talents to use!

On all occasions the secret is Cold Reading and/or the use of a Mentalists clipboard or similar method of obtaining information without the spectators knowledge prior to the show.

In other words what follows are merely presentational ideas, which can be used to gain you TV/Radio & Published media publicity.

HOSE PIPE READING

Hose Pipe reading is used for psychic insights into people's relationships and affairs of the heart.

It is used both to predict when someone will meet the man or woman of their dreams and also to discover the long-term compatibility of existing partners.

A rubber hosepipe is used and basically is thrown into the air by the person wishing an answer to their relationship question.

When the Hose lands on the floor, we look at the patterns it makes and the distance between one end of the Hose to the other and it is this, which gives us information to tell the client.

The idea behind this being that one end of the Hosepipe is MALE (the end which water comes out of) and the other end is FEMALE (end which fits onto tap) hence the reason why a Hosepipe is so good for relationship/romantic issues.

Also it is Water that runs through a Hose pipe and as we human beings are made up of around 90% Water, the Hose pipe is yet again the ideal tool to use for psychic divination on romance matters.

When it lands on the floor after being thrown into the air by the client, you can refer to the distance between the MALE and FEMALE ends of the Hose as being the indicators of how long it will be before they meet their ideal partner.

Or this same point of reference could be used to reveal how long it will be before they will move their relationship with an existing partner onto the next step, maybe getting engaged or married.

The number of times the Hose overlaps itself in the middle when it lands on the floor could be referred to as the number of obstacles in their path to true love.

Use your initiative and this idea of Hosepipe reading for relationship issues will prove very popular for TV shows, especially around Valentines Day!

I have personally demonstrated Hose pipe reading on TV shows broadcast on Nickelodeon & RTL and I am aware that a fellow Psychic used with my permission the idea to get themselves onto Granada Tonight (ITV) and other TV shows around Valentines Day 1998.

TEA BAG READING

Tea Bag reading has been devised to bring a modern day slant to the age old tradition of a psychic reading the tea leaves and the patterns they make in your cup after its contents have been drunk.

In our modern world people have become either too lazy or too busy to take time to brew a proper pot of tea using tea leaves and that's why the use of tea bags has become so popular.
I have noticed that the way people make a cup of tea and the state their tea bag is in at the end reveals an awful lot about them and that is how I discovered that tea bag reading works!

For example a relaxed, calm & happy person might squeeze their teabag out gently before removing it from the cup and casually disposing of it in the bin.

Whereas a stressed, worried and unhappy individual might literally take their frustrations out on the teabag and squeeze it so hard and for a prolonged period of time that it becomes a small deformed shadow of its former shape!

So that's the idea for teabag reading, the way people squeeze the bags when making their tea and also the manner in which they then dispose of them, or in some cases try and make two cups from one bag all reveal a lot about that person.

The brand of teabag and flavour of teabag they use could also reveal lots about their personality and attitude to life.

You could also explore the idea that whether the person uses a cup or a mug reveals things and that perhaps the bigger the mug/cup they use the bigger their ego is?

Think about it I'm sure you can have a lot of fun with this one!

PYRAMID HAT POWER

The reputed psychic power of the Pyramids is infamous and it is this rich history of the Egyptians and the mystique surrounding the ancient pyramids that was the basis for Pyramid hat power!

Read a book on Pyramid Power and you will discover that in experiments it has been discovered that an apple placed under a Pyramid shaped wire frame lasted significantly longer than an identical apple placed nearby before rotting.

Apparently Pyramids have amazing preservation qualities which are illustrated and highlighted by the fact that the Egyptians choose to bury their dead in the Pyramids, helping them to become "Mummy's" with ease.

It is also believed that Pyramids draw Natural psychic & healing energy from the Universe around them and amplify the intensity of this for the good of all the Pyramid contains.

If you like, this means the tip (point) of the pyramid acts as a receiver or Ariel through which all the Psychic energy from the universe is absorbed and as this energy floods down to the base of the Pyramid it becomes amplified more and more as the Pyramid gets wider and wider towards its base!

I therefore realised that it would be a good idea to make Pyramid shaped hats which people could wear when they were ill, the Pyramid would draw the universes Psychic healing energy to it and it would then be passed through the pyramid and into the person wearing the hat to help them recover!

I have also discovered that these Pyramid hats can be worn by workers in factory's and this will, as once featured on American TV show "World Weekly News" enable the wearer to become far more productive in their job!

Working on the premise that Pyramids draw psychic energy to them and that there are countless reports world-wide of people having Psychic experiences who have visited and entered the Pyramids in Egypt also makes the use of Pyramid Hat's ideal as a novel presentational slant for many Mentalism routines.

You could have two spectators wearing Pyramid Hats, one being the transmitter and one being the receiver in a demonstration of telepathic ability, which is enhanced due to them wearing the Pyramid Hat!

Then one spectator draws a simple image and projects this image to the other spectator who amazingly manages to draw exactly the same image on their pad.

Incidentally this drawing duplication effect will be explained later in this manual and is indeed the effect I use as an apparent demonstration of Pyramid Hat Power!

PARANORMAL BANANA BENDING

Remember the old stunt of removing the skin from a Banana to discover that it is already sliced?

Well for the Banana stunt you just stick a needle through the skin and wiggle it from side to side before removing it from the same hole.

This slices the Banana in half at the point where the needle was inserted and leaves no tell tale signs on the skin. The Banana looks normal but when the skin is undone will fall apart into two separate pieces.

A whole bunch of Bananas can be gimmicked in this way and then a spectator can be given a free choice of Banana, which they remove from the bunch.

You can explain that in EEC Countries and under new European Laws it is illegal to sell Bananas which do not have a big enough bend in them, which as a matter of interest is as bizarre as it sounds TRUE!

Being inspired by Psychic metal bender Uri Geller you have devised a way to make the previously unsuitable for sale (not bent enough) Bananas saleable by mind over matter!

You show the chosen Banana to camera and then start to rub it as you concentrate your Psychic energies into it and as you do so THE BANANA VISIBLY BENDS!

Well at least that's the way it looks to TV viewers as you simply hold the Banana face on to the camera so that people are looking into the bend, which makes the Banana look much straighter than it actually is!

Try this in front of the mirror, holding the Banana so the curved side points outwards towards your body and the side facing the mirror is the inner side of the bend or to put it another way the mirror image is that of someone looking into the bend.

Then as you rub the Banana and apparently do your psychic thing you simply turn the Banana slowly from the position it is in, to one where it ends up held with the bend pointing down towards the floor.

Do this correctly and it actually does look like the Banana is bending a bit and has become more bent than it originally was!

You can then tell the spectator to point out their finger and imagine all the psychic energy in their body flooding out through their finger like a laser beam.

At this point they are told to imagine slicing the Banana in half with the laser beam without damaging its skin in much the same way Doctors can use Lasers to operate on our internal organs without cutting through our skin!

Now the Banana can be un-peeled by the spectator who like the audience will be amazed that the Banana has become sliced into two separate pieces.

Yes I know you think I'm mad and that this would not fool anyone, let alone pass as genuine Psychic Powers, however I can assure you that done correctly it does work and DOES AMAZE – and this is because of the correct way it is done and the context within which it is performed.

I usually use this as a lead in for a more serious metal bending routine and would advise you to do so as well.

ASTROLOGY FOR PETS

I think the title for this idea says it all. Many TV & Radio shows have a resident Astrologer for human beings as do nearly every newspaper and magazine, so why not an Astrologer for pets?

You could have your own weekly TV/Radio slot or regular published column by way of which you reveal what the future holds for members of the animal kingdom.

Comments such as: "This week will be the start of new adventures for Leo Dogs as your owners finally decide to take you on a different route for your walks!"

"Rabbits born under the sign of Taurus will experience some minor health problems this week so rest up and take things easy!"

Yes I know I've lost the plot, but this could AND WILL WORK for someone who uses his or her imagination a little.

Model your Astrological readings to those that appear in magazines and newspapers, with the only difference being that within them you mention that these things will happen to popular household pets of that star sign!

This idea may seem a little surreal, but I'm certain that someone will get their own regular TV and Radio slot by doing it!

CONCEPTION WINDOWS

Conception Windows is the scientific sounding name which I gave to my idea of using Astrology to help people conceive more easily or to conceive a baby of their choice!

For over a year (1999 – 2000) I had on the website of British lifestyle magazine Iqmagazine.com a regular column dealing with "Conceptions Windows" and I can assure you that this idea generated much media interest.

I know almost nothing except the basics about Astrology and so for this idea to work you need to recruit the services of a trained Astrologer.

This Astrologer will preferably be one who shies away from the limelight as in exchange for payment you will on a regular basis ask him/her to calculate using Astrology certain things and then you will be the one to reveal them on TV/Radio shows and in the media.

This idea although not entirely new, was given a new lease of life by me thanks to the CONTROVERSIAL manner in which I presented it to the media and the scientific sounding name for it of Conception Windows.

To get instant media attention you must use a press release with a controversial heading such as "Babies For Sale!", this will catch their attention, as would the headline "Babies To Order".

You then explain that by using Astrology you can tell a couple the information they need to have a Bespoke Baby (Tailor Made Baby) or in other words the Baby of their dreams.

Using the Male and Females dates, times and places of birth combined with the details of the actual baby they wish to conceive Astrology is used to determined the actual date and time upon which sexual intercourse needs to take place for this to happen.

Obviously it is not 100% guaranteed that they will conceive on this first occasion and so they are told to abstain from sex (or use protection) on all other occasions except the monthly dates given upon which conception of their desired baby due to Astrological and Planetary forces is possible!

This technique can also be used in third world countries, perhaps by way of the Internet to advise couples when to conceive in order to give birth to only MALE BABIES which due to infanticide would save thousands of lives each year.

These lives would be saved as in many third world countries any female babies that are born are KILLED AT BIRTH! This
Life saving angle is a very strong one to use and WILL get media attention.

This technique can also be used in the same way to avoid unwanted pregnancies and therefore avoid ABORTIONS and ADOPTIONS, which need not occur.

After all some babies are unfortunately aborted because health difficulties are detected, but using Conception Windows the couple are more likely to conceive a healthy child and thus AVOID ABORTION!

In the same way a mother who discovers she is to have triplets may not be able to cope and this may lead to adoption for some children, an occurrence which again could be avoided by Conception Windows by ensuring sexual intercourse takes place on a date and at a time when only one child will be conceived!

So infanticide, Abortion & Adoption, along with the idea of being able to have the baby of your choice are all angles from which media interest can be generated.

The "Bespoke Babies" angle is perhaps one of the most controversial, imagine being able to ensure by way of Conception Windows that the time you conceive is one that:

- ❖ Will ensure you give birth to twins, triplets, Quads or indeed the number of babies of your choice.

- ❖ Will enable these aforementioned babies to be IDENTICAL twins, triplets, quads or more as desired.

- ❖ Ensure that the baby you have is MALE, which in the case of infanticide avoids unnecessary deaths!

- ❖ Ensure the sex of your baby will be FEMALE.

- ❖ Ensure the future personality and temperament of your as yet unconceived child by ensuring it is born with a certain star sign.

- ❖ Conceive a child which will be predisposed to certain talents, for example one more likely to become an Olympic swimmer!

- ❖ Give you dates upon which you can have sex without the need for conventional contraception without the huge risk of becoming pregnant.

- ❖ Give infertile couples or those experiencing problems dates/times upon which to have sex to SERIOUSLY increase their chances of conceiving in the natural way!

In short **CONCEPTION WINDOWS** opens up a world where people need only give birth both when they want to and also to a child which fits their requirements completely in every way.

Those of you wishing to use this idea are advised to track down a suitable Astrologer in your own local area who is prepared to furnish the required information and calculations as and when needed.

However should you be unable to or not wish to spend time searching for such a person then e-mail me on ***sales@hypnotictraining.com*** And I will put you in touch with the British Astrologer, which I used to calculate the information for me when writing my column for Iqmagazine.com.

Incidentally this idea

WILL MAKE SOMEONE MILLIONS

WILL THAT PERSON BE YOU?

Couples could be charged a sizeable consultation fee to calculate exactly when they should have sex (what date & time) in order to produce a baby to fit their requirements exactly.

All this could be done over the Internet with the couple paying by credit card and filling in an on line registration form and questionnaire of their needs.

You could then e-mail them back the **CONCEPTION WINDOWS** which are correct for them, by that I mean the correct times and dates for the next twelve months which would lead if pregnancy occurs to the baby of their choice.

The website itself with a controversial enough name such as "babiesbydesign.com" or "babiesforsale.com" would help to generate media publicity of your business and its activities.

I personally just used **CONCEPTION WINDOWS** to give **FREE** advice to couples by way of the Iqmagazine.com column and then as a result of this was able to sell mail order Astrology reports which were advertised at the foot of my column as being the ideal Birthday gift.

I personally would not extract money from people in the ways suggested however I have seen GENUINE examples of this idea working to help couples and so I can recommend the concept.

Using the Internet for Credit card sales and then getting the website publicised by TV/Radio and Media publications by making them aware of the controversial nature of the business would make you very rich indeed.

WILL YOU BE THE ONE TO MAKE A MILLION?

FROM – CONCEPTION WINDOWS?

IF SO DON'T FORGET WHO GAVE YOU

THE IDEA – MY COMISSION IS 10% - OK?

SOME FINAL THOUGHTS

The Cold Reading methods necessary to effectively present the ideas contained in this section are all explained in detail within the Navel Reading section of this manual.

You may think that some of the ideas in this section are either too bizarre or too controversial as to be of practical use in the real world!

Well I have got news for you, these ideas like everything that is contained within the pages of this manual have unless otherwise stated all been tried, tested and proven to work in the real work.

I know that some of the ideas in this manual will not appeal to you, however I hope that the ones that do will far outweigh this!

My intention, in this manual is and has always been to teach you all I know that is of benefit to anyone working in the Mentalism and Psychic Industries who needs more Publicity, a higher profile and ultimately a vastly improved income.

These ideas have enabled me to establish myself as a regular Psychic Performer on numerous TV & Radio shows and if they help you to achieve the same whilst earning a fortune into the bargain then my efforts will have all been worthwhile.

CHAPTER ELEVEN

STUNTS FOR THE MEDIA

In order to become a regular on TV & Radio shows you will need to get the viewers and listeners involved in such a way that the broadcaster will be bombarded with calls about your Psychic Talents and as such will ask you back sooner rather than later.

It is also far easier to get on TV & Radio shows in the first place if you have just appeared in the printed media, a copy of this recently printed article sent to the shows researchers and/or producers by mail, fax or e-mail will often lead to a TV/Radio follow up interview.

If you have ever seen Uri Geller or indeed myself on a TV show then you will already have a good idea of what I mean, but in any case here are some stunts and ideas which can be used to ensure you become a regular face on TV & Radio shows and in the printed media.

This increased media profile will then lead to more live show bookings and ultimately increased performance fees which of course is our desired aim.

RETURN FROM THE DEAD

With this stunt you tell the viewers or listeners at home to get a pen, a blank sheet of paper, an ashtray and a lighter or matches ready as later on they can take part in an experiment to prove that there really is life after death!

Later in the interview you tell the viewers/listeners to write down onto the piece of paper the full name of a deceased relative or friend with whom they would like to make spiritual contact.

They are then told to set fire to the paper and allow it to burn away in the ashtray, whilst at all times looking into the flames produced by the burning paper.

You tell them that just so long as they stare at the flames and concentrate on their loved ones name, they will receive instant spiritual contact from their friend or family member.

You then say "Anyone watching/listening who carries out this experiment and makes contact with their loved ones please call the station and tell us what happened on (then give their number) and perhaps we will get you on a future show!"

That's it really except to say that as with all stunts of this nature it is best if you DO NOT tell the shows producer, researcher or presenter that you will be doing it as then they cannot possibly do anything to stop it being transmitted (assuming it's a live show).

Also by finding out the shows direct dial telephone number you can instantly (from memory) give this number out to the viewers or listeners and as a result their phone lines will be jammed.

You can guarantee that their phone lines will be jammed for a few reasons:

❖ Because you would have around a dozen of your friends and family who are located in different areas of the Country call up and claim to have had a spiritual experience as a result of the experiment.

❖ Because members of the public want to be on TV and the Radio and as such will ring up claiming something has happened when it hasn't in the hope that this may lead to their 15 minutes of fame.

❖ A small percentage of people will allow their mind to play tricks on them and will genuinely believe that something has happened.

❖ Consider that the show probably only has two or three phone-lines & that from the thousands or millions of people watching/listening if only 0.5% of them responded then that would be hundreds of calls and the phone lines would be jammed for hours.

Stunts which prompt the viewing/listening audience to both participate in an experiment and then to call in will always lead to the phone lines being jammed and those who have seen Uri Geller perform on TV will know that he uses this fact to great effect.

The shows producers, researchers & presenters will all be so impressed by the chaos caused and the interest shown in you by their audience that they will make sure they get you back onto their show VERY – VERY – SOON!

This "RETURN FROM THE DEAD" stunt can also be used in printed media publications, again the readers are told to do exactly the same thing and then upon having a spiritual experience they should contact the publication.

The only difference being that in this case you must tell the publication what you are going to do and in the case of Daily newspapers state an actual time that day when they must carry out the experiment.

With magazines which may have a shelf life of up to a month you should mention an actual date and time (towards end of its shelf life) that the experiment should be carried out.

For some reason making a specific time and date when everyone reading the article should carry out the experiment makes it seem all the more believable that something special will happen and if they start to believe this then their mind WILL play tricks on them and something WILL HAPPEN!

URI GELLER LIVES ON!

The idea of this stunt is to use it when you are on a show giving a demonstration of metal bending.

As you hold the Spoon or Fork in your hand you would look into the camera and say "I want everybody at home to really concentrate on this Fork as then our combined energies together will make it bend!"

Then once the Fork has visibly bent and snapped into two pieces (explained elsewhere) you say something such as "Wow all you wonderful people at home must have been concentrating really hard for that to happen!"

"In fact sometimes when people concentrate as hard as that strange things happen in their own homes!"

"Perhaps the cuttlerly in your Kitchen draw has developed bends or the keys on your key-ring have become distorted"

"Maybe that broken watch has started working again or something else strange has happened whilst you were staring at me on your screen!"

"If anything strange whatsoever has just happened please call and let us know on (their number) as we'd love to hear from you!"

Once again the Psychology behind this stunt as with most stunts of this nature is that as detailed for "RETURN FROM THE DEAD".

CAN YOU READ MY MIND?

You explain to the viewers/listeners that you have drawn a simple drawing of an object onto a piece of paper before the show started and then you sealed it inside an envelope.

You then give that envelope to the shows presenter and tell them to look after it and not open it until next time I appear on the show (this makes the viewers think you have already been invited back!).

"I want the viewers at home to look directly into my eyes (you look straight at camera) or listen closely to my voice (in case of being on radio or for blind viewers) and I will count to three."

"As I count to three concentrate on me and tune into my mind as I shall be trying to project the image I have drawn and sealed into the envelope to you!"

"1 – concentrate, 2 – see that image clearly in your mind now and on 3 – please draw the image you have seen onto the back of a postcard and send it to us at (their address) and in the very near future I'll be back on the show to reveal how many of you got it right!"

There is no secret to this stunt other than you draw a simple drawing of a house like a child would, you know a simple house, with four windows, a door and a chimney.

The law of averages is on your side and the fact is that lots of the people who do reply will get the object right, certainly the 50 or so friends/family who send postcards in on your behalf will be correct and this itself warrants a reappearance on the show.

The way your patter is worded makes it difficult for the show not to rebook you, as their viewers/listeners will want to know if the object drawn by you is the same as the one they received.

And the large quantities of postcards arriving at the station over the next few days will keep your name at the forefront of the producer's minds, proving by the audience's response to the stunt that you were popular with them!

Remember a stunt such as this needs to be pulled without giving any of the shows production team any form of prior warning as otherwise they will try to stop you asking the viewers/listeners to contact them as from previous experience they will be aware of what chaos this causes!

HELP US WIN THE MATCH

In this stunt you display a large Orange coloured Spot to the shows viewers and/or newspaper/magazine readers.

They are told that the spot is Orange as the colour Orange is a powerful combination of the colours Red and Yellow combined.

You further explain that you have energised the Orange spot with your Psychic energy and that if everyone concentrates on it for 30 seconds seeing clearly the result they wish to achieve then it can become 100% Total Reality.

You count to three (when on TV/Radio) and get the audience to concentrate on the Large Orange dot as you say "Concentrate clearly and England will win their important match today!"

This stunt is so adaptable and becomes newsworthy in almost every sporting event that I love it to bits as does Uri Geller who like myself has used this and stunts similar an awful lot in the past!

The fact is in sporting event finals there is also a 50/50 % chance that the outcome you wish will happen and if your side don't win, it's not your fault – oh no its down to those people who did not concentrate properly.

STARE INTO MY EYES

The idea behind this is to have the viewers stare into your eyes as you face the camera or to stare into a close up photo of your eyes in the case of media publications as they concentrate on what they wish to achieve and say it out loud three times.

For example this could like the Orange Dot be made newsworthy by linking it in to getting people to try and make their team, side or player win the event.

However you could also use it at such times as National No Smoking Day by telling them to look into your eyes and say loudly and clearly three times "I AM A CONFIDENT, HAPPY, CALM & RELAXED HEALTHY NON SMOKER!"

Those people who would have naturally stopped via will power alone will later attribute their success to the fact they stared into your eyes and this could lead to future media coverage as on air or in the article you tell them:

"Those people who have now after looking into my eyes lost all desire for Tobacco or Cigarettes and feel they will now continue to be the confident, happy, calm & relaxed non smoker that they have now become, please contact us on (their number)"

TV & RADIO PSYCHIC READINGS

If you are asked onto a Live TV or Radio shows to give Psychic readings to the viewers or listeners over the telephone then don't panic.

All the Cold reading techniques you'll need to use are explained in the Navel Reading section of this manual.

Also you will find that in the case of TV/Radio shows the callers will be asked what area of their life it is they are calling about and do they have any specific questions to ask the Psychic.

This will be done by the researchers who answer the phones before that caller is put through to you on air and indeed this information will either be in the case of Radio shows displayed on a screen in front of you as the caller is connected or in the case of TV shows will be told to you through your studio ear-piece.

When neither of these things is to occur you quite simply ask the caller "In what area of your life can I help you today?"

This open ended question makes them answer you with a detailed reply which feeds you all the information you will need to, in conjunction with the cold reading methods give a very accurate appearing reading!

In otherwords in the case of TV/Radio phone ins there is far less guesswork required on your part than on many other occasions.

NEWSPAPER/MAGAZINE COLUMN

Dispensing spiritual advice by way of a regular newspaper or magazine column is the easiest form of "Psychic" work there is by far!

All the people mentioned in the column and to whom you are apparently giving Psychic advice would have written to you via the publication telling you exactly what their problem is and asking for your help.

You therefore already know what the problem is and merely need to give a common-sense logical sounding answer with an element of reassurance to the person who sent their question.

With a little initiative you can mention details which the person has revealed to you in their letter as part of your reply to them in such a manner that anyone else reading the article will think you have revealed this information thanks to your Psychic Powers.

OK I know the person who sent the letter will not be fooled by this, but the MAJORITY of people will be! Also don't forget that the person who wrote in will be more interested in hearing your common-sense advice.

Don't forget to make lots of predictions for the future, as these at the time cannot be proved one way or the other and will sound due to the detailed information you give to be precise psychic insights into that person's life.

For columns like this you usually call yourself a Psychic Agony Aunt/Uncle.

URI GELLER OUTDONE!

Imagine being able to walk into the offices of any National Newspaper and asking to see one of their journalists.

Imagine then getting him to examine a fork, which he finds to be completely normal.

Imagine now telling him you are the world's newest and by far greatest psychic phenomenon and that your talents make Uri Geller look stupid.

Imagine now giving him the fork to hold in his own hands as you say "Those people who accuse Uri Geller of trickery are probably right as why does he not make things bend in your hands like I do?"

Imagine that as you say this the very Fork that the Journalist has just examined starts to dramatically bend whilst held in their own hands with you stood a good distance away.

Imagine now that he can examine the Fork once again, as can all his colleagues at the newspaper who will all find that it is a bent fork, which cannot be bent back into a straight position by mere physical force alone!

Imagine the reaction this would cause from the Journalist and his colleagues in the office, then imagine how eager they would be to get the photographer down to take photographs of you for inclusion in the next days edition!

And finally imagine what would happen and how much TV work would result if you visited ALL THE OFFICES of ALL THE MAJOR newspapers in one day and did exactly the same thing to them all resulting in feature appearances in all of them the next day.

NOW STOP IMAGINING as thanks to an ingenious state of the art set of gimmicked Forks this is all possible exactly as I have just described.

This is a new magic effect, which has just been released in April 2001 and is called **"BENDING FORK"**

You are supplied with two special Forks, which can be examined, and seem completely normal, and yes the bending does take place IN THEIR hands with you NOWHERE NEARBY!

One of the Forks allows a straight Fork to visibly bend whilst held in their hands whilst the second one allows a previously bent and then examined fork to visibly straighten whilst held in their hands.

The **"BENDING FORK"** package is not cheap and retails for around $800-00 a set, however this is good for us with the foresight to obtain major National scale FREE PUBLICITY with it as the high price (compared to many other effects) will help keep this exclusive to the select few for some time!

Incidentally the "Bending Fork" set will pay for itself many times over when you consider that not only will it generate publicity for you as described, but also it can be used during your live stage shows as well!

USEFUL MAGIC RESOURCES

In various sections of this manual I refer to items which can be purchased from magical supply stores many of which advertise on the excellent Internet Sites of *www.magicweek.co.uk* and also *www.magictimes.com*.

Others can easily be found by visiting *www.google.com* and then for your search subject enter "magic dealers" and a huge list will come up.

The top of this list will be The Magic Dealers Association Web Page and via this site you can visit literally dozens of on line stores selling many books, videos, gizmos, gadgets and props of use to Psychic Entertainers like ourselves!

AUDIO TAPE HEADLINE PREDICTION

This is another reputation maker, which again requires an expensive piece of equipment. This must be purchased from one of the magical dealers you find on the web!

Imagine recording onto an audio-tape your verbal prediction of what the National Newspaper headlines will be in two weeks time.

Imagine then putting this tape into its plastic box and sealing it shut with sticky tape before locking it into a metal cash box, which is then locked into a bigger metal cash box in order that no one can tamper with the contents.

Imagine then packaging this up and sending it by Recorded Delivery (where recipient has to sign for collection of goods) to the editor of a leading National Daily Newspaper.

You are waiting at the Newspapers offices when the parcel Delivery Company arrive to deliver the package and witness it being signed for and left with them.

You are now able to speak to the editor and explain that you sent the parcel and DO NOT want it opened until the exact date you state in two weeks time as it contains a prediction of what that newspapers headlines and main stories will be on that day.

Before leaving the newspapers offices you get the editor to sign a contract agreeing that he will not tamper with the prediction, will stick it in the newspapers vaults for safe keeping and will then bring it along with him on the evening in question to the relevant television station or live performance venue.

Imagine then on the night in question appearing on a LIVE TV show and LIVE on air having the newspapers editor open the package and then the two metal cash boxes (as on air you give him the keys) and then finally he cuts open the seal on the tape case and places it into the audio tape recorder in front of him.

He then presses the play button, the tape begins to play and your voice is heard to come from the speakers revealing not only that days newspaper headlines and main storys but also many major news events from the past two weeks along with the previous two weeks winning National Lottery Numbers.

The tape is then removed from the player and given to the newspapers editor to take away and play back as many times as he wants and they will genuinely find that upon the tape which was mailed too them TWO WEEKS BEFORE THE TV SHOW (which can be proved by delivery companies records & receipts) is your voice containing numerous CORRECT predictions of what would happen during that 14 day period.

Don't you think that this would get that newspaper to cover the story?

Don't you think they would run stories leading up to the revelation of your predictions on the TV show and also after the event detailing how you were 100% correct?

Don't you think a LIVE TV show would jump at the chance of having you on to reveal the prediction on the day in question?

EXACTLY! – Anyone with half an ounce of sense will have answered YES to all these questions!

And that's precisely why the "Audio Tape Headline Prediction" can when used correctly make you an international household name!

You could also mail an audio tape prediction in the same way to the editors of the local/regional newspaper in each of the areas that you are to perform your live show at in the near future and then this would lead to both pre-show and post-show publicity in every area that you visit!

It would of course also make for the show stopping ending to your live show when your mailed two weeks previously predictions are revealed to be correct!

SO WHAT'S THE SECRET?

Well quite simply for the cost of between $400 to $1500 you purchase a very special yet very normal looking tape player from a magic dealer.

The audiotape sent to them in advance is a blank tape, upon which NOTHING is actually recorded, which is one of the reasons it is packaged up so securely so that nobody will tamper with it and find this out!

On the day that the tape is to be played on the TV SHOW you simply record your verbal "Predictions" into the secret section of the tape player.

In other words hidden within the player is a section upon which you can record your voice.

Then when the blank tape is placed into the player and the play button is pressed the Hocus-Pocus takes place.

You see the player is manufactured in such a way that when the Play button is pressed what actually happens is that your voice which was recorded onto the secret section of the player is played back and is actually what the audience hear!

As this secret section plays back it is at the same time being recorded onto the blank tape which was placed into the normal looking player and so once your CORRECT PREDICTIONS have been heard, they are then genuinely recorded onto the tape!

This means that the editor can then take the tape away with him and whenever he plays it back will hear exactly the same as they just did when they heard your voice coming from the secret section.

This concrete's the impression into their mind that you recorded the predictions onto the tape two weeks before the predicted events happened as it is indeed THE VERY SAME AUDIO TAPE.

From everyone's point of view this is a test conditions display of genuine Psychic Powers and if you can't generate TV/Radio, Newspaper and Magazine publicity for yourself using this special prop then you may as well change career now as the possibilities are endless!

You can predict a whole seasons Football results, who will win political elections, what the winning Lottery numbers will be and in fact anything which the public has an interest in and already is a newsworthy event.

By predicting the outcome of events, which are already of themselves, newsworthy you instantly make your stunt of predicting the outcome newsworthy, it becomes a PUBLIC INTEREST story and much media coverage can then be obtained.

THE BLINDFOLD DRIVE

Imagine alerting Journalists from all the National Newspapers, Leading glossy magazines and all the TV/Radio news shows that a lunatic will be driving **BLINDFOLDED** through the city at 12pm (lunchtime) and that this is an event they should not miss.

Imagine then five minutes before this time calling the POLICE and telling them a BLINDFOLDED person is driving down the main street of the city and they should investigate.

Imagine then being arrested by the POLICE for dangerous driving on the street in question which just so happens to be where all the TV/Radio, Newspaper & Magazine Journalists, Photographers and film crews are!

Imagine that when you get out of the car having been stopped by the Police, both the Police and the Media witness the following items being removed from your head:

1. A Large Black Bag is first removed from your head

2. Under this over your eyes is a Blindfold made of CAST IRON, which is painted black.

3. When this is removed it is seen that over your eye sockets with surgical tape are stuck large cotton wool pads.

4. These are then removed to reveal solid coins stuck over your eyes using Dough such as that bread is baked with!

DON'T YOU THINK THIS WOULD MAKE THE NEWS?

Then when you are released from the Police Station you contact all the Media you invited who will have already started running the story and tell them YOU WERE NOT driving dangerously as you have x-ray vision and are Psychic!

Before they think you have gone stark raving mad you offer to appear on their show to demonstrate your Psychic Powers at which time you appear and demonstrate an equally mind blowing stunt such as **"BENDING FORK"** which I mentioned earlier.

Now be honest, don't you think that would get you major National publicity and help make you a household name?

SO HOW'S IT DONE?

The short and simple answer is that despite the way things appear YOU CAN SEE PERFECTLY WELL and therefore can drive!

Yes the coins over your eyes and the dough holding them in place are real!

The cotton wool pads are held in place with surgical tape and indeed the blindfold genuinely is made of Cast Iron.

And as for the bag over your head, well when placed over someone else's head they will be unable to see anything.

The Bag Blindfold and Cast Iron blindfold are both items, which can be purchased with full instructions from magic dealers, and you should be able to purchase them both for less than $80-00 for the pair!

With these items instructions for using the cotton wool pads, surgical tape, dough and coins should automatically be included.

If not you are well advised to purchase the book "Thirteen Steps to Mentalism" by Tony Corinda which has an excellent chapter in it on Blindfolds which will reveal all you need to know!

Incidentally this book is invaluable reading for anyone who wishes to pursue a successful career as a Mind Reader and Psychic Entertainer.

HITTING THE HEADLINES

To ensure that a stunt such as this hits the headlines you need to both do everything you can to ensure the media show up at the correct time and also have a back up plan.

I would prepare a press release on my computer the night before the stunt is to take place and then on the day in question I would make sure I was up at 6am and do the following:

1. I would firstly send by e-mail a copy of the press release to the **NEWS DEPARTMENTS,** and **THE FEATURES DEPT** and **THE EDITOR** of all the National Daily & Sunday newspapers, the leading magazines and of course all the National Television and Radio news stations, along with the major "News & Features" agencies in the area. This e-mail would have no contact details on it and would just make them curious when they read it.

2. At around 9.00am (by which time all offices will be manned) I would call each of the companies and tell them to check their e-mails if that hadn't already, but not to worry as details of the most important news event to happen today will be sent to them by fax within the next 30 minutes.

3. Then during the next 30 minutes I would send a paper copy of the same press release by fax to each of the three departments at each of the companies who were sent the e-mail.

4. By now they will have received both an e-mail and fax telling them that the event will take place today and it should be no later than 10.30a.m. They will all be awaiting your final phone call as the press release merely says what will happen and that it will happen on a major street in their city BUT NOT THE EXACT LOCATION.

5. Then at around 11-00am I would have a few female friends call them all up telling them the exact location, which just gives them time to get there, but leaves it last minute enough that they WANT to cover the story as their CURIOSITY, has been aroused.

6. I would also as a back up plan pay two trusted friends to show up at the right location at the right time. One of these friends would film events as they happened on a Digital Video Camera (which can be hired) and the other would take photographs of things as they happen on a digital stills camera.

7. This means that if turnout by the media is disappointing the moment you have been arrested the story itself has then become bigger due to Police involvement and this will enable your trusted friends to sell their Video footage to National News shows and copies of the photos to the National newspapers. Obviously only those who did not attend in person would buy these things off your friends posing as freelance journalists, but here the motivation IS NOT money but maximum media coverage.

8. At this point any media who call the Police will be able to confirm that someone has been arrested for driving down a busy street in the city whilst blindfolded.

9. You will probably get a fine off the Police, however you may get away with just a caution as once your in the Police station your defence is that **YOU WERE NOT DRIVING DANGEROUSLY** as you could see perfectly well! You could then agree to show them how you can see through the blindfolds if they agree not to tell the press how it was done!

10. If they agree then show them how its done and you may get away with a caution, if they don't agree demand that the matter goes to court, pointing out that this will bring you even more media publicity and make them look stupid in court as you will prove you could see perfectly well and as such were not driving dangerously.

11. Needless to say if the matter went to court all the media would be alerted that the Psychic who drove blindfolded through the city was to be in court that day and of course they would attend court to follow the story which gets you even more publicity.

12. In court you would point out that it IS NOT ILLEGAL to drive whilst wearing dark sunglasses just so long as you can still see the road and therefore it should not be illegal for you to drive blindfolded if you can still see the road and as such drive safely.

13. You as your defence in court would then be blindfolded by the prosecution in the same way you were that day and could then proceed to Juggle, walk round obstacles and read a book proving beyond doubt that despite being blindfolded you can still see!

14. Having proved that you can see in these circumstances which are the same as on the day in question I am very confident that if the case ever did get to court in the first place you would be released without charge, however don't take my advice on this – seek LEGAL ADVICE FIRST!

15. Were you to be charged a fine could be paid easily by the money generated from the media coverage, OK you might lose your driving license, but once you're a household name which a stunt such as this could make you paying a driver would be easy and with such Press Coverage as this type of court case would have any form of custody would be near impossible as in court you have proven that you could see (without giving away secret) and as such are far more likely to be charged with wasting police time.

16. ***THE BOTTOM LINE IS THAT YOU'D GAIN MILLIONS OF POUNDS WORTH OF PUBLICITY AND CAPTURE THE PUBLICS IMAGINATION MAKING YOU A TRUE HOUSEHOLD NAME!***

However as I say anyone using the contents of this manual does so at their own risk and I shall not be held responsible for any potential repercussions occurring as a result of anyone using any of the stunts or routines as suggested by me in this manual as they are supplied for information purposes only.

However I can say in all honesty that a stunt such as this leading to a High Profile court case which you would probably win WOULD MAKE YOU A HOUSEHOLD NAME!

Well let me get that right it would set the ball rolling to a string of TV/Radio, Newspaper and Magazine interviews and it would then be down to you to do things of an even more impressive nature such as **"BENDING FORK"** and the **"Audio Tape Headline Prediction"** in order to concrete your new found reputation as the Worlds Leading Psychic into the publics mind.

INTERNET = SUCCESS

In my opinion anyone setting up in business with the aim of becoming a successful Psychic Entertainer would be committing commercial suicide if they did not have their own site on the Internet.

My Internet sites can be visited at *www.hypnotorious.co.uk* and *www.hypnotorious.com* and should give you a good idea of the kind of site I use to achieve my web presence.

Take my word and personal experience for it when I say that more and more these days TV/Radio Show Producers and also Newspaper/Magazine Journalists are using the Internet as a research tool!

Employ the services of a good professional website design company and not only will they design your site, but they will also promote it to all the Internet search engines, which in turn will ensure that thousands of people get to see your site on a weekly basis.

Indeed potentially your site is available 24hrs a day, seven days a week, 365 days a year by anyone with access to the Internet in any location of the world.

Not only will your site prove invaluable in promoting your Live Psychic shows and personal one to one readings, but also it will help you to sell your mail order products/services by the truckload – visit my site of *www.hypnotorious.com* and look at the "New Products" & "Videos Courses" pages which will show you how I use the Internet to make money from mail order sales.

Once your Internet site has been designed and is on line you can then use it in many ways some examples of which are as follows:

1. Advertise your website and its contents FREE on the 100's of newsgroups, message boards, free advertising sites and special interest forums and this will help increase the traffic (visitors) to your site. Obviously the more visitors that your site gets the more likely it is that someone will then book your services. Think of your site as being like your shop window, it needs to look good and people need to know it exists before they can buy anything from inside.

2. You can send e-mails to the numerous entertainment's agencies listed on sites such as *www.entsweb.co.uk* informing them briefly of your UNIQUE services and inviting them to visit your Internet site which then does the sales pitch for you!

3. You can send e-mail style Press Releases to the TV/Radio, Newspaper and Magazine journalists listed on sites such as *www.ukmedia.com* or *www.mediauk.com* enticing them to visit your site which should speak for itself as you are THE WORLDS ONLY – Navel Psychic, Pawologist or whatever your current publicity ploy is!

4. You can contact people with similar sites to yours, although obviously not of direct competition and exchange links with them. This means that in exchange for you advertising their site on the links page of yours they will do the same on their site and thus send web surfers to you! Visit the links page on my site of *www.hypnotorious.com* and you will see what I mean.

Please do not underestimate the power of the Internet, used correctly it can make you a Millionaire from Merchandising and that's good as all the Bizarre talents I've detailed in this manual have Mail Order sales potential built into them!

My web page has led to numerous TV/Radio, Newspaper and Magazine Interviews, not to mention lucrative Live shows in destinations such as Bahrain – Thailand – Tenerife - Barbados – Greece – Ibiza – Benidorm & Ireland amongst numerous others.

The point I'm trying to make is that in today's modern age having a web page is essential in the quest for fame!

Another advantage is that when shows have been booked by clients in foreign countries they can visit your site and download your show posters, advertising flyers and photos that they can then instantly print out and start using at their end to promote your show.

This saves both time and money in sending things to them by airmail, you can also have your promotional video available for viewing on your site, which is something I'm working on at this time

IGNORE THE WEB AND YOU ARE STUPID!

CHAPTER TWELVE

FURTHER SECRETS & IDEAS

In this final section of my manual "The Bizarre Paranormal World of Jonathan Royle I shall be revealing to you secrets of some of the routines I use in my Psychic shows and some other useful ideas and information which will make your quest for Psychic fame all that much easier!

E-Z WAY TO ASTROLOGY

By far the easiest way to learn to do Astrological readings of people is as follows:

- ❖ Write down each of the twelve star signs.

- ❖ Next to these write down to each of the twelve signs the name of a family member or close friend or at worst work colleague who has that particular starsign.

- ❖ Remember which person relates to which starsign and vice versa and then your job of learning basic Astrology is done!

When you are doing readings and find out what the persons starsign is, you quite simply recall which friend or family member you know has that same star sign and then proceed to reel off information about them.

In other words as you know your friend or family member inside out, their personality, their bad habits, and their likes/dislikes etc and they have the SAME STARSIGN as the person now sat in front of you, they should therefore have much in common!

I've been using this simple technique for years and have found through personal experience that by describing the character traits, personality, likes/dislikes and bad habits etc of the person you know well with the same sign as your client you will be 99% correct almost 100% of the time!

Obviously you reveal this information to the client sat in front of you as if it is your expertise of Astrology that leads you to say this about them and certainly you do not mention the connection to family/friends!

Learn Astrology this way and you'll be giving simple starsign readings in less than an hour!

PICTURE TRANSMISION

EFFECT

Two Volunteers from the audience are invited up on stage and are seated so that they are a good distance away from each other with one volunteer seated on either side of the stage.

They are each given a large drawing pad and a marker pen and you then explain that one of them is the Psychic Transmitter who will draw a simple picture on their pad when you ask them to and that the other person is the receiver and will start drawing the first thing that comes into their head at the same time.

You ask both spectators to open their drawing pads and then you say "On the count of three I want you both to start drawing at the same time, transmitter you will draw and project as I've instructed and receiver you will draw the first thing which comes into your head!"

You then count to three and both spectators start drawing, the amazing part is that when both pictures are compared both of them have drawn pictures of EXACTLY THE SAME THING.

Thought transmission and reception has been achieved!

EXPLANATION

Firstly you need to buy two large drawing pads, the type that are spiral bound at the top end.

Open the cover and using a razor blade or art knife score the paper so that it can later be torn out of the pad easily at this dotted line, leaving any paper above the dotted line still inside the pad.

When both pads are prepared in this manner you next write on the top of the pages you have just prepared the phrase:

"TRANSMITTER – PLEASE DRAW A HOUSE!"

This must be on the paper ABOVE the scored line as then it will remain inside the pad when the sheet below it is ripped out later in the routine and nobody in the audience will be any the wiser about the written instruction from you to the volunteers!

Both pads are prepared in exactly the same way and then your ready for performance time.

Both spectators are brought on stage and seated a fair distance apart so as to imply a scientific test conditions experiment is about to take place.

You then proceed as follows:

"On the left hand side of the stage we have a wonderful female volunteer called (their name) and on the right hand side a male named (their name)"

"Could you please just both confirm that you have never met me before?" (they reply that this is correct)

"Could you also confirm that you have never met each other before?" (Again they reply that this is true)

"And finally could you confirm that nothing has been prearranged this evening and that you have no idea what we are about to attempt?" (Again answer will be that this is true)

"Well Ladies and Gentlemen you see before you on stage two wonderful people from the audience who are about to take part in an experiment of telepathy!"

"In a few moments I shall give you both a drawing pad and a marker pen and on the count of three, then and only then I want you to open your pad, Look clearly at the page before you and the moment you get the urge start drawing a simple object onto the pad!"

"One of you will be the transmitter and the other the receiver, so transmitter I want to project what you are drawing from your mind to the other volunteers mind at the same time as you draw it!"

"And receiver you will just notice that an image will jump into your mind and its this image you will start drawing, hopefully it will be the same as that being projected towards you!"

"OK open your pads and stare at the blank page before you (This makes them both notice the bit which says Transmitter – Please Draw A House) getting ready to draw on the count of three"

"1,2, and on 3 start drawing – that's right transmitter project your picture as clearly as you can and receiver draw whatever it is the mental commands are instructing you to!"

"OK put the final few touches to your SIMPLE drawing and then please tear the page you have just drawn on out of the pad below the easy to rip dotted line!"

Up to here your wording has been such that neither the audience or on stage volunteers are sure who is the receiver and who is transmitter and that's the way you want it to be.

When the spectators open their pads and see the instructions "Transmitter – Please Draw A House" they believe that this is telling them they are the transmitter and that they have to draw and transmit a house to the other spectator.

They assume the other spectator has instructions telling them they are the receiver, however as we know they both are led to believe they are transmitters and so they both end up drawing a house.

Then they are told to remove the pages from the pads below the dotted easy to tear lines, this means that when the pictures are shown to the audience as matching, the written instructions from you will not be seen as they are still inside the pad.

From the moment the pictures have been removed from the pad you can start referring to the spectators on stage in such a way that you refer to the female as being the transmitter and the male being the receiver.

The two on stage volunteers will assume this is just a slight error or mix up on your part and so say nothing, and the audience believe that these were the peoples jobs and so in the context the test has been presented find it amazing that the receiver has managed to draw the same picture as was being transmitted to him!

The whole secret of this is to phrase things and present things in such a manner that everybody assumes certain things are happening in certain ways or that certain people have very different parts to play in the experiment.

The truth being that they both have exactly the same role to play which is why they end up drawing exactly the same picture.

The audience are all amazed by this and even the two on stage people are amazed both of them thinking that the person opposite them has managed to read their mind!

This effect can psychologically be made even stronger by having the drawing pads removed from the plastic carrier bag which the Theatre Manager brought on stage during the "Base Chakra Projects the Answer" routine as detailed in the Navels section of this manual.

This makes the audience automatically assume and believe that you have never seen, touched or tampered with the two drawing pads which apparently you have just touched for the first time when removing them from the plastic bag!

E-Z MAGAZINE TEST

EFFECT

Two on stage volunteers remove two magazines purchased for you before the show by the Theatre manager from the plastic carrier bag, which they came in.

You now face the audience whilst the two spectators are seated BEHIND you in such a manner that YOU CANNOT see them at all and all they can see is your back.

You tell the two spectators to open their magazines onto any page of their own free choice, which they then do!

You next ask them to write down any word they see on either of the two pages before them onto the sketchpad they have which they just used for the Transmitter/Receiver routine!

You say "Can you just pick only one word from the magazine and write it onto your sketch pad – yes or no?" (They answer yes)

They are then told to fold their pieces of paper into four and to put the magazines back into the plastic bag.

At this point you start feeling the vibes and suddenly tell the female that she was thinking of the word **FASHION,** she then opens her sheet and shows it to the audience as proof that your revelation is correct.

The routine ends with you telling the man he choose the word **GAMBLING** and indeed when he opens his sheet to show the audience it proves that this your second revelation is 100% correct drawing thunderous applause from the audience.

EXPLANATION

Quite simply you have tampered with two magazines, one woman's magazine is tampered so that rather than normal pages each page has been blanked out by you and in the centre of each page is one word only in big letters and that is FASHION!

The same is done with the mans magazine so each page bears one word only and that word is GAMBLING.

This means that wherever they open their respective magazines does not matter as each and every page gives them only one option of picking just one word and of course that is the word you already know.

The man is told to remove the men's lifestyle magazine from the bag and the female told to remove the ladies lifestyle magazine.

As they were removed from the same plastic bag that the theatre manager brought the cards up in for the "Base Chakra Navel Routine" the audience automatically assumes and believes that they were bought for you.

This means that thoughts of you using gimmicked magazines will never enter their head.

A routine such as this may seem too simple as to be effective but with the correct presentation it will amaze the audience, and only two people (those on stage) will ever know how its done.

Incidentally in my experience these people on stage never tell anyone how it was done as you have on stage praised them and made them look clever for projecting and receiving information and for being very intelligent volunteers.

To now tell people how simply it was done would make them look silly and daft to their friends – therefore your secret is safe!

PSYCHIC METAL BENDING MADE EASY

I will now reveal to you some of the easiest methods there are to perform Psychic Metal Bending stunts which look equally as amazing as anything you'll ever see Uri Geller perform.

I'm only going to be giving brief details here, but with a little common sense and a little practice by yourself in front of a mirror of what I reveal you will be Metal Bending in no time!

The bottom line secret of any Metal Bending technique is that you either switch the straight (unbent) item for a duplicate bent item using sleight of hand, giving the impression that this now bent item is the same one you started with.

Or you have tampered with the Key, Fork or Spoon before the show to make it weaker or last but not least you use a method to divert attention, physically bend the borrowed item and them use sleight of hand to make the bend appear apparently visibly in front of their eyes.

Otherwise you are using faked Keys or Cutlery such as the items supplied in the **"BENDING FORK"** set mentioned and recommended earlier in this manual.

In order to be able to bend borrowed Keys, Spoons, Forks & Nails I would recommend that you purchase the books "Gellerism Revealed" by Ben Harris and "Key Bending" by Walker M. Both of these are available from Many Magic Dealers and teach you impromptu ways to bend borrowed objects!

On the subject of Key Bending effects I would advise you to buy "Hell Bent Extra" by Bob Solari which is an excellent effect in which a Key chosen by the spectator bends dramatically.

Also Key bending wise a special device called **"PERFECT KEY BENDER!"** invented by Guy Bavli is available from magic dealers for around $40-00. This gimmick enables you to both bend and then re-straighten borrowed keys in the most amazing ways!

Those serious about learning Metal Bending would also be well advised to purchase The Training DVDS entitled "metal bending" by Patrick Kuffs and also "Psychokinetic Silverware" by Banachek as between these two you will be performing miracles which make Uri Geller look stupid!

The Fork technique I use for Metal Bending is to before the show bend one of the times away from the other three so that when the fork is held with its back to the audience, the bent tine is pointing out towards you.

When this Fork is picked up and shook towards the audience or camera the bent tine is not visible and the fork appears normal in all ways, then as you slow down the speed at which you shake the fork backwards and forwards the bent tine starts to become visible and from the audiences point of view it looks as though the tine is visibly bending away from the others.

This illusion of the tine visibly bending away from the other's can now be made to look even more dramatic by turning the fork sideways on to the audience as you slow down the pace of shaking it even more and visually the illusion is that of the tine bending visibly away from the others!

I first saw this performed in this manner by David Berglas on Channel Fours "Secret Cabaret" show during 1990, however I understand it may be the creation of that genius Mentalist Steve Shaw also known as Banachek.

I then Pick up a spoon and as I rub it the metal of the spoon appears to turn all rubbery, the bowl of the spoon starts to flop over and then the spoon snaps into two separate pieces.

To achieve this the spoon must be prepared before the show, to do this you bend the bowl of the spoon backwards and forwards at its neck and keep on doing this until you hear and see the metal crack slightly which happens just before the neck is about to snap off.

This is something you will have to do a few times until you get the hang of stopping as soon as you see/hear the crack in the neck develop and then bending the neck straight so it still looks like a normal untampered spoon from a short distance.

When it comes to ShowTime the spoon looks from a short distance normal and can be held by its handle in the normal way, however due to the preparation even the slightest pressure on the bowl will make it bend dramatically.

You can then take hold of the spoon by its neck (where the crack is already) and with your free hand bend the bowl back and forth until you feel the bowl snap off completely.

Keep the fact the bowl is now separate from the neck/handle hidden under your fingers, which cover the gap.

You can now allow the bowl to flop forward as if the metal has turned to rubber and then when you release your grip/pressure on the base of the bowl it will fall to the floor as if the metal has at that very second snapped.

Practice this in front of a mirror and very quickly you'll learn how to make it look like you pick up a normal spoon, rub it and make it start to bend and then allow it to visibly turn to rubber as It finally snaps into two pieces!

For those already with knowledge of metal bending here's a final thought to set your creative minds off in an entirely new direction.

Colour Photocopiers (laser copiers) make good duplications of coins and keys, which look like they are real metal!

Imagine copying both sides of a coin and then placing one of these copied coin faces on either side of a thin (coin thickness) piece of flat sponge or foam rubber, before finally colouring the edges a natural coin colour.

From a short distance the object would look normal and yet whenever desired could be bent in half visibly giving the effect that a solid metal object had turned to rubber.

You could then use sleight of hand to switch this gimmicked coin for a genuine coin which you have bent in advance enabling you to apparently hand out the coin they have just seen you visibly bend for examination.

Colour laser copies could also be taken of both sides of a key and then stuck either side of a key shaped (and key thickness) piece of foam rubber or sponge and then coloured along the edges in the same way.

Switched for a genuine metal pre-bent key by sleight of hand after the audience has visibly seen you bend the gimmicked key you would have a very powerful key bending effect on your hands.

FINAL THOUGHTS

Well that's it for "The Bizarre Paranormal World of Jonathan Royle" and I am sure that if you use the ideas I've taught you then International Media Fame and Fortune can and will be yours!

For now I wish you the best of luck in your quest and don't forget that Hypnotism & Suggestion are also very powerful techniques for any Psychic Entertainer to understand and have in their toolkit and as such I'd advise you to get my 513 Paged paperback book "Confessions Of A Hypnotist" which is subtitled "Everything You Ever Wanted To Know About Hypnosis but Were Afraid To Ask" – it can be obtained from where you purchased this book and retails at the time of writing this at £19.99 which is around $35.

Considering that it will teach you Everything that you'll ever need to know about Stage Hypnotism and also Hypnotherapy this is a bargain not to be missed as Hypnotherapy tapes can be released for profit and sold under the guise of them being Psychic Mind Power Development Tapes, something which Uri Geller has himself done successfully many times in the past!

CHAPTER THIRTEEN

HYPNO-TRICKS

(SECRETS OF PSEUDO HYPNOTIC STUNTS)

Within this Chapter I will teach you many Fake Hypnotic Stunts which with just a little thought and imagination on your part can be presented as demonstrations of your Psychic Mind Control Powers.

In short if you ask a volunteer to co-operate and close their eyes and then you say something such as "In order for this to work you must keep your eyes tightly closed at all times unless I say otherwise!" then as they will want things to work they will play along.

However as you combine saying this with running your hand over their face in a Hypnotic manner, the audience perceives this as if you have placed the volunteer into some kind of Instant Hypnotic Trance.

Then when the volunteer returns to the audience and is told what they have just done, they too will be as amazed as the audience as they will have no idea how they were able to have needles thrust through their body with no pain or be supported across the backs of two chairs as concrete blocks are smashed across their chests!

The key secret is that your patter should always sound like that a genuine Stage-Hypnotist would use as then the audience will come to believe that you are a genuine Hypnotist and that the things you are doing are a result of you having placed your volunteers into some kind of Instant Hypnotic Trance!

Most of these demonstrations can be performed anywhere, anyplace, anytime and as they can be performed on anybody, including the world's biggest sceptic they are ideal for challenge situations.

Best of all as they use no genuine Hypnosis, you can advertise yourself as a "Mind Magician" and avoid the need of applying for any form of Council Permission to perform your shows!

By changing the patter just a little, these demonstrations can also be presented as experiments in Psychic Mind Energy or whatever other names you wish to call them!

So let's get started with one of my favourite experiments entitled:

WEAK ARM – STRONG ARM TEST

EFFECT

Volunteer one clenches their right fist and then with their fist in this closed position places their right arm outstretched straight in front of them.

They are told to close their eyes and imagine clearly a time in their life when they felt very weak unloved & unwanted.

They are told to now notice how weak, how drained and how NEGATIVE this makes them feel.

"Feeling weak, drained and negative from the tips of your toes to the tips of your fingers!"

You tell them to TRY to keep their arm straight out in front of them as they allow these NEGATIVE emotions and feelings to flood their entire body from tip to toe.

Then you count to three: - 1,2, and on 3 you cue a 2nd volunteer upon the stage to push down the first persons right arm which they find they are able to do with the greatest of ease.

It is explained to the audience that under normal circumstances the 1st volunteer would have been able to keep his arm much stiffer, much straighter and out in front of him for much longer despite volunteer number two pushing down on his arm.

It is explained that this demonstrates how Negative emotions in our minds can lead to Negative effects in our bodies and as a consequence often lead to unnecessary illnesses and disease.

The good news however, is that by using a form of treatment such as Hypnotherapy we can remove all negative emotions from our bodies and therefore end up with a far more healthy life.

To demonstrate this you have Volunteer number 1 close their eyes once again and have them imagine the warmth represented by the colour Orange that is now flooding into their body.

They are told that just so long as they see the colour Orange clearly that in a few moments time something which was just a few moments ago so difficult will now become so ridiculously easy to achieve.

They are told to notice the inner strength they now feel which is making each and every muscle group in their body from the tips of their toes to the tips of their fingers STRONGER than they have ever been before.

Volunteer number one is then told to resume the same position as before with their right fist clenched and their right arm held outstretched straight in front of them.

Volunteer number two is then told "OK on the count of three just TRY to push his arm down and notice how difficult it is for you and how much STRONGER he has become, 1, 2, 3, That's it just TRY to push down his arm.

Volunteer number two is allowed to continue TRYING for a few seconds or so and then is told to relax. Then volunteer one is told to relax also and take their new-found strength with them.

When asked volunteer one WILL SAY how weak he felt the first time and indeed how much stronger he felt the second time around.

Volunteer two when asked will genuinely comment how much more difficult she found it to get his arm to budge the second time around.

EXPLANATION

Everything is done and carried out 100% exactly as I have just explained, with only a few points being of particular relevance as follows:

The first time around volunteer one has to hold their arm out in front of them from the very start of the demonstration and so it is little wonder that their arm is tired by the time volunteer two comes to push it down.

Also the first time around the psychological effect of thinking of negative things will genuinely make volunteer one feel weaker – its quite simply a simple form of SELF-HYPNOSIS which makes this work without fail with any willing & co-operative subject.

The suggestion of "TRY to keep your arm out straight in front of you!" suggests by that single word TRY that they will be unable to do so!

This is a technique known in Hypnosis as "The Law of Reversed Effort" which states that the harder they TRY to do something the less success they will have!

And finally with reference to the first time round where volunteer one is made to feel weak, because you cue volunteer two to push their arm down on the count of three without person one hearing you it will then come as a shock when it happens!

Because volunteer one does not know when his arm will be pushed down or indeed expect it to happen at all, it will be a complete surprise to him when this happens, he will be caught off-guard and will not have chance to tense up his by now already very tired arm.

The moment this first demonstration is done both volunteers are told to relax as normal. This gives volunteer one time to rest his arm ready for the second time!

This time volunteer one stands with his arms by his side and eyes closed as you tell him to think of the positive times in his life when he felt STRONG, confident and on top of the world.

He is told to notice that as he clearly sees these things in his minds eye so at the same time he starts to feel STRONGER in each and every muscle group from the tips of his toes to the tips of his fingers.

You then start to explain to the audience that its time to make volunteer one much stronger and healthier by the power of Hypnosis and you go into your Mumbo Jumbo at this point!

The moment volunteer one has started to visualise the colour Orange clearly in their mind, then and only then you get them to resume their original position of having their right arm straight out in front of themselves with the fist clenched.

Volunteer one is told "Notice how much stronger you feel, notice how much stronger you are and how much stronger you have become!"

Volunteer two is then told "On the count of three I want you to TRY and push his arm down as you did before, except this time notice how much harder it becomes for you to achieve this."

Then you count 1,2, and on 3 – Just TRY to push down his hand, that's it Just TRY, TRY (continue like this for a few seconds and then say) And now everyone just relax once again.

This time volunteer one has been warned when the pushing will begin and has time to tense their arm, also this second time around it is upon volunteer two that the Law of Reversed effort is used by suggesting to her to TRY and push down his hand.

SUMMING-UP

Do exactly what I have just explained in exactly the way I have said to do it and this demonstration will work EVERY time. Yes the levels of success will vary, but in general 9 times out of ten the visual difference will be VERY DRAMATIC!

And in the other 10% of cases it will still be visual enough to show that "Hypnosis" has indeed made the man stronger the second time around.

This works due to a combination of The Law of Reversed Effort (TRY), the verbal suggestions given to them and the things they think of (self-hypnosis), and the fact that second time around the man (volunteer one) has prior warning of when the woman (volunteer two) will TRY to push down his arm.

He has of course also had a minute or two to rest his arm between tests and this time only places his arm outstretched in front of him at the last second, thus not giving it time to get tired as in the first instance.

This may not sound very impressive when described like this on paper, but visually its very dramatic and makes for a good TV or Stage Show demonstration which both the audience and those whom participate in the experiment will find AMAZING!

BUCKET OF ICE TEST

EFFECT

It is explained to a volunteer seated on stage, that in a few moments time their right arm will be placed into the fish tank next to them which is full of Cold Water and Ice.

They are told to remove their hand from the Iced Water the very second that they feel it is too cold or painful to keep their hand in it any longer.

They are told to close their eyes and you then lift up their arm and place it into the tank of Iced Water without warning.

From the second their hand enters the Water until the very second they remove their hand is timed by a stopwatch which is held and operated by a 2nd Volunteer from the audience.

The time is noted and Volunteer one is told how long they managed to keep their arm under water before the "Hypnosis" begins.

Volunteer One is told to close their eyes and relax as you start the Psychic Mumbo Jumbo.

You suggest to them that "In a few moments time when and only when I count to 3, then and only then I will place your right arm into the water tank beside you."

"This time you will notice that from the very second your hand enters the water you WILL FEEL calm, relaxed and confident in every way!"

"You will notice that something you once thought would be so difficult now becomes so ridiculously easy and you will feel NO DISCOMFORT whatsoever!"

Then you go into the think of the colour Orange Blurb and feel the warmth Patter mentioning to the volunteer that:

"Just so long as you keep seeing the Colour Orange brightly in your minds eye whilst feeling that warmth flooding your entire body YOU WILL FEEL NO DISCOMFORT whatsoever and will be able to keep your hand in the tank for much longer with the greatest of EASE!"

1. Relaxed, Calm & confident.
2. feeling warm & strong inside and on
3 Just notice how, unlike last time you feel no discomfort whatsoever.
   (As you count three you place their hand back into the water)

At this point Volunteer number two starts the stopwatch and prepares to stop it the very second that volunteer number one removes their hand from the water again.

The times are compared and it is noticed with much amazement from both those involved and the audience that She was able to keep her hand under water for CONSIDERABLY longer the 2nd time around!

She is given a towel to dry her arm and returned to the audience to thunderous applause.

EXPLANATION

Basically if you do exactly what I have explained in the way I have explained it, and say what I have said in the way that I said it then this WILL WORK with great success for you.

The volunteer hypnotises themselves through their belief that "Hypnosis" will work, as don't forget you asked only for volunteers who were willing & co-operate whilst having very good powers of Intelligence, Imagination and Concentration.

Your suggestions to them as detailed in the "effect" section are worded such as to Hypnotise them further into the belief that this will work.

The fact they have had their hand under the cold water once means that the second time around it is not so much a shock to their system and this alone will allow them to keep their arm under for longer than before.

Also second time around the idea of pain is NEVER allowed to enter their head. You see first time around they are told "Remove your hand from the water the very second it becomes too PAINFUL to keep it there!"

This suggests to them it will be painful and with this in their mind it won't be many seconds before they remove their hand from the water.

However second time around the word pain is NEVER ever mentioned and instead they are told to notice HOW LITTLE DISCOMFORT they will feel and how much easier it will be this time.

Lastly the fact they know how many seconds they kept their hand under first time around will usually make them determined to beat this second time around and in a focused state of mind such as this – SUCCESS WILL BE ACHIEVED.

For this experiment I find it works better if the volunteer with the stopwatch is a male whilst a female is used to place her hand into the water tank!

The tank by the way is nothing more than a reasonable sized fish tank, which is filled with 50% cold water, and 50% Ice cubes!

Incidentally it's a proven scientific/medical fact that women have a higher pain threshold than men and that's another reason why I use a woman for this "Bucket of Ice" test.

PSYCHIC STRONGMAN TEST

As a demonstration of "Hypnosis" this experiment has been used by me on countless Television shows, and indeed this test is so good that it has been used by top psychic performer Uri Geller on many of his world-wide TV shows to date, although obviously Uri didn't present it as "Hypnosis" as we will do!

EFFECT

A large volunteer is seated on a stool/chair and four other volunteers are asked onto the stage to participate.

The man on the chair is told to sit upright with his hands on his lap, whilst the four other volunteers are told to interlock the fingers of both hands so that the fingers of the left hand are against the back of their right hand and vice versa.

With their hands interlocked in this position they are then instructed to place their two Forefingers so that they point outwards with their fingertips away from their interlocked hands.

With their hands like this two people are told to place their outstretched forefingers underneath the seated volunteers armpits (one under his left armpit and one under his right).

And the other two volunteers are told to place their outstretched forefingers under the seated mans kneecap area, again one under the left side and one under the right.

On the count of 3 they are all told to TRY and lift the seated man as high as they can noticing as they do how difficult this is to achieve. 1,2,3 – OK just TRY.

They attempt to do this either with no or very little success, which demonstrates how hard the following test, will be to achieve.

The four volunteers who are stood up all overlap their hands in the air so they go, right, right, right, right, left, left, left, left in order so all four people now have their right hands on top of each other in the pile and then their left hands above these!

At this point you instruct each of the volunteers to close their eyes and get them to concentrate on the Orange Colour and the warm feeling for a few seconds.

As you do this it is suggested to them all that "In a few moments time we are going to lift this man again and this time something you once thought would be so difficult WILL become so ridiculously easy!"

"Just so long as you think of the colour Orange at all times you will find that he becomes as light as a feather and that you become as strong as an Ox!"

"On the count of three I want you to all open your eyes, remove your hands from the pile and put your hands back together as they were before so that your fingers are interlocked onto the backs of your hands with only your Forefingers pointing outwards away from you.

Then immediately resume your positions as before, so your fingertips are under the mans armpits and kneecaps as you had them before and then the very second I shout NOW – that very second YOU WILL LIFT HIM UP with the greatest of ease.

1 – Confident, Calm & relaxed, 2- Strong as an Ox and on 3 Resume your positions this very second. (Allow them all to do so and then say) NOW – Lift him up – higher and higher and higher!

This happens and yes the man is almost thrown through the roof the second time to everyone's amazement, before being returned to his chair.

EXPLANATION

Don't even ask me to explain why this works – but believe me it does! I can honestly say that I've been using this test both on TV and Live Stage shows for a number of years now and it has NEVER gone wrong.

Admittedly the patter I use is worded following the rules of NLP and as such actually does have a positive psychological effect on the volunteers.

However even if you carry out this test without using the patter I've suggested then, as you will find for yourself, this test will still work!

The most bizarre thing about this test is that at the end the seated person will swear that they actually felt themselves get lighter, whilst the four other volunteers will swear they felt themselves get much stronger.

Don't underestimate the visual & psychological impact this test has on an audience as I have always found it to be an excellent applause puller, which is long remembered by the crowd!

THE HUMAN PLANK TEST – (FULL BODY CATALEPSY)

EFFECT

A tall volunteer is apparently placed into an Instant Hypnotic Trance and after you have given him a few simple suggestions his body becomes as stiff and rigid as an Iron Bar!

To prove this fact to the audience you place the mans rigid body across the backs of two chairs so that his neck is balanced on the back of one and his ankles are balanced on the back of the other.

Then when the applause has died down, you sit on his unsupported midriff and lift your legs into the air to prove how rigid his body has become!

Then you can stand on a chair and then step onto the centre area of his body and stand on him/her, so that your entire weight is supported by their now stiff rigid body!

Should the occasion be right you could even balance a concrete block on their chest area and then smash it up with a sledge hammer, whilst to everyone's amazement, the volunteers body remains stiff and rigid!

Or you could even place a plank of wood onto their chest and a heavy anvil onto this, which can then be hit repeatedly in time to the music by you and another volunteer, proving beyond doubt by way of your "Anvil Chorus" that the spectator is Hypnotised and is indeed as stiff as an Iron Bar.

My Hypnotic tutor Delavar, even went to the extremes once, by having an Elephant place its front feet onto the volunteers chest whilst they were supported across the backs of two chairs!

I'm sure you can see what I meant now, when I stated that this is by far the most impressive demonstration of apparent Hypnosis that you could ever present and yet it uses no actual Hypnosis whatsoever!

EXPLANATION

A fairly tall volunteer is used as visually this looks more impressive when they are placed onto the backs of the chairs, however other than this, the only other important point is that the volunteer whether male or female must be wearing trousers of some kind.

It would also be wise to ask for a volunteer who does not suffer from back problems or have any other potentially serious health problem, this both makes the demonstration look even more dangerous in the audiences eyes, but also it ensures that you end up with a fairly fit and healthy volunteer.

Firstly I ask the volunteer to lie down on the stage so they are laid down outstretched on their back.

I then position the two chairs in front of the laid down volunteer so that the back of one chair comes in line with the area just above their ankles and the other is in line with the area just below the shoulder blades.

Incidentally the chairs are positioned so that the backs of them are facing inwards towards each other and the seats are pointing outwards, so that someone can still place their body weight on the chairs in order to stop them falling over.

Two volunteers are now positioned one in front of each chair so that they can stand with one foot on the stage and one foot on the chair seat so that their body weight stops the chairs from falling over.

The volunteer is then asked to stand up and asked to close his eyes as you say:

"Just close your eyes NOW and just so long as you keep your eyes tightly closed at all times, then you will find that you feel no discomfort whatsoever and that in a few moments time you will have become the world's strongest man!"

At this point I let the theme from Superman start playing as it hypes the audience and on stage volunteers up even more as I tell the volunteer off mike (so that the audience cannot hear) that they should put their hands down by their sides and grab tight hold of their trousers on the area just below their bum and keep a tight hold of this area on both sides at all times, then on the microphone so I can be heard I say:

"That's it Sir, Feet together, Hands down by your sides and just so long as you keep firmly in this position at all times, then from this moment forward keeping your eyes tightly closed at all times you will realise that each and every muscle in your body from the tips of your toes to the tips of your fingers is becoming stiff rigid, locked, glued, welded and cemented in place so that its almost as if your entire body is now like a solid Iron Bar!"

"Because you now realise that you are Superman himself, the worlds strongest man and from this moment forward just so long as you keep tight hold at all times and just so long as your eyes remain tightly closed, then you will feel no discomfort whatsoever as you are the world's strongest man!"

"OK 3,2,1 and just let yourself fall gently backwards into my arms as you remain stiff rigid, holding tight at all times, eyes remaining closed at all times, you are the worlds strongest man!"

As this last sentence is spoken, I stand behind the person and gently pull them backwards towards me so that I can then place my arms so that they go, one under each of the volunteers armpits, enabling me to lift them up easily from that end, whilst I instruct another of the onstage volunteers to lift the person up by their ankles and help me position them on the backs of the chairs.

This part of the operation should prove fairly simple as you have already positioned the chairs correctly in advance, so it should prove simple to balance the volunteer on the two chair backs, so that at one end they are supported just under the shoulder blade area and at the other end they are supported just above their ankles.

From an audience point of view this looks very much like the person is supported by their neck and ankles, and although this is not actually the case, it is how 99% of your audience members will recall things after the event!

Once the volunteer is in this position I simply say:

"Ladies and Gentlemen the world's strongest man!" and then I pause as this acts as an applause cue which gets the audience clapping.

The moment they do stop clapping, I tap the volunteer on the underside of his back, in effect pushing his body upwards as I say:

"Stiff, stiffer, stiffer still, just like an Iron Bar, just so long as you keep tight hold and keep your eyes tightly closed at all times!"

I then sit down on the volunteer, so that I am sat with my bum on their upper leg area as close to their groin as possible as this allows for even weight distribution to occur, and as I lift my feet off the ground, I stretch my arms out and say loudly:

"Ladies and Gentlemen The Power of the Mind!"

This usually acts as a cue for the audience to applaud and the moment they stop clapping I get off the volunteer and move behind them so that I can now stand onto another chair and then stand on top of the volunteers body.

I position myself so that when I stand on them, my right foot goes onto the area just above the volunteers Knees and my left foot is placed onto their chest (not their stomach) so that my weight is evenly distributed across them.

At this point I extend my arms and say:

"Ladies and Gentlemen (pause) HYPNOSIS!"

And again this acts as another applause cue, and because this for some reason is perceived as being more impressive than sitting on them, it will draw even more applause.

147

I then get off them and with the help of the other onstage volunteer, I get hold of the top area of their body, whilst the other person gets their ankle area and I say:

"On the count of three lets lift him up off the chairs and lay him gently on the floor, 1,2, and on 3 just lift!"

Once the volunteer has been laid down on the floor I quickly say:

"Eyes remaining tightly closed at all times until I say otherwise!"

I then say thanks you to all the other onstage volunteers and send them back to the audience to a round of applause and then there is just me and the Superman volunteer left on stage!

At this point I go up to them place my hand on their shoulder and say:

"I'm only talking to you if I am touching you on the shoulder, in a few moments time when I count to three, then and only then, your eyes will open, normal feelings will return to all areas of your body and you will return to your normal self in every way!"

"So on 1, everything I have suggested to you tonight completely cancelled out in every way, and on two normal feelings returning to every muscle and every area of your body and on 3, wakey, wakey, rise and shine!"

At this point I help the volunteer to stand up and get them to take a bow before returning to the audience to a huge round of applause!

THE SECRET

Quite simply standing feet together, hands by your side, grab tight hold of your trousers at the area just below your bum and then have someone position you across the backs of two chairs as I detailed earlier and you will discover the secret for yourself.

You see once across the chairs, your head tips back over one chair and your feet hang over the other, which both make the centre of your body arch upwards like a cantilever bridge.

Add to this the effect of grabbing tight hold to the area of your trousers just below your bum and this makes your body arch up even more!

Then just so long as you position yourself where I have instructed when sitting or standing on the person, your weight will be distributed across their body and down the backs of the chairs, in exactly the same way as weight is absorbed by a cantilever bridge, all the patter etc is just pure presentation and is what makes the audience perceive this demonstration as genuine Hypnosis, when in truth it is just a clever scientific trick!

A square plank of wood could also be placed around the area that you would sit and onto this can be placed an Anvil as detailed earlier.

The secret of this being, that the Anvil would be made especially for this stunt so that it was no heavier than an average person (8 stone) as then the effect on the volunteer regards to weight is only the same as someone sitting on them.

If you and your assistant both take a metal hammer and take it in turns to swing these down onto the Anvil, it looks very impressive, and if done in time to the music does indeed become a sort of "Anvil Chorus" but the blows are softer than they appear to be and are absorbed by the "Cantilever Bridge effect!"

The concrete block stunt is how the audience perceives it, however the slab is really a brittle and easily broken sandstone or such like, which with a few gentle taps from a sledgehammer will shatter into bits and fall to the floor off the volunteers chest.

And whilst we don't advise it, you could duplicate Delavar's Elephant stunt by enlisting the help of a good Elephant trainer and some specially made chairs.

The chairs would be made of metal so as to be sturdier, but most important of all they would be made at a height, which matched the height that is necessary for the secret of the Elephant stunt to work.

The secret being, that when an Elephant stands on its two back legs, that is where 99% of its body weight is balanced, so when the Elephant apparently rests its front legs on the volunteers body, in actual fact all of its weight is on its back feet and it just looks as if its front feet are resting on the persons chest as the chairs have been made at the correct height for this to be possible!

Just like all of the other routines and stunts in this manual, we take no responsibility whatsoever for anyone trying out what we reveal herein, as we are detailing these secrets for educational and information purposes only, you have been warned!

THE BLOWTORCH STUNT

EFFECT

A male volunteer from the audience is asked to remove his shirt, he then stands upright with his feet slightly apart so that he is firm and steady and then you pass your hand over his face, he closes his eyes and apparently goes into a trance!

You then lift up his right arm and leave it rigid stuck out at the side of him and then do the same with his left arm so that he looks like a human letter T.

A few Hypnotic suggestions are given to him and then you produce a blowtorch and light the flame, which brings gasps from the audience.

To everyone's amazement you then run the large flame of the burning blowtorch over the arms and chest of the Hypnotised volunteer and they feel no pain whatsoever!

They can then be awoken from Trance and take their applause!

EXPLANATION

The truth is that the burning blue flame of a blowtorch would cause instant skin damage and severe burns, however the yellow flame of a blowtorch, will cause no damage if run over the body at an even steady pace so that it does not remain in one spot too long.

Take a lighter and run the yellow part of the flame steadily and evenly over your hand and you will see what I mean.

The blowtorch is therefore gimmicked, so that the airholes are permanently blocked up and so that it can only ever burn with a Yellow flame, which is relatively safe if run over the body in an even steady manner, just like the lighter is run over your own hand!

However to an audience it looks very impressive indeed, the only thing to be careful of is if the volunteer is very hairy, as the flame WILL burn the hairs off their body and if this starts to happen you will have to rub the area you have just been over with the blowtorch with a wet cloth quickly so that it puts out their burning hair before it gets to hot!

I suggest that you experiment on yourself first if you ever intend to use this demonstration and then you will know exactly what I mean.

The rest is just pure presentation to make it look like the person has been hypnotised to feel no pain and suggested patter is as follows:

"Well thank you very much indeed for volunteering Sir, in a few moments time we shall turn you into the world's strongest man!"

You then run your hand over the volunteers eyes as you say:

"And now just close your eyes and just so long as you close your eyes and keep them closed whenever I tell you to, then and only then this will prove to be 100% successful and will cause you no discomfort whatsoever!"

The volunteer because of the way this is worded will close their eyes and the audience perceives this as though you have placed them into some kind of Instant Trance.

Then off microphone (so audience don't hear) you say to the volunteer, "Be a good Sport mate, do as I say and we'll make you a Star!"

150

Then you say on microphone (so audience can hear) as you place your hand on the person's shoulder,

"Keeping your eyes tightly closed at all times unless I say otherwise, in a few moments time when the music begins to play, then and only them you will open your eyes and have an overwhelming desire to remove your shirt as if you were one of the world's greatest male strippers, however the moment you have taken your shirt off you will stop and wonder what the hell you have been doing and the moment I say sleep you will instantly close your eyes again and keep them closed unless I say otherwise!"

You then turn to the audience and say:

"Ladies and Gentlemen, Please welcome, better than the Chippendales, better than Adonis, it's the Wimpendale!"

At this moment the music begins to play such as I'm Too Sexy by Right Said Fred and the volunteer will open his eyes and take his shirt off, which by the audience is perceived that you have turned him into a stripper by Hypnosis!

Then the moment he has taken his shirt off, the music stops and you once again run your hand over his eyes as you say:

"That's brilliant and just close your eyes once again, relax and keep your eyes tightly closed at all times unless I say otherwise!"

Then you lift up his right arm and extend it out at the side of him as you say:

"Just allowing your right arm to remain stiff rigid out stretched at the side of you as you imagine now it's a solid Iron Bar!"

This tells the volunteer to keep his arm there in that position, but is perceived by the audience as if he has no choice but to do it as if he is reacting to a Hypnotic suggestion.

The same thing is then done for his left arm as you say:

"Just allowing your left arm to remain stiff rigid out stretched at the side of you as you imagine now it's a solid Iron Bar!"

and then you say:

"Just so long as you keep your arms in this position, and just so long as you keep your eyes tightly closed at all times then you will feel no discomfort whatsoever!"

151

Then you light the blow torch and run it over his arms and chest in the manner explained before, you continue doing this for around a minute and then turn the blow torch off, face the audience and say:

"Ladies and Gentlemen Mind Over Matter!"

This acts as an applause cue, and as the audience applauds, you tap the volunteer on the shoulder as you say:

"OK now wakey, wakey, *OPEN YOUR EYES!*"

This concrete's the idea that he was in some kind of Trance to start with!

You then simply give the man his shirt back and send him back to the audience to a huge round of applause as you say:

"Ladies and Gentlemen please give our wonderful brave volunteer a huge round of applause as he returns to his seat in the audience!"

THE HUMAN PINCUSHION EXPERIMENT

EFFECT

A volunteer is placed into an Instant trance and then two Hypodermic Needles are removed from their packages and one is pushed through the back of the volunteers hand, whilst the other is pushed through their arm.

The needles are then removed and the volunteer feels no discomfort whatsoever as they are awoken from trance!

EXPLANATION

Quite simply you get someone from the audience who is not scared of needles.

The secret is that the fleshy skin on the back of his hand is pinched by your fingertips of one hand (which he will feel) and then you say:

"Notice now that the area I have just pinched is turning numb and you feel no discomfort whatsoever!"

As you say this the first needle is pushed through this fleshy skin area of the back of their hand just at the point where you have been pinching.

The truth is that the needle being pushed through this fleshy bit of skin is felt far less than the sensation of you pinching the loose, fleshy area of skin in the first place, which is the same area that the needle is pushed through.

Once the needle is through you can let go of the fleshy area and the needle will visually appear to be stuck through more of their hand than actually is.

When you come to remove the needle, you pinch the skin up again between your fingertips and in this position pull the needle out in a steady motion.

The same thing can be done with the fleshy skin area of arm, near the point on the inside of your arm where your elbow bend is and of course this is done in the same way.

The most painful thing the volunteer actually feels is you pinching their skin before the needle is inserted or removed and as they are warned that you are about to pinch their skin this does not bother them.

As their eyes are closed the needle going in and out does not alarm them, and as the needles are sterilised (new ones for each demonstration) there is no health risk involved.

As with many of the secrets revealed in this manual we take no responsibility for your actions but would advise that you try these secrets out on yourself (with a friends help) before ever attempting at your own risk in public.

The perception of the audience is that you have placed them into an Instant Trance (you just ask them to close their eyes as in the blowtorch stunt) and then that you have via Hypnosis anaesthetised their body so that they do not feel the needles going through their body.

The truth is that the needles hurt far less (especially as they are Hypodermic) than the action of you pinching and pulling on their loose skin areas in the first place!

THE ANIMATED ARM EXPERIMENT

EFFECT

A volunteer is chosen at random from the audience and joins you on the stage where they are seated next to you behind a table in full view of the audience.

A second volunteer is also chosen from the audience and seated at the table as a close up independent witness to the proceedings.

The first volunteer is then apparently placed into an instant trance state and their hand is apparently glued to the table by "Hypnotic" suggestion.

In this state with their eyes closed, you seem to control their mind in some way, because as you point at their hand and lift your own arm into the air, at the same time their arm rises into the air in a most uncanny manner!

153

You then pause for a short while in this position and when you then start to move your arm downwards without saying a word, so the volunteer also moves their hand back down to the point where it is once again glued to the table.

The second volunteer is then asked to point their finger at the first volunteers hand and told to say nothing but do the same as you just did when and only when they decide to.

Sure enough despite volunteer number one having his eyes closed, when volunteer two decides to lift his arm into the air, volunteer number one does the same at exactly the same time.

And when volunteer two decides to lower his arm again, amazingly so does volunteer one, even though they cannot possibly see what is going on and nothing has been said to alert them to what is happening.

The first volunteer is then awoken from trance and both people are sent back to the audience to a huge round of applause!

SPECIAL NOTES

The effect of this routine looks the same as the one performed by Top British Mentalist Derren Brown during his Live Shows and also on one of his "Mind Control" TV Specials, however I have decided to include my performance method herein as mine uses absolutely no Hypnotic Trance and indeed the Linguistic wording is different in order to achieve apparently the same effect, without the volunteer needing to be placed into any form of actual Hypnotic Trance.

Should you be able to find a copy for sale on e-bay, then I'd recommend that you purchase at any price a copy of Derren's Excellent book "Pure Effect", but please note it is only the original self-published spiral bound version which contains his own handling and method for the routine which he has entitled "Lift" and as this edition is very rare, it is very hard to find to say the least, however the time and expense will prove well worth your while, as will obtaining any of Derren's other excellent works from his site of *www.derrenbrown.co.uk*.

EXPLANATION

This demonstration must either be performed seated at a table which has a tablecloth draped over it, which reaches to the floor so that nobody can see either yours or volunteer number ones feet, or it can be performed whilst stood up at a bar in a pub, just so long as the Landlord will allow you to go to the staff side of the bar so that once again the viewing public are unable to see either your or volunteer number one's feet!

If the audience could see your feet, this could give the secret of it all away as you will be directing the volunteer on exactly when to lift their arm up or put it back down on the table by pressing down on their foot with your foot to signal that they should lower their arm and by releasing the pressure on their foot to signal that they should lift their arm up into the air.

To apparently place the first volunteer into a trance I simply take hold of their right hand and place it over their face as I say:

"As I move your hands towards you, just let your eyes close, that's it just close your eyes and relax, just so long as you keep your eyes tightly closed at all times then this experiment will have a very good chance of working"

I then remove their hand from their face and lower it to the table as I say:

"And as I lower your arm down and place your hand flat on the table, so you keep your eyes tightly closed at all times and allow yourself to relax completely"

"Don't say a word at any time, just let your eyes remain closed, allow yourself to relax and listen to every suggestion that I give you!"

"Noticing now that pressure *(as you say this your foot presses down on their foot under the table and remains there, whilst on top of the table you are apparently pressing their hand firmly to the tabletop)* as your hand glues itself to the table top and remains there at all times whilst you can still feel this pressure *(as you say "this pressure" your foot presses down firmly on theirs to signal to them in a non-verbal manner that it's the pressure on their foot that you are on about!)* Its almost as though your hand is locked, glued, welded and cemented to the table top at all times whilst you can feel this pressure *(again as you say "this pressure" above the table you are apparently pushing down on their hand to reinforce things, but under the table you are pressing down firmly on their foot again to reinforce the fact that you mean the pressure on their foot!")* and whilst you can feel this pressure *(repeat the foot pressure again under table as you appear to press on hand)* your hand will remain glued to the tabletop at all times, however when and only when you feel this pressure *(repeat the foot pressure as you appear to press on their hand)* disappear, then and only then you will allow your hand to rise up into the air, keeping your eyes tightly closed at all times! Just nod your head if you understand *(when they nod you know they have understood the foot cues)* However you will also notice that whenever this pressure reappears *(again do foot signal as appear to press on their hand)* that then and only then you will allow your hand to lower down back to the table until it is glued back to the table top! Just nod your head if you understand! *(Again when they nod you know they have understood the meaning of the foot cues!)* As I now remove my hand from yours, that pressure *(do foot signal)* remains there and so your hand remains glued to the table top until that pressure *(foot signal again)* disappears!

At this point volunteer one is sat their with their eyes closed as if they have been placed into a trance and they should now be at a point that they realise that whilst your foot is firmly pressing on theirs (as it is at this time) they must keep their hand on the tabletop, however when you remove your foot from theirs so that the pressure is released they must them lift their arm up into the air.

You should be able to work the rest out now from the description I gave you of how things look to the audience, in essence when you point at their hand and lift your arm up, this is the same time as you release the pressure on their foot so that the volunteer lifts up their arm which looks very spooky indeed.

Then when you lower your arm is the same time as you replace your foot onto their foot and press down which signals them to also lower their arm and hand down back to the tabletop.

When volunteer two points at Volunteer one and apparently takes control of them the secret is exactly the same, the moment you see volunteer two move their arm upwards you release the pressure from number ones foot, and the moment you see them move their arm back down you replace the pressure so that volunteer one places their hand back down to the table.

I am sure you now understand why the audience must not be able to see either your foot or volunteer number ones foot at any time, hence the reason for the draped table or standing behind a bar as detailed earlier.

You then simply place your hand on the apparently Hypnotised volunteers shoulder and say:

"When I click my fingers you will then open your eyes, you'll feel your normal self in every way and you will forget to remember and remember to forget everything that has just happened!"

You then simply click your fingers and apparently awaken the subject before sending them both back to the audience as you say something such as:

"Thank you Sir, you've been a wonderful volunteer and enabled us to witness the true power of the mind, you are a very special person indeed and as such an experience is such a special and person one, I trust that you will keep the inner personal details of your experience to yourself!"

This seems innocent enough to the audience, however it's a nice way of telling the volunteer not to tell anyone what has really gone on and by praising their ego in this manner, they will keep things to themselves.

One other important point is to pick two people who don't know each other and who are seated in different areas of the room as that way they are less likely to talk to each other afterwards.

Even if they do though, as volunteer one had his eyes closed all the time, he will have been very disorientated and will not really have a clue what has gone on as his version of events is a totally different one than from an audience perspective.

This is what we in the business call the "Dual Reality" principle!

Try this out as I have stated and I am sure you will find that this gets amazing reactions from your audience and that they find it very spooky indeed!

THE EYE TEST

A wine bottle with a loose fitting cork is placed onto the table, you apparently place a man into trance and awaken him believing that he is drunk, he is told to place his left hand over his left eye and then to extend his right arm in front of him. You count to 3 and tell him to try and push the cork down into the top of the bottle using only one finger and the more he tries the more he keeps missing as he is of course Hypnotically drunk!

The secret of this is that most all people will find it impossible to hit the cork with their extended forefinger when one eye is closed. But when presented like this the audience perceives it as if you have made the person drunk by Hypnosis.

In order to be able to actually do this yourself to show it can be done when you are soba, you must aim for a spot a couple of inches to one side of the cork, give it a try and you will soon see what I mean!

STRONG WOMAN TEST - A

You get a woman to stand and face the audience, get her to raise her two arms straight out to the sides, then ask her to bend her elbows and touch the fingertips of her hands together. In this position you can now get two men, they each grab hold of one of the ladies forearms and try as they might they will be unable to pull the woman's hands apart! This can easily be demonstrated as turning her into the world's strongest women or perhaps as turning the two men into the world's weakest men!

STRONG WOMAN TEST – B

Ask a women to place her hand flat on the top of her head (palm downwards) and to push her palm/hand onto the top of her head with all her might. A man is then told to try and remove her hand from her head by taking hold of her forearm! Again this is practically impossible and can be presented as if the result of Hypnosis!

STRONG WOMAN TEST – C

Get a woman to place her hand under her arm, back of the hand under her armpit and in this position it is also practically impossible for anyone to remove her hand from under her armpit by pulling on her forearm!

DRUNK TEST

Get someone to hold both their hands out in front of them, hand wide apart and ask them to extend both their forefingers. Tell them on the count of three you want them to quickly bring their hand together and push the tips of their fore fingers together. Count to 3 and they will try with no success, however you can do it as you are not "drunk" which is of course what you have apparently suggested to them!

You ca do it because you demonstrate doing it slowly, but when the volunteer tries to put their forefingers together, they will experience great difficulty as they have been asked to do it quickly and due to the fact they are attempting to perform a none too easy action under circumstances that the average person will find unnerving.

HYPNOTIC PULSE STOPPING

A great demonstration for a Pseudo-Hypnotic Act is to apparently stop your own Pulses by the power of self-Hypnosis!

With volunteers holding each of your wrists, so that they can feel your Pulses, first one stops and then the other, then one comes back and then the other in a most spooky manner as you Hypnotise yourself!

The secret is that a small rubber ball is held under each of your armpits, this can be held in position with a strap so that it can remain there throughout the show.

Slight pressure on the rubber ball under your armpit will cause that pulse to stop, therefore done in turn you can make one pulse and then the other stop and then bring them back one by one apparently as a demonstration of self-hypnosis.

The audience member's confirming that your pulses have stopped and then started again!

THE WEAKNESS TEST

Ask a man to clench both his hands into fists and then to place one fist on top of the other. The idea is for him to push them both together (one down on top of the other fist) to stop anyone pushing them apart.

You then apparently make him weak with hypnotic Suggestion and using only the tips of each of your forefingers, you easily push his fists apart! This is simply achieved by snapping one finger of either hand against the back of each of the man's two fists as this will separate them every time!

SUPERHUMAN STRENGTH TEST

Take a female and have her stand upright with both her arms outstretched and then place both her palms flat against a wall. Once in this position have a man stand behind her and place his left arm flat on her left shoulder, try as he might and push as hard as he can, he will be unable to push her against the wall. This looks particularly impressive when you line up a row of say 8 men behind the women all of whom place their left hand flat on the persons left shoulder in front of them. Even with a row of eight people in this position pushing on each other against the woman, they will be unable to push her against the wall. You can present this as either the woman becoming super strong or all of the men becoming weak!

HYPNO-HEAT

In this stunt you apparently remove the foil wrapper from some chewing gum, dampen it against the side of a glass and stick it to someone's forehead as you suggest to them that they are Hypnotised and as such the foil will get red hot, so burning hot that they will have no choice but to remove it from their head and sure enough in the matter of a few seconds this happens to everyone's amusement!

You will need two packs of gum, one cinnamon (use Big Red from Wrigley's) and the other a different flavour of the same make and size!

Open the Big Red gun (Cinnamon) and remove a stick, take the other flavour and wrap one of those sticks up in the foil removed from one of the Big Red (Cinnamon) sticks and then place it into the sleeve of the non Cinnamon flavour packet so that it looks like it is just one of them!

The secret is quite simply that the Cinnamon flavour from the wrapper cause the skin to get hot when it gets wet!

So when you are ready to perform this, remove the gum and offer it to a friend to eat who will for example confirm it tastes like normal mint gum (which indeed it is).

Take the empty wrapper and wet the inside of the aluminium foil on the side, which has the Cinnamon coating (not the shiny side).

The easiest way to do this is rub it on the side of a beer glass, which is damp or has condensation on it.

Then just stick the foil on the volunteers head and from here on its all just acting as in about 40 seconds time their head will feel so hot that they will have to rip the foil off as you are suggesting they will do!

CAN'T WALK STUNT

Tell someone to stand by a wall with their right side facing it and to place their right foot against the wall, with their left foot about 6 to 8 inches away from their right!

You now apparently hypnotise them and tell them all strength has vanished from their legs!

To prove this, the subject is asked to raise his left foot without changing the position of his right foot and indeed he can't!

Then apparently awaken him from trance and ask him to step forward with his left foot, he will then be able to walk back to the audience as normal!

STUCK IN CHAIR

Place someone into a chair, have him or her lean well back, place the tip of your forefinger onto the person's forehead and then tell them to try and stand up. They will be unable to do this, especially if their legs are outstretched in front of them as they sit leaning back in the chair!

GIRL THAT CANNOT BE LIFTED

One minute a man can lift up your skinny female assistant and the next he becomes so weak under Hypnosis that he cannot possibly move her!

The secret is to use a skinny assistant, the girl stands sideways to the audience, her arms tight against her body so they are bent up at the elbows.

Now a man steps behind her and has to lean down to take hold of her elbows to lift her by them, this he does and manages to lift her up and then put her back down.

When you want the man to look weak, your assistant who is working with you and is in on the trick, pushes or sways her body backwards just a bit.

This unknown to the man trying to lift her or the audience, throws him off balance slightly so that he does not have his full lifting power and can no longer lift her.

CAN'T BE LIFTED – VERSION B

Get a big strong man to lift you the performer up by the waist, once he has done this get him to hold you in the same position again, but he is to stare you in the eye as you mentally make him weak by telepathic hypnosis. This time he will be unable to lift you and this is for two reasons, a) He has to keep staring up to look you in the eye and b) As he is trying to lift you, the tips of your forefingers are gently touching both sides of his neck, one side touching his Carotid Artery (very lightly only) and for some reason this stops people being able to lift you up!

BROOMSTICK TEST - ONE

This effect is quite startling as it uses the strength of several people. You can use a broom handle, snooker cue or walking stick to perform this effect. Hold this in your open hands about eight inches in front of the shoulders and the same height as your shoulders, the arms being bent at the elbows.

The portion of the arm (from shoulders to elbows), is against the side of your body. The broom is placed into the performers cupped hands and the palm should be facing the audience.

The Broom handle should be placed between the thumb and palm but **NOT HELD IN PLACE** – One or more people are invited to come forward and push against the broom.

The performer now stands on one foot (right foot is suggested), left foot slightly folded back to aid in your balance.

You now challenge the volunteers to push against the broom so that they try to push you completely off balance.

They may grip the broom in any position they wish (but force must be equally distributed) and push with all their might, however they will not be able to push you off balance.

The broom must be placed on a dead level and held there. You must concentrate on holding the broom in position and you will find that only a tiny amount of resistance is required.

In this position its impossible for any number of spectators to push you off balance and so you can present this as if you've hypnotised them all to become very weak indeed!

There will often be a tendency on the volunteer's part to push the broom upwards or downwards, guard against this, do not allow them to jerk or suddenly push.

Because the Broom handle is on the same level as your shoulders, the volunteers pushing can gain absolutely no leverage to counterbalance the slight muscular effort that you exert against their efforts.

This requires practice but is a mind-blowing demonstration when mastered.

BROOMSTICK TEST – TWO

The performer places the palms against the handle of a broomstick held in a vertical position and requests that any volunteer try to push the broom down onto the floor. This is found impossible to do, as they cannot move it down even an inch, yet the performer apparently only supports the broom with open hands!

The secret is that you take the broomstick, with the handle uppermost, keeping the broom in a vertical position, you face the volunteer, keeping them somewhat to your left.

You extend your right hand, fingers extended along the handle of the broom (nearest floor), allowing the handle of the broom to cross open palm along from base of thumb to about tip of your third finger.

The left hand now takes a position further up the handle on the opposite side of the broom, so that when the hand is open. The fingertips will be about 3 inches above the waist.

The handle of the broom passing over open left palm in a similar position and manner to that of the right hand.

You will now find that with the hands in this position the broom is held firmly as though your fingers were encircling it.

Now instruct the volunteer to grasp the upper part of the handle of the broom and without jerking, but rather with a steady downward pull, to try to move the broom down until it touches the floor.

Make sure the volunteer does no jerk and caution them about twisting or hanging on the broom.

If you have an obviously strong person assisting, be sure to allow the hands to assume a position further apart than the one mentioned, it can sometimes be necessary to allow a distance of 24 inches to successfully offset the effort exerted by a muscular assistant.

No matter how strong they are though, you can always prevent them from putting the broom down to the floor. If you use judgement and experience in placing your hands you will always have the greater power of leverage.

The pressing of the two hands towards each other has a tendency to bring the broom into a position that the downward pressure will be null and void whilst they exert themselves to the utmost.

You are rarely required to use but a small amount of your strength to combat this. Always insist on the spectator keeping his hands close together as the further away his hands are from yours and the closer together his hands are kept, the easier this stunt is to perform.

You'll find all of these Hypno-Tricks along with numerous others demonstrated and explained in full on my Ten DVD Home Study Couse "There's No Such Thing As Hypnosis" which is available from *www.hypnotherapycourse.net*

CHAPTER FOURTEEN

ROYLE'S ULTIMATE MENTALISM ROUTINE?

Every Psychological & psychical ploy, verbal patter lines relevant to its success and of course the methodology of the effects themselves are all explained in great detail.

What follows is a 100% fair and honest description of what takes place and what the audience see, however please note in actual performance the routine is even most impressive than it sounds here, as no words can do justice to the visual and psychological beauty of the routines perfection.

Read on for the most amazing Mentalism routine I've ever had the joy of performing which I Jonathan Royle developed in conjunction with an underground ideas man David Turner and have honed to perfection so that you can slot it directly into your show.

This routine has been honed to perfection and was inspired by a combination of ideas by Max Maven, Ali Bongo, Al Koran, Aldo Colombini, Simon Arrason, Marc Paul and numerous other tops names.

CHAOS – REALITY

EFFECT

In Clear view of the audience the Psychic Entertainer picks up a clear tub containing screwed up balls of paper which he explains there are 18 of which are all blank.

Then he picks up a large writing pad and a black marker pen and is seen to draw a large cross onto the first sheet, which is then torn off, screwed up and added to the box.

This is then repeated with a second sheet, the audience seeing the black cross being drawn onto the sheet and then seeing the cross on the sheet as its screwed up and added to the box of paper balls.

The performer now has a box containing 20 screwed up balls of paper of which the audience know that TWO contain a Large Black Cross on their interior and have been told that the other 18 are blank inside.

After explaining that you will make everything in the next experiment as random as possible, you draw attention to a large envelope which has been in full view of the audience from the start of the show and state that you'll be coming back to that later.

You then throw the contents of the clear plastic container into the audience so that the 20 paper balls fly out amongst the crowd and you tell the audience that whoever is nearest to a paper ball on the floor should pick it up and open the ball to see if there is a black cross inside.

Eighteen people find no crosses and so are told to sit down, however two people find black crosses inside their papers and as such are requested to come and join you on stage.

For the sake of this example we'll say that one of the people is Female and one is male, although obviously the actual outcome would be different at each and every show due to the random nature of selection.

Its is explained that the shows organiser (The Company Boss for example) has in his possession some decks of playing cards which he obtained before the show and has been keeping safe until they were needed.

The Company Boss is introduced on stage and confirms that he got the random selection of decks of cards before the show and has been keeping them safe until they were required now!

He is instructed to place the plastic carrier bag of cards onto the table, take out the receipt, place it in his pocket and take a bow as he leaves the stage to another round of applause.

In this example, lets say that the on stage Male is then handed the plastic bag and told to empty the contents out onto the table discovering that the bag contains several decks of playing cards all of which are of different designs and of different back colours.

The performer asks the volunteer to select a deck of cards again in an apparently chaotic and random manner so that the end result lets say for this example is that a Red Backed Bicycle deck is chosen to be used in the experiment.

The on stage Female is also asked to select any deck of cards by simply picking up whichever deck she wants to use off the table.

The female is then told to remove cellophane from the box, remove the cards from the deck and remove the cellophane from the cards, then hand you the deck which you proceed to shuffle up into a random order before handing them back to her.

She is then instructed to cut the cards several times so that nobody could know what order they are in and told to give out 5 cards to members of the audience which she does at random.

She then returns to the stage and you tell those in audience to look at their cards and just remember the number or letter on the corner of the card as you will attempt to get this correct as you tell them to project this number or letter to you using their third eye, projecting it like a blue beam of light towards the stage as they stand up in front of their seat.

One by one you get the Letters or Numbers correct, each time the person sits down to indicate that the number or letter is correct its another applause cue for the audience.

After the third person you stumble on the fourth and say you'll come back to them later, then of course you get the fifth person correct and they sit down.

You return to the fourth person and tell them to concentrate more clearly and then suddenly you blurt out "I See the Two of Diamonds – It's the Two of Diamonds"

This is confirmed to be correct and because you've finished by getting the suit and also number or letter it heightens the applause even more!

You explain this was just a warm up for the hardest chaotic and most random experiment that you have ever attempted, which is next.

The man is then told to remove the cellophane from his deck and his deck from its case, check they are all different, give them a shuffle and then hand them to the lady on stage who is also to give them a thorough mix up and shuffle.

This happens and then the lady is told to replace the cards into the box and place a strong elastic band around them from top to bottom to stop the cards falling out if they were thrown out into the audience.

When she has done this she is told to toss the cards out to anybody in the audience as again this keeps the Chaos and total randomness theme going.

The person who catches them is told to remove the cards from box and shuffle them so they are in an entirely random order, then they are to replace them in the case and replace the elastic band as it was, before tossing the deck to someone else.

The performer explains this will happen a total of three times in all and when the final of the three randomly selected seated audience members has done his or her mixing the cards are replaced by them into the box, the elastic band replaced and the cards thrown back up to the stage, where they land on the floor and remain for now untouched.

The Man on stage is then told to guard the large envelope prediction with his life and ensure that nobody gets anywhere near it.

The female on stage is now told that she will create the final element of Chaos and Randomness, the box of randomly chosen and randomly shuffled and mixed cards is then picked up, the female positioned on the correct area of the stage and the cards removed from the box and handed to her to hold.

She is instructed to place the cards behind her back out of site and give them one final mix, which she does.

Then you explain that you want her to cut a small section off the deck or in otherwords take about a third of the deck and in a few moments when you count to three, on the count of three she is to immediately bring out the hand holding the approx. third of the deck and throw the cards up into the air letting them fall randomly and visually to the floor.

You count to three and she does this for the first time, this is then repeated a second and third time, until the entire deck is all over the stage, some cards face up and some cards face down.

The female is then told to collect up all the cards which are face up, pick them up from the floor and place them on the table before you, which she does as you recap briefly on the whole randomness and chaos of the selections and situations which have occurred so far.

Once all the cards which landed face up are on the table she is told to look at the cards and think of just one of them, which she does.

THEN WITHOUT ANYTHING BEING WRITTEN DOWN – YOU TELL HER EXACTLY WHICH CARD SHE WAS MERELY THINKING OF AND THE AUDINECE WILL GO MAD WITH APPLAUSE.

The audience think the experiment is over, however there is still much to come....

The Man is then instructed to open the envelope and remove its contents, this he does and finds a second envelope, he is told to do this and he finds a third envelope and finally inside this he finds a large folded prediction which has a smaller envelope paper clipped to it.

You ask for the small envelope to be handed to you, which it is and say you'll come to that later.

The lady is told that the man will read each section of the prediction out one by one and that after reading each section she is to check the cards on the table and confirm to the audience if the prediction is right.

The man reads the prediction and for example it says:

1. **THERE WILL BE A TOTAL OF TWELVE CARDS FACE UP**

2. **ONLY FIVE OF THESE CARDS WILL BE BLACK**

3. **OF THE BLACK CARDS THERE WILL BE THREE SPADES AND TWO WILL BE CLUBS.**

4. **THE REMAINING CARDS WILL BE RED AND CONSIST OF THREE DIAMOND CARDS – AND THE REST WILL BE HEARTS.**

5. **EXCEPT FOR ONE CARD WHICH TONIGHT I FEEL WILL BE A JOKER.**

ALL OF THESE STATEMENTS ARE FOUND TO BE 100% CORRECT

Once again the Audience go wild with applause as you send the Man back to his seat, but tell him to remain standing where he is at his seat in audience so everyone can see him.

When the applause dies down the lady is handed the smaller envelope and asked to tear it open, remove the contents and throw the envelope away, which she does.

She is then told to read out the contents slowly and clearly in a loud voice so all can hear and the man in the audience is told to sit down if the information about him is correct.....the prediction is read and for example it says:

I Jonathan Royle do on this evening of Saturday November 27th 2004 get the feeling as I sit writing this in my Hotel before going to tonight's show, that a strange series of events will happen as follows:

1. A Man Approx. 5ft Ten in Height wearing jeans and a striped jumper will end up assisting me on stage – I also feel the names Trevor and Joanne are linked to this man.

   AT THIS POINT MAN CONFIRMS THIS IS CORRECT AND THAT HIS NAME IS TREVOR AND HIS DAUGHTERS NAME IS JOANNE.

2. His birthday will be August 13th and he will have 2 rings on his fingers.

   THIS AGAIN IS CONFIRMED CORRECT

3. My second assistant will be a Lady and her Birthday will be January 7th

   SHE CONFIRMS IT'S CORRECT

4. My Male assistant will have randomly chosen the Red Backed Bicycle deck of cards and at this point will hopefully sit down as my predictions will have been correct and the audience will give him a round of applause.

HE SITS DOWN AS THEY APPLAUD

5. My second assistant who will now be reading this hopefully correct series of predictions will be highly intelligent, with a great sense of humour, they are a trustworthy, caring individual and I feel I can rely on them to throw the cards randomly into the air so that my earlier predictions will be correct.

THIS OF COURSE IS CORRECT

6. And finally I'm sure I can rely on the audience to give my second volunteer a huge round of applause as they take a bow and make their way back to their seat!

PERFECT APPLAUSE CUE

Thus the routine ends with the second person leaving the stage to thunderous applause, leaving you alone on stage alone.

At this point you ask the Companies Boss to stand up and remove the receipt his has in his pocket and look at the receipt.

You then proceed to reveal details about the receipt you could not know such as the Store Managers Name, Vat Registration number and such like, how much money was handed over and how much change was given, before asking him to take his seat as you say goodnight, take your final applause and milk the crowd for a standing ovation.

Oh and don't forget that in actual performance there are many Physical and Verbal Psychological ploys used which make the routine even more powerful and amazing to watch than any written description of the effect could do it justice!

SO HOW IS IT ALL DONE THEN?

Many of the individual sections which make up this routine have already been explained within the pages of this book and as such you would be well advised to read the following sections again to get a total understanding of how this routine works:

❖ THE BASE CHAKRA PROJECTS THE ANSWER = This is explained in the Navel Mind Reading Chapter of this book.

❖ THE RECEIPT TEST = Again this is explained in The Navel Mind reading chapter of this book.

❖ NAVEL COLD READING = Some Cold Reading can be worked into this routine to make it even more impressive and as such please re-read the Navel Cold Reading Chapter of this book.

❖ E-Z ASTROLOGY = See Chapter Twelve and discover how to easily add simple Astrology readings to this feature length Stage Routine.

AND NOW YOU NEED TO READ THIS:

THE PAPER BALLS WITH BLACK CROSSES FORCE

The original idea of this force was I believe from the mind of Max Maven and was intended for use when for example you wanted to get two spectators onto the stage who you had already done some pre-show work with, but get them on stage in such a manner that it seemed like a totally random choice.

To do this you'd have 18 screwed up balls of paper in a plastic tub and tell the audience it contained 20.

Then you'd toss all the balls out into the audience and ask people stood near one to pick it up and stand up in front of their chair.

At this point as instructed previously your two "stooges" stand up with their paper balls in hand which they have just removed from their pockets during all the confusion.

It is visibly clear to the entire audience that 20 people are stood up with paper balls in hand which ties in with what you said earlier.

You then ask them to unscrew their paper ball and sit down if the paper is blank, but stay standing if they find a black cross.

Needless to say the two spectators you have done pre-show work with have the black crosses and as such they remain standing, appear to have been chosen at random and are then asked to come and join you on stage.

At this point you'd make a statement something like:

"Can you please just confirm that prior to meeting here today, we have never met before?"

They of course will state this is true as prior to meeting in that venue on that day you have never met them before, their answers that this is true give the audience the impression however that nothing has taken place before the show!

You could then continue by saying:

"I want you both to think clearly of an animal, a vegetable and a mineral, are you thinking clearly of these things?"

They of course answer yes and for example these may be the things you got them to write down on a clipboard before the show, more about clipboards and their use in a moment.

You then say:

"And would it be true to say that is impossible for me to know what you are thinking of at this moment?"

Of course they will state that this is correct because as far as they are concerned you don't know what they wrote on the paper which was on the clipboard, which they then removed, folded up and placed in their inside pocket.

To the audience however it again creates the impression that nothing has ever been set up, you've never met or talked to the people before and ultimately makes your revelation of the information obtained from the Carbon Clipboard seem a million times more impressive when presented in this manner.

For a more detailed insight into using clipboards in Psychic Work please re-read the "Pawology" Chapter of this book.

MY ADDITIONS TO PAPER BALLS BLACK CROSS FORCE

Now you know the basic idea behind the paper ball force, you'll need to get an A5 writing pad, an A5 Artists pad and two black marker pens to make use of my additional Psychological ploys.

Remove the lid from one of the marker pens and leave it for a few days to dry out, you don't want the pen to work when its nib is moved over paper, you just want it to look like your drawing a black cross onto the paper.

Next take the writing pad and remove 17 sheets of paper, which are then screwed up into balls and placed into the clear plastic ice-cream tub or similar container.

When it comes to performance time, you will blatantly lie and state that there are 18 blank paper balls in the container, which once the audience have watched you apparently draw two black crosses on paper and add those to the tub concrete's into their mind the idea that the box contains 20 paper balls before you toss them all out into the audience.

Next take the marker pen which works and draw a large black cross onto the top sheet of paper, then remove this sheet from the pad, screw it into a similar sized ball and place this into your pocket as this is the one which you will give to the spectator who you talk to before the show and arrange to be your "instant stooge".

Next draw another large black cross onto the top sheet of the writing pad and finally remove one sheet from the artists pad which is made up of slightly thicker paper and using a thin line of glue stick, fix this page over the black cross page of the writing pad.

The end result should be one whereby the top sheet of the pad is blank and due to the thickness of the paper the black cross on the sheet underneath it does not show through.

When it comes to show time, you casually pick up the pad purposely letting the blank face of the pad be seen by the audience which will register in their minds as being blank without you having to draw attention to it verbally.

You then face the pad so its towards yourself and nobody can see what you are drawing upon it as you pick up the black marker pen which as you may have guessed by now is the one which does not work and has completely dried out.

You then apparently draw a large black cross onto the top sheet of the pad, in truth you make the action of drawing a cross so that your hand movements are consistent with what the audience would expect it to look like and so that the on stage volunteers can hear the nib moving against the paper, which are all psychological ploys which when people try to backtrack will make it next to impossible to work out how the routine was done!

You then tear of the top sheet of the pad and using one hand screw it into a ball and toss it into the container with the other balls.

Next you apparently draw another black cross with the non working pen, and again your actions look correct and they can hear the nib on the paper, which when you put the pen down and turn the pad towards the audience in a casual manner so that they can see the large black cross convinces them 100% that the pen was genuine and embeds into their heads the idea that you drew large black crosses on both sheets of paper.

You then tear off this sheet and screw it into a ball before finally adding it to the tub with the other balls.

At this stage the audience are convinced (including the instant stooge) that the box contains a total of 20 paper balls, two of which they believe they have seen you draw black crosses on and 18 of which you have told them are blank which ties in perfectly with what they are about to witness and come to believe is a totally random and honest selection process.

You toss the paper balls into the audience and tell them that if a paper ball lands near them they are to pick it up and stand up.

You have previously told the "instant stooge" that when people start picking up paper balls is the time he should get the black cross ball from his pocket and pretend to pick it up from the floor before standing up with it in his hand.

The confusion and distraction caused by people picking up the paper balls which were really thrown is more than enough misdirection to cover this deception.

You will then end up with 20 people stood up in front of their chairs which is exactly what the audience expects and as such seems totally fair and random.

You then ask them to unscrew their paper balls and those who have blank sheets are told to sit down which of course 18 of the people then do, as in truth you only threw 19 balls into the audience and 18 of these were blank.

You will now be left with two people stood up, one of whom is your "instant stooge" and one who truly is a completely random selection and its this point which makes the rest of the routine even more mind-blowing and impossible to trace back as one psychological ploy seems to rule out how the next method could ever have been used and so on throughout the routine and that's why when combined together the end result and audience reaction you'll get with this routine is far greater than the sum of its total parts.

These two people are then the ones who are asked to come and join you up on the stage for the next part of the routine in the order it is detailed at the start of this chapter.

THE NEXT SECTION OF THE ROUTINE

Its is explained that the shows organiser (The Company Boss for example) has in his possession some decks of playing cards which he obtained before the show and has been keeping safe until they were needed.

The Company Boss is introduced on stage and confirms that he got the random selection of decks of cards before the show and has been keeping them safe until they were required now!

He is instructed to place the plastic carrier bag of cards onto the table, take out the receipt, place it in his pocket and take a bow as he leaves the stage to another round of applause.

For exact details of how to handle this refer to **"The Base Chakra Projects The Answer"** in the Navel Mind Reading Chapter of this book.

In this example, lets say that the on stage Male is then handed the plastic bag and told to empty the contents out onto the table discovering that the bag contains several decks of playing cards all of which are of different designs and of different back colours.

The performer asks the volunteer to select a deck of cards again in an apparently chaotic and random manner so that the end result lets say for this example is that a Red Backed Bicycle deck is chosen to be used in the experiment.

The on stage Female is also asked to select any deck of cards by simply picking up whichever deck she wants to use off the table or by selecting it out of the carrier bag.

The female is then told to remove cellophane from the box, remove the cards from the deck and remove the cellophane from the cards, then hand you the deck which you proceed to shuffle up into a random order before handing them back to her.

She is then instructed to cut the cards several times so that nobody could know what order they are in and told to give out 5 cards to members of the audience which she does at random.

She then returns to the stage and you tell those in audience to look at their cards and just remember the number or letter on the corner of the card as you will attempt to get this correct as you tell them to project this number or letter to you using their third eye, projecting it like a blue beam of light towards the stage as they stand up in front of their seat.

One by one you get the Letters or Numbers correct, each time the person sits down to indicate that the number or letter is correct its another applause cue for the audience.

After the third person you stumble on the fourth and say you'll come back to them later, then of course you get the fifth person correct and they sit down.

You return to the fourth person and tell them to concentrate more clearly and then suddenly you blurt out "I See the Two of Diamonds – It's the Two of Diamonds"

This is confirmed to be correct and because you've finished by getting the suit and also number or letter it heightens the applause even more!

You explain this was just a warm up for the hardest chaotic and most random experiment that you have ever attempted, which is next.

AN IMPORTANT NOTE

In this example the woman has an entirely free choice of deck, however the man who is first to choose a deck and in this example is our "Instant Stooge" has his deck forced onto him so that the final written prediction in the small envelope is correct when it states:

My Male assistant will have randomly chosen the Red Backed Bicycle deck of cards and at this point will hopefully sit down as my predictions will have been correct and the audience will give him a round of applause.

This force can be done by your favourite method, the Magicians Choice being a good one, however to add to the apparent random chaos of the whole routine I use the Pick Any Two Eliminate One (PATEO) force devised by Roy Baker.

Let's say there are five different decks of cards in the carrier bag and we know we want to force the Red Backed Bicycle deck on the man you would proceed as follows:

You pick up any two decks (but not the force deck) and ask the spectator to pick one that they want to have placed back in the plastic bag.

This then brings the total down to four decks, the spectator is then asked to pick up any two and you apparently pick one at random to ditch into the plastic bag, of course in truth it is only random if he picks up two decks which are not the force deck.

If he picks up the force deck then you pick the deck which is not the force deck to be placed into the carrier bag and this leaves three decks on the table of which one is the force deck.

It is then your turn and again you pick up the two decks which are not the force deck so it does not matter which he discards.

You'll then be left with two decks only of which one is the force deck and obviously you choose to eliminate the one that is not the force deck leaving him with the deck which is already predicted on the final prediction.

This seems like a totally fair selections process and will be hard for the audience or him to remember exactly what happened which again makes the whole routine even harder to back track on or work out after the event.

As for the female she genuinely can randomly select any deck she wants and that part of the routine is easily explained by the secrets used in **"The Base Chakra Projects The Answer"** the routine then continue as follows:

The man is then told to remove the cellophane from his deck and his deck from its case, check they are all different, give them a shuffle and then hand them to the lady on stage who is also to give them a thorough mix up and shuffle.

This happens and then the lady is told to replace the cards into the box and place a strong elastic band around them from top to bottom to stop the cards falling out if they were thrown out into the audience.

When she has done this she is told to toss the cards out to anybody in the audience as again this keeps the Chaos and total randomness theme going.

The person who catches them is told to remove the cards from box and shuffle them so they are in an entirely random order, then they are to replace them in the case and replace the elastic band as it was, before tossing the deck to someone else.

The performer explains this will happen a total of three times in all and when the final of the three randomly selected seated audience members has done his or her mixing the cards are replaced by them into the box, the elastic band replaced and the cards thrown back up to the stage, where they land on the floor and remain for now untouched.

The Man on stage is then told to guard the large envelope prediction with his life and ensure that nobody gets anywhere near it.

The female on stage is now told that she will create the final element of Chaos and Randomness, the box of randomly chosen and randomly shuffled and mixed cards is then picked up, the female positioned on the correct area of the stage and the cards removed from the box and handed to her to hold.

She is instructed to place the cards behind her back out of site and give them one final mix, which she does.

Then you explain that you want her to cut a small section off the deck or in otherwords take about a third of the deck and in a few moments when you count to three, on the count of three she is to immediately bring out the hand holding the approx. third of the deck and throw the cards up into the air letting them fall randomly and visually to the floor.

You count to three and she does this for the first time, this is then repeated a second and third time, until the entire deck is all over the stage, some cards face up and some cards face down.

The female is then told to collect up all the cards which are face up, pick them up from the floor and place them on the table before you, which she does as you recap briefly on the whole randomness and chaos of the selections and situations which have occurred so far.

Once all the cards which landed face up are on the table she is told to look at the cards and think of just one of them, which she does.

THEN WITHOUT ANYTHING BEING WRITTEN DOWN YOU TELL HER EXACTLY WHICH CARD SHE WAS MERELY THINKING OF AND THE AUDIENECE WILL GO MAD WITH APPLAUSE.

Everything as stated here happens exactly as it looks to the audience except for one very important and major point, which is the key to most of the rest of the routine and happens at this point:

The female on stage is now told that she will create the final element of Chaos and Randomness, the box of randomly chosen and randomly shuffled and mixed cards is then picked up, the female positioned on the correct area of the stage and the cards removed from the box and handed to her to hold.

This is when the deck that has been thrown back from the audience is switched for an identical looking Red Backed Bicycle deck and is another reason why we had to force that deck on the man in the first place so that it would match the fake deck which is in our jacket pocket.

As for the switch the more blatant you are with it the better as it's the last thing the audience will ever be expecting at this point even if they are magicians and that's the real beauty of the Psychological Structure and order of this routine.

I simply pick the real deck up off the floor then walk towards the female so that I approach her from the side and end up stood almost behind her as I reposition her on the stage in preparation for her next "important" role.

This is logical and psychologically and visually seems 100% normal, however it gives you all the cover in the world to drop the real deck into your pocket and remove the special deck in its place which is then in your hand as you walk away from the female having repositioned her on the stage for the next bit where she will end up throwing cards into the air.

SO WHAT'S THE SPECIAL DECK WE NEED

Well for the example as it appears here your special deck would be made up of 40 Double Red Backed Bicycle Cards and Twelve double faced Bicycle cards which would have the same face on each side as follows:

THE DOUBLE FACED CARDS

Joker/Joker

Three Spades/Three Spades
Seven Spades/Seven Spades
Queen Spades/Queen Spades

King Clubs/King Clubs
Eight Clubs/Eight Clubs

Two Diamonds/Two Diamonds
Nine Diamonds/Nine Diamonds
Jack Diamonds/Jack Diamonds

Three Hearts/Three Hearts
Eight Hearts/Eight Hearts
King Hearts/King Hearts

It will be noticed that these 12 Double Faced cards are such that they make the prediction in the first envelope correct 100% of the time as follows:

The man reads the prediction and for example it says:

1. THERE WILL BE A TOTAL OF TWELVE CARDS FACE UP

2. ONLY FIVE OF THESE CARDS WILL BE BLACK

3. OF THE BLACK CARDS THERE WILL BE THREE SPADES AND TWO WILL BE CLUBS.

4. THE REMAINING CARDS WILL BE RED AND CONSIST OF THREE DIAMOND CARDS – AND THE REST WILL BE HEARTS.

5. EXCEPT FOR ONE CARD WHICH TONIGHT I FEEL WILL BE A JOKER.

ALL OF THESE STATEMENTS ARE FOUND TO BE 100% CORRECT

In short this prediction will be 100% correct every time as when the woman tosses the deck into the air in three separate sections whichever way round the cards turn and whichever way round they land, each and every time there will only be 12 cards face up as the other 40 cards are double backed cards and as such will always look as though they are face down.

That gives you the secret to that bit of the routine which was inspired by a Card Castle effect in Luke Jermay's Book "Building Blocks" and also by Ali Bongo's effect which is best known as Simon Arrosons "Shuffle Bored".

THE NEXT PART OF THE ROUTINE

In performance this part comes before the prediction effect which we have just explained and is as follows:

The female is then told to collect up all the cards which are face up, pick them up from the floor and place them on the table before you, which she does as you recap briefly on the whole randomness and chaos of the selections and situations which have occurred so far.

Once all the cards which landed face up are on the table she is told to look at the cards and think of just one of them, which she does.

THEN WITHOUT ANYTHING BEING WRITTEN DOWN – YOU TELL HER EXACTLY WHICH CARD SHE WAS MERELY THINKING OF AND THE AUDIENECE WILL GO MAD WITH APPLAUSE.

Well we already know that there will always only be 12 cards face up and in this example we know that they will always be these cards:

So take a very good close look at the list and see if you can work out why this particular selection of 12 cards is so important and why this example selection makes the merely thought of card revelation so easy to perform...

THE DOUBLE FACED CARDS

Joker/Joker – (THE COLOURED ONE)

Three Spades/Three Spades
Seven Spades/Seven Spades
Queen Spades/Queen Spades

King Clubs/King Clubs
Eight Clubs/Eight Clubs

Two Diamonds/Two Diamonds
Nine Diamonds/Nine Diamonds
Jack Diamonds/Jack Diamonds

Three Hearts/Three Hearts
Eight Hearts/Eight Hearts
King Hearts/King Hearts

It's easy because you need only make a statement such as:

"I get the feeling that Your thinking of a Red Card"

The law of averages is on your side here as there are more Red Cards than Black cards for her to look at.

If as will often be the case you are right, you would then continue by taking a stab at the suit by saying:

"I get the Feeling your thinking of a Heart"

If the answer is correct fine you now just need to work out which heart, however if the answer is no at least you now know it's a diamond card and its just a case of working out which one before the final revelation is made.

In both Groups of Red Card (Hearts and Diamonds) you'll notice they are made up of one Picture Card, One number card with a value below Five and one number card with a Value above Five.

As there are two cards (including the picture card) with a value above five I say:

"And Now I'm getting the vague impression coming through that the card your thinking of is higher than a number five is that correct?"

Ideally the answer would be NO at this point as then you'd instantly know which card that they must be thinking of as there is only one of that suit with a value below the number five!

So this is where you pause and then dramatically say:

"Yes I feel your thinking of a Red Card, It's a Heart Card and I feel it's the Three of Hearts"

If they'd said no when you said :

"I get the feeling that Your thinking of a Red Card"

Then you'd pause for a second after they say no and say:

"Yes that's right your thinking of a red card dyed Black"

This makes a gag out of things and allows you to change course to work out which Black Card it is which as there are more Spades than Club Cards I'd say:

"I get the Feeling your thinking of a Spade"

Most of the time this will be right, but if not at least you now know the card must be a club and by using the statement of:

"And Now I'm getting the vague impression coming through that the card your thinking of is a number card is that correct?"

From this answer you'd know if it was The King of Clubs or the Eight of Clubs and could then dramatically reveal the correct card for example as follows:

"Yes I feel your thinking of a Black Card, It's a Club Card and I feel it's the Eight of Clubs"

You could narrow the volunteer's selection even further right from the start by simply saying:

"Just look at any of the face up cards, but make it a number card, and see that number card your thinking of clearly in your mind"

A casual Phrase such as this rules out the Joker and also all of the Court cards so their choice is narrowed down to one of seven cards.

Personally I let them have a choice of any of the cards as by using the questioning technique whereby it seems that your making a statement you can very quickly eliminate cards from the list and work out what card they are thinking of.

It does not matter one little bit that you'll be told that some of your statements are wrong, **INDEED THIS MAKES THE EFFECT STRONGER** as it illustrates that this truly is difficult to do and is not a trick which works every time.

And remember this at the stage you get them to think of one card and then read their mind, nobody in the audience **(or apparently you)** have any idea how many cards were actually face up or what they are and as such any thoughts of you being able to work out what they are thinking of with a few questions are way out of the window and again its because of the Psychological structure of this entire routine that the **WOW FACTOR** is so high!

Get together the cards on the list and practice having people think of just one and then making statements (which are actually questions) to enable you to work out which card they are thinking of and you'll soon master the art of "pumping" as we call it in the business.

Remember what I said in the Cold Reading section about phrasing things as if your making a statement, and remember that because of the context of where this happens in the routine, nobody will think anything is strange if you get the odd thing wrong before **MAKING THE CORRECT REVELATION.**

AND NOW FOR THE FINALE OF THE ROUTINE:

The audience thinks the experiment is over however there is still much to come....

The Man is then instructed to open the envelope and remove its contents, this he does and finds a second envelope, he is told to do this and he finds a third envelope and finally inside this he find a large folded prediction which has a smaller envelope paper clipped to it.

You ask for the small envelope to be handed to you, which it is and say you'll come to that later.

The lady is told that the man will read each section of the prediction out one by one and that after reading each section she is to check the cards on the table and confirm to the audience if the prediction is right.

The man reads the prediction and for example it says:

1.   THERE WILL BE A TOTAL OF TWELVE CARDS FACE UP

2.   ONLY FIVE OF THESE CARDS WILL BE BLACK

3.   OF THE BLACK CARDS THERE WILL BE THREE SPADES AND TWO WILL BE CLUBS.

4.   THE REMAINING CARDS WILL BE RED AND CONSIST OF THREE DIAMOND CARDS – AND THE REST WILL BE HEARTS.

5.   EXCEPT FOR ONE CARD WHICH TONIGHT I FEEL WILL BE A JOKER.

ALL OF THESE STATEMENTS ARE FOUND TO BE 100% CORRECT

Once again the Audience go wild with applause as you send the Man back to his seat, but tell him to remain standing where he is at his seat in audience so everyone can see him.

When the applause dies down the lady is handed the smaller envelope and asked to tear it open, remove the contents and throw the envelope away, which she does.

She is then told to read out the contents slowly and clearly in a loud voice so all can hear and the man in the audience is told to sit down if the information about him is correct.....the prediction is read and for example it says:

I Jonathan Royle do on this evening of Saturday November 27th 2004 get the feeling as I sit writing this in my Hotel before going to tonight's show, that a strange series of events will happen as follows:

1.   A Man Approx. 5ft Ten in Height wearing Jeans and a striped jumper will end up assisting me on stage – I also feel the names Trevor and Joanne are linked to this man.

     AT THIS POINT MAN CONFIRMS THIS IS CORRECT AND THAT HIS NAME IS TREVOR AND HIS DAUGHTERS NAME IS JOANNE.

2.   His birthday will be August 13th and he will have 2 rings on his fingers.

     THIS AGAIN IS CONFIRMED CORRECT

183

3. My second assistant will be a Lady and her Birthday will be January 7th

   SHE CONFIRMS IT'S CORRECT

4. My Male assistant will have randomly chosen the Red Backed Bicycle deck of cards and at this point will hopefully sit down as my predictions will have been correct and the audience will give him a round of applause.

   HE SITS DOWN AS THEY APPLAUD

5. My second assistant who will now be reading this hopefully correct series of predictions will be highly intelligent, with a great sense of humour, they are a trustworthy, caring individual and I feel I can rely on them to throw the cards randomly into the air so that my earlier predictions will be correct.

   THIS OF COURSE IS CORRECT

6. And finally I'm sure I can rely on the audience to give my second volunteer a huge round of applause as they take a bow and make their way back to their seat!

PERFECT APPLAUSE CUE

Well that's how the audience will remember it, now let's look at what really has happened.

In this example, the man was our "Instant Stooge" and before the show we have found out from him the following:

❖ By Observation what his height is roughly and also we've made a mental note of what he is wearing, how many rings on his fingers and such like.

❖ We can casually ask him his date of birth and a couple of names important to him or we could obtain these using a Clipboard **(see earlier advice)** so that when the prediction is revealed even your so called instant stooge is amazed and wonders how the hell you read this information from his mind!

❖ On some occasions when a clipboard has not been practical I have used a Centre Tear or Billet Switch **(See Corindas 13 Steps to Mentalism available from *www.magictricks.co.uk)* to obtain the information.

❖ The bottom line is that we know all of the information that gets revealed about him **BEFORE THE SHOW** and as such can genuinely write this on the prediction in advance of the show.

❖ We also know for a fact that we will force the Red Backed Bicycle deck on him and as such can also write in that information in advance of the show.

AND HERES THE REALLY CLEVER BIT

There are actually Two Predictions, both of which are identical in every respect as far as information regarding our male "instant stooge" is concerned, but both of which are different regarding predictions for our second volunteer who truly is picked at random, so let's look at what gets revealed about them:

1. My second assistant will be a Lady and her Birthday will be January 7th

2. My second assistant who will now be reading this hopefully correct series of predictions will be highly intelligent, with a great sense of humour, they are a trustworthy, caring individual and I feel I can rely on them to throw the cards randomly into the air so that my earlier predictions will be correct.

Well let's look closely, other than having got her date of birth correct and it clearly stating she would be a lady, everything else mentioned about your second randomly selected volunteer could apply to absolutely anybody whether male or female and as such can be written on the prediction in advance of the show.

The only difference between the two predictions that you write up before the show is that one says:

My second assistant will be a Lady and her Birthday will be

And the other one says:

My second assistant will be a Man and his Birthday will be

Other than that everything else on both predictions is identical.

You will then need Two Small Wage envelopes, some carbon paper and some cellotape.

Cut a piece of Carbon paper so that it just small enough to slide inside one of the wage envelopes and be stuck into place on one side of the envelope.

The second wage envelope is then also prepared in this same manner.

The two predictions are then prepared as stated earlier and the slips are folded so that the blank area after the phrase **Birthday will be** is in line with the carbon paper when placed inside the wage envelope.

You can then make some pencil marks on the exterior of the envelope to remind you what area of the outside of the envelope relates to the blank section on the slip inside where the randomly selected volunteers birthday is yet to be written.

As you may have guessed this final piece of information will get there thanks to the use of a nail writer such as a Swami Gimmick or Boon (see *www.magictricks.co.uk*) which will be used in the usual thumb writing fashion to write the persons birthday on the exterior of the envelope in the correct place which causes a carbon copy of your writing to be transferred onto the correct blank area of the folded prediction which is inside the envelope.

The Predictions are now sealed and onto the flap in black marker pen you right the two words **MY NAME** which will aid in the psychological misdirection later.

Both of these wage envelopes are then placed into a slightly larger envelope which is then sealed and they must be placed inside so you instantly know which is the prediction saying the random person is a male and which is the one saying female.

This larger envelope then has the folded paper prediction for the cards face up section of the routine paper clipped to it and is put inside the other envelopes which are mentioned in the description of the effect and placed on view as the Major Prediction to be used in this routine.

Its visual if the biggest envelope is A4 and then the one inside is slightly smaller and then final of the three is A5 size.

Anyhow when the man has opened the three envelopes and finds the folded paper predictions paper clipped to another envelope, you stop him and remark how those envelopes had been in full view since the start of the show and how nobody could have tampered with them and such like.

You then ask him to hand you the envelope which as we know contains two wage envelopes inside it, but remember noone has any idea what's inside it at this point.

You instantly tear it open and remove whichever wage envelope is correct based on whether your random volunteer was male or female and then casually pocket the larger envelope which still contains the other wage envelope inside it.

You then keep this wage envelope in view at all times as you ask the man to read out the folded paper prediction he has in his hand.

This gives you all the time in the world to use the thumb writer to write the randomly chosen volunteers birthday into the blank space via the carbon inside the envelope, and of course by this stage you know what the man or woman's birthday is as you will have casually asked both volunteers this when they came up to the stage and then done a short Astrology Reading for them which impresses your audience even further.

But by this point the audience will either have forgotten that they ever told you this information or will remember but still find it amazing that you'd apparently predicted it all before the show.

You can then when it comes to handing the wage envelope to the person left on stage use the gag of saying;

"We'd never met before tonight and yet I wrote something on this envelope before the show began, can you please read out what it says?"

They will read the two words **"MY NAME"** and this will be perceived by the audience as if they are confirming that somehow you wrote that persons name on the envelope before the show actually started, whereas the onstage volunteer sees it just as a joke which makes them giggle, yet this giggle looks to the audience as if the person is "shocked" or "amazed" that you'd predicted this information in advance.

THEN QUICKLY BEFORE THEY CAN SAY ANYTHING ABOUT THE GAG CONTINUE

"Would you now please tear open the envelope and reach inside and remove the slip of paper and just throw the envelope away"

Yes they might see the carbon stuck on the inside of the envelope but they won't have a clue what its there for and due to the overlapping of many different principles and psychological ploys this won't help them work out what has gone on!

In truth Nobody has ever noticed as on stage they are so nervous and tend to do exactly what they are to do and remember that by getting them to throw the envelope away after removing the slip, the evidence is now back in your possession and to the audience this removes all suspicion from the envelope as people assume if anything were special about it you'd not treat it this way.

THE ROUTINE THEN ENDS WITH

You then finish with the Receipt test as mentioned earlier and will have concluded a truly mind-blowing display of Psychic Entertainment.

FURTHER POINTS

As already mentioned some of the other routines I explain herein can also be worked into the routine and if this is done you have a complete show at your fingertips which promoted correctly can earn you a fortune!

Regards the double faced cards, when I first did this routine I just stuck some cards back to back to make my own crude double faced cards and it did not seem to matter as all the cards face up will be of same thickness when the volunteer is picking them up and as such they don't feel any different.

Oh and the Double Faced cards are distributed into 3 areas of the deck, 4 together, then 4 together and then the final 4 together.

These are stuck into deck in such a way so that they are roughly one section in each third of the deck, this means when she cuts off a third and tosses it into the air about 4 cards will end up faced up each time.

She is told to cut three times and throw in three lots as otherwise I've found the deck tends to stick together and you don't get enough of a visual mess on the stage to have the true Chaos Psychological & Visual effect which is a large part of what makes this routine so strong.

You can get the person to pick the face up cards up and place them on a table, don't worry nobody notices they are double faced due to the fact they are not looking for it and have not got a clue what is going on.

However if your paranoid about this then just have the person kneel on floor and sort out the face up cards and place them in a row on the stage, this stops them picking the cards up high off the ground which may flash them to audience.

But in truth I've never found this to be a problem!

To end don't forget that the plastic bag if made into a double bag can be used as a change bag and as such is ideal for switching billets collected from the audience for ones you have prepared yourself making it easy for you to do a Killer Questions and Answers Routine **(see 13 Steps to Mentalism)** as you've effected the switch of the entire audiences billets using an ordinary every day item which will not be suspected by anyone!

WITHIN THE STRUCUTRE OF THIS ROUTINE ARE TECHNIQUES AND PLOYS WHICH YOU CAN USE TO PERFORM MANY OTHER MENTALISM ROUTINES WHICH I AM SURE YOU WILL NOW BE ABLE TO DEVISE FOR YOURSELF

Have fun using any part of this routine or indeed all of it together as I suggest and have used myself on many occasions with great success.

And if you have any ideas for additions to the routine, please email them to me at *hypno@hypnotorious.com* and I may include them in a future manual?

GOOD LUCK AND ENJOY BEING A MENTALIST

CHAPTER FIFTEEN

ROYLE REVEALS – HOW TO BE AN ALTERNATIVE and/or MAINSTREAM COMEDIAN USING HIS 5 CARD REPEAT ROUTINE

Within the pages of this Chapter I shall be revealing my own personal tried, tested and proven to work routine for a true classic of magic!

Paul Daniel's is famous for his "Six Card Repeat" and Wayne Dobson scored a TV hit with his "Five Card Repeat" version.

The method for performing this effect that I shall reveal within these pages is, I believe of my own creation! By that I mean I have taken an existing method and improved it to be far more practical to the Commercial Professional Performer.

Furthermore the Comedy Patter routine detailed within these pages is one that I have now been regularly working before paying audiences for well over a decade, and I can honestly say that this routine has always served me well.

The Comedy Patter routine as detailed herein has been worked by me extensively in front of both Mainstream and Alternative Comedy audiences with great success.

I have used this routine twice when supporting Jimmy Cricket on his "Laughter Show" and have audience tested it regularly at Alternative Comedy venues when working with the likes of Lee Evans, Steve Coogan & Logan Murray to name but a few!

In fact it was this routine which won me the Heats, and got me into the finals of year 2001, Bachelors Cup A Soup Extra Comedy Challenge. (A high profile Alternative Comedy Competition and an unheard of feat for a magical performer!)

As always I mention these things not with the intention to sound big headed, but rather to illustrate how much faith you can indeed place into the Patter Routine, which follows.

This Patter owes much to the two routines mentioned earlier *(those by Daniel's & Dobson)* and also to Comedy Heroes of the past including the late Max Wall, to whose funeral I was very proud and privileged to be invited!

Whilst I would openly admit that none of the one liners in this manuscript are in any way original or new, I would defend my actions of releasing this routine due to the original manner and order these gags have been placed into.

Also for those wondering what is this doing inside a book about becoming a Psychic Entertainer & Consultant, the answer is simple!

You see my past as a Magician is well known in England, so whilst working as an apparently "genuine" Psychic I found it wise to get any objections out of the way right at the start of my show and I did this by drawing attention to the fact that I started out as a Magician before becoming a Psychic.

After all the name of the game is Entertainment with a Capital E and I've found that the routine which follows not only breaks the Ice with your audience, but once you have got them laughing and on your side they grow to like you as a person and then you can get away with practically anything and everything for the rest of the show.

I shall start by detailing the Comedy Patter Routine, then reveal my own method for performing this classic effect and shall finish by teaching you some secrets of the Professional Stand up Comedian which any magical entertainer will benefit greatly from learning!

So here we go then guys & girls!.....

THE COMEDY PATTER ROUTINE

(I use this as my opening routine and as such once the compere has introduced me I walk on stage, arrive at the microphone and launch into the Comedy Routine that follows!)

Good Evening Manchester! **(Wait for response)** well that's a bit sad isn't it? Lets try that again and this time sound like you're at least a little pleased to see me, or don't you do impressions? **(Slight pause)** Good Evening Manchester! **(pause)** that's much better, but theirs no need to shout I'm not blind! **(Pause)** stupid...yes!....Blind no!

Well Ladies & Gentlemen, they say that an audience can smell fear **(pause)** especially if you've just shit yourself before you walk on stage! *(At this moment I pull on the bum area of my trousers to visually emphasise the gag)* Yes its true I was very nervous when I arrived here tonight, so nervous in fact that before I came **(pause)** no I don't mean like that love *(pretend to look at a Women in the audience as though she has interpreted this as a masturbation joke)* I mean before I came here tonight!

Yes before I came here I phoned my good friend Bob Monkhouse *(or other famous comedian)* and asked him how to get over my nerves. We're like that *(at this point visually show two of the fingers of your right hand crossed)* you know me and Bob Monkhouse! Oh yes we've both got Arthritis.

Very good advice he gave me actually. He taught me how to use the Marbles and Cream Cracker method to get over my nerves, oh yes he did! Apparently all you need to gain confidence, as a Comedian is a Jacobs Cream Cracker and six marbles.

He told me to make a small hole in the centre of the cracker and then to place it over my willy whilst I stood in front of a full length mirror with three marbles in each of my cheeks, making six marbles in all. Then he told me all I had to do was stand in front of the mirror like this and play with me willy whilst I kept on saying the phrase Good Evening Ladies & Gentlemen.

Now apparently doing this helps you to lose all your inhibitions and as such you become far more confident and as a result a better comedian. So there I am Naked in front of the full-length mirror, Cracker over me Willy and one-eyed trouser snake, or should I say Monster in hand? *(Here I mime doing this)*

In this cheek I've got three marbles *(push left cheek out with fingers to illustrate)* and in this cheek I've got another three marbles *(illustrate by pushing other cheek out with fingers)* and then I start playing with myself as I say Good Evening Ladies & Gentlemen. *(Again mime doing this as you actually say the phrase)* and as you can imagine I sounded ridiculous because of the marbles in my cheeks, so I swallowed two marbles to see if that would be any better and again I said "Good Evening Ladies & Gentlemen"

(again as always with this phrase I mime the playing with my willy bit as I push my cheeks out with my fingers and say the phrase so that I really do sound stupid) but it was no good so I swallowed two more marbles *(here mime swallowing them)* and again "Good Evening Ladies & Gentlemen" *(again miming the actions)* but still no good so I decided to swallow the last two marbles.

(mime it and then say clearly) and then I said "Good Evening Ladies & Gentlemen" and suddenly I felt full of confidence **(pause)** and apparently that's because, When you've lost all your marbles **(pause)** and your still fuckin crackers **(pause)** then you're a comedian **(pause)** Thank You!

(At this point without fail I have always found that the audience will applaud you loudly) No don't, don't **(pause)** don't stop! Actually on second thoughts save it for the end because I've got a week finish.

Incidentally that's the last joke I shall be doing tonight involving masturbation, so darling *(look at a pretty female near the front)* if you hear me do any more jokes on masturbation **(pause)** I'd like you to come up here on stage and pull me off!

Nice to see so many friendly looking faces in the audience tonight **(pause)** Alright Jack, How's your back? *(Appear to wave at someone)* All right Peg, How's your leg? *(Appear to wave at someone)* All right Rick **(pause)** How's your **(slight pause)** neck problem doing?

I nearly didn't make it to the show tonight, I just managed to fly in from the Bahamas **(pause)** I didn't catch an aeroplane **(pause)** I just got thrown here in a freak Whirlwind! **(Pause)** I'm sorry about that last joke, I know it was rubbish, but I only did it because they told me to do some Tropical Material! *(Sounds like Topical).*

Speaking of Aeroplanes if you ever get on one, make sure you are sitting at the back **(pause)** after all when did you last hear of a Plane backing into a Mountain? **(Pause)** Actually safest place of all is to sit inside the Black Box!

THIS IS THE PART OF THE ROUTINE WHERE IT'S EASY TO ADD MANY MORE AUDIENCE INVOLVEMENT GAGS AS EXPLAINED LATER!

Yes being a Comedian is a very strange job, people are always coming up to you and saying "You can use this joke" or at parties they always surround you demanding "Come on then tell us a Joke!"

I mean you don't get that in any other profession, imagine it your at a party you don't go up to a plumber and say "Come on then fix me taps!" or up to a Politician and say "Come on then tell me some lies" or heaven forbid up to a Gynaecologist and say "Can you have a quick look at the wife for me?"

Incidentally Ladies if any of you are suffering from any problems down below come and see me after the show **(pause)** I'm not a qualified Gynaecologist, but I'll have a damn good look for you!

Seriously though I've always wanted to be a Comedy Magical Entertainer ever since I was young, in fact the first strange thing I did was the day I was born **(pause)** I came out of the woman in the bed next to me mum!

My dad looked down at me and said **(pause)** Rover **(pause)** well he'd always wanted a dog. He said "Rover" you'll go far **(pause)** and I did **(pause)** that night he locked me in the Guards van on the 8-15 train to London Euston.

Yes I've had a very sad childhood, orrr *(as say this beckon to audience to join in with the sound of sympathy)* no sadder than that *(beckon again and the audience will do the sympathy sound again but louder)* – **(pause)** well maybe not quite that sad.

At the age of six I was left an orphan **(pause)** I ask you at the age of six what did I want with an Orphan? At the age of seven I lost both my parents **(pause)** what a card game that was **(pause)** I've never played cards since **(pause)** I'm scared of winning them back!

It was terrible being me when I was young **(pause)** come to think of it, its still terrible being me now I'm old. I never got any decent presents at Christmas *(beckon to*

audience as you did earlier and they will again make the noise of sympathy – orrr!)
One Christmas my dad gave me an empty shoebox, he told me it was an Action Man
deserter. The next year he bought a wet the bed doll in Oxfam, then he shaved its hair
off and told me it was an Action Man coward!

It was a hard childhood, me, my brother and my sister had to share a bed, and two of
us wet the bed **(pause)** I slept in the shallow end. I remember one night in bed me
sister said to me "show me yours and I'll show you mine" to which I said "well I've
got one of them and you haven't – ha – ha" *(mime showing your willy to her)* to
which she said "well I've got one of them, and mummy told me that whilst I've got
one of them I can have as many of them as I like!"

Before you start worrying I won't be doing any jokes tonight about Incest, I think it
would be totally in bad taste to say something like "Incest" – a wonderful game all
the family can play! **(Pause)** And my dads right behind me on that one!

Yes we were a poor family when I was young, so poor in fact that me mum & dad
used to buy me my school uniforms from the local Army & Navy store! I can tell you
its no fun going to school during a war wearing a Japanese snipers suit!

Mind you at school I was the teacher's pet **(pause)** she kept me in a little cage in the
corner. And as I grew up things went from bad to worse, especially when we had to
play Rugby at school, after the game everybody would laugh at my tackle in the
showers. I've never liked Rugby since I've always thought it's a game played by men
with odd shaped balls!

I was very unlucky when I was young, especially when it came to my relatives! I was
so unlucky that one day I bought my Granny some After Eight mints **(pause)** and she
died at quarter too!

My Granddad was even unluckier than me **(pause)** he died drinking a can of Long
Life! Then I reached that tricky age when I started to ask me parents that awkward
question of where did I come from. My dad told me that babies were delivered by the
Stork, to which I asked him "In that case who fucks the stork?".

Eventually he admitted that the stork had nothing to do with it, and in fact in truth it's
all over a Lark in a field! In the end He did tell me about the birds and the bees
(pause) the next day I went out raped a seagull and got stung by a wasp. **(Pause)** I
thought I was Pregnant for Three Weeks!

Yes very protective my parents were, they wouldn't even let me near a Naked Flame
until I was 18! Then I discovered that my Willy and a rubix Cube have a lot in
common **(pause)** the longer you play with them, the harder they get. The first time I
came I thought I'd broken it.

One day my dad caught me having a wank in my bedroom, he walked in and said
you'll go blind if you keep reading that, to which I said "Dad I'm Over here!".

Anyway I told him straight I wasn't reading the magazine, I was just looking at the pictures.

And before I knew it the time had come to see the School's career officer. When he asked me what I wanted to do I said, "I want to be a comedian!" **(Pause)** Oh how he laughed! **(Pause)** their not laughing now though **(pause)** I don't like the way I said that!

Then I left school, I had no O Levels, I had no A Levels **(pause)** but I did have three spirit Levels! **(Pause)** well the teachers always said I was well balanced.

As you've probably guessed I was a late starter and I've never really had much luck with the girls. In fact I'm really unlucky with women **(pause)** I had a girlfriend once who was half-Swedish and half Gypsy **(pause)** she was up all night massaging my clothespegs.

Then there was the girl who was half-English and half French **(pause)** she only shaved under one armpit *(here I lift up one arm to visually emphasise the gag)*.

Eventually I lost my virginity to a Feminist Prostitute **(pause)** she insisted on paying half. She asked me if I wanted a Blow Job and I said "OK but only if it won't affect my dole money!".

In the end I got so fed up with Women that for a short while I tried being Gay. I went into a Gay church once **(pause)** to be honest I only knew it was a Gay church when I realised that only half of the congregation were kneeling.

Did you know they have now started selling Gay Dolls in Leather Outfits at most major toyshops? You'll find them on the shelf right behind Action Man! Its no use buying one though, because when you take the lid off the box **(pause)** It just won't come out!

Then there was the time when I went into a Butchers and asked for a large salami sausage, which he started to slice up **(pause)** to which I said, "What do you think my arse is a money box?".

Then I tried being Bi-Sexual, but that didn't last for long **(pause)** I couldn't stand getting rejected twice. Next I found out about Lesbians, apparently Lesbians are attracted to Women **(pause)** in that case I must be a Lesbian trapped in a mans body.

For my Eighteenth Birthday a load of me mates took me to Amsterdam for a party and I visited my first sex shop. They sold loads of books on better sex, all the girls were buying titles like "Sex Without Fear" and "Sex Without Guilt". In the end I bought myself one called "Sex without Partners" **(pause)** it's a handbook! In fact they have now started selling it in WH Smiths, they've put it on the shelf with all the other Do It Yourself Manuals!

Whilst in Amsterdam I bought myself an Inflatable sex doll and what a disappointment that was. I gave mine a love bite on the neck **(pause)** then it farted and flew out of the window.

I noticed they had lots of different types of Condoms on sale, Coloured ones, Flavoured ones, even glow in the dark ones. I was a bit confused so the guy running the shop gave me some good advice, apparently you should never leave the curtains open whilst having sex with a Luminous condom on, because to anyone walking by it looks like you are opening and shutting a fridge door repeatedly **(pause)** and if your having real fast sex then it looks like your strobing!

And as for flavoured Condoms, well I bought one that was cheese & onion flavour, my girlfriend at the time got pissed and accidentally started giving me oral sex before I'd put it on **(pause)** but still never mind she didn't notice the difference.

The ones, which really get me, are the coloured condoms, now obviously the black ones are so your partner can imagine you're a well endowed foreigner, but as for the green ones what are they all about? I thought it might be an alien abduction sexual fantasy thing and then my girlfriend explained that its so that she can get me to wear it, stand on the edge of the bed and say, "Ho Ho Ho – I'm The Jolly Green Giant!". **(Pause)** "But don't squeeze the sprouts!".

They sold a wide range of mucky videos as well, I can tell you some of them were pretty disgusting! One of them featured a man having sex with a sheep **(pause)** apparently its not Baaad *(here say the word bad drawn out so it sounds like a sheeps Baa noise)*. Which reminds me, what do they call a sheep tied to a Lamppost in Wales? **(Pause)** a Leisure centre!

Another video involved a man getting caught by the police whilst having sex with a Horse. In court the judge let him off because apparently he was in a stable relationship at the time.

I was unfortunate enough to meet one of the stars from those animal sex videos once and I said to him "How low can you get?" to which he quickly replied "Well I tried a Hamster once!".

And the best video of all was the one starring Mr. Bobbit, you know who I mean that American guy who had his Willy sewn back on after his wife had cut it off and thrown it out of the window during a row. Imagine that, she's just cut off his Willy, thrown it out of the window and your walking down that very same street. You could slip and go flying on that stray Willy, imagine the embarrassment as you check into the local hospital with a broken leg and the nurse asks you what has happened? Imagine it guys having to reply "well I've slipped on a Willy" **(pause)** to which she says "whose yours?"" and you reply "I wish!".

I've recently had an audition for a Porn Movie myself **(pause)** they put me on the short list **(pause)** still I'm not to bothered if I don't get the role **(pause)** after all its only a small part!

The most shocking thing I saw though were some of the sex toys they were selling! I just couldn't believe it one woman who was slightly stoned came in and asked for the big red vibrator on the wall to which the shop assistant said "Don't be stupid love that's the fire extinguisher!".

And that's to say nothing of the woman who brought her vibrator back to the shop demanding a refund because she claimed it knocked all her teeth out during oral sex!

They were selling those Viagra tablets as well, which help you to get a big stiffy. With each Viagra tablet you bought they gave you one free anti-depressant, which you are supposed to take at the same time. Then when you go out on the pull if you don't trap off with a women **(pause)** you don't give a Fuck!

I went to one of those Coffee shops as well, you know the ones where they sell that maryjane. To be honest I'm stupid when it comes to drugs, I don't know the difference between smoking drugs and injecting them! **(pause)** I can't tell you the number of times I've burnt my arm with a spliff. *(Here visually mime trying to inject drugs into your arm with a red-hot burning cigarette).*

To earn extra money I used to make donations to the Local Sperm bank for which you'd be given £15 a visit! The guy who owned the Sperm bank was very unlucky, his first three customers were useless **(pause)** two of them came on the bus and the other one missed the tube!

I remember well one visit I made to the sperm bank, there I am in my cubical, todger in one hand, jar to catch me spunk in the other, and a table full of adult magazines to get me errect **(pause)** and then I noticed these loud groaning noises coming from the next cubicle. My curiosity got the better of me and so I looked over the top of my cubicle to be shocked by the sight of a guy being given Oral sex by three beautiful nurses. **(Pause)** I went straight to the manager to complain **(pause)** oh yes I did. I asked him why it was that I got a table full of mucky magazines to arouse me, whereas the guy in the cubicle next to me was getting the personal attention of three pretty nurses, to which he replied quickly **(pause)** well that's simple really sir **(pause)** Your not a member of BUPA!

Eventually I got over my wild and adventurous phase in life and returned to pursuing my dream of becoming a famous Magical Comedy Entertainer. One day I read a book and it said that a Comedian says things funny **(pause)** whereas a comic says things in a funny way **(pause)** well if that's true **(pause)** then that makes me a magician!

In fact to start the magical proceedings this evening I'd like to show you the very first trick that I ever saw, well I didn't actually see it for real, it all happened in a dream. So can we have some dream lighting please? *(At this point you look up at the lights as if they are meant to be dimmed – the gag being that they remain exactly the same, and then after a short pause you say)* You just can't get the staff these days.

And can we have some dream music please *(at this point some dreamy/cheesy sounding background music comes on to accompany you during the rest of this routine)* Yes it all happened in a dream, and I have some very strange dreams **(pause)** no not those type of dreams love! *(Appear to tell off another female in the audience for getting the wrong impression then after a short pause say)* stop making up your own jokes!

Oh yes I have some strange dreams, one night I dreamed I was awake, then I woke up and found out that I was asleep. Then there was the night I dreamed I'd become a Homosexual **(pause)** it was my own fault I fell asleep on a camp bed **(pause)** which reminds me of the politician who dreamed he was doing a speech in the House of Lords **(pause)** then he woke up and found out he was!

Anyhow in this dream I woke up one morning, I thought it was Dawn **(pause)** but I was wrong it was Samantha. The curtains were drawn, but the furniture was very real. I got out of the wrong side of bed **(pause)** don't you just hate it when you wake up with the mattress on top of you?

Then I walked over and looked out of the window and there was a heavy Jew *(sounds like Dew)* on the grass **(pause)** he'd obviously been chucked out of the sinagod for swearing.

And then I noticed a German Shepherd Shitting on my Lawn **(pause)** and then the dirty bastard let his Dog do the same thing!

So I moved away from the window and I asked my girlfriend to call me a cab and she said "Jonathan you're a cab!" In the end I called myself a cab, the cab pulled up with a jerk **(pause)** the jerk got out and I got in.

I knew the driver was going to be easy, she had a mattress strapped to her back. And as for her sister, well she was so popular that when she died **(pause)** she had to be buried in a Y shaped coffin!

As we were driving along she was going *(here make sound of a car engine and mime turning the steering wheel, then after a short pause say)* but then she stopped because she got a sore throat.

She asked me to wind up the window, so I turned to the window and said "You can be a really stupid window at times you can!".

On the way we got lost so we stopped to ask directions and discovered that there was this farmer there digging his field **(pause)** he was going YO Field!

Eventually we arrived at the Squitz Hotel, it's like the Ritz except the foods not quite so good. As I walked in the man asked for my name, I guess he didn't like his own. I went inside and found that there was a magician on stage performing with his assistant **(pause)** some people have just got no shame.

197

And that's the moment my desire to become a magician began, that very moment he did his first trick using 1,2,3,4,5 cards *(as you say this cards are counted)* he threw away 1,2, cards, gave them a flick as it's the flick which works the trick and then he counted the cards again and there were still 1,2,3,4,5 cards and the whole audience went "Good God Man!" **(Pause)** but obviously you weren't that audience.

I tell you what guys and girls we'll try that again and I want you all to join in and say "Good God Man!" – OK? So he showed 1,2,3,4,5, cards, threw away 1,2, gave them a flick as it's the flick that does the trick and counted them again to show 1,2,3,4,5 cards and the whole audience *went (here pause and gesture to the audience and they will say "Good God Man!" then pause for a few seconds and say)* The first time I saw that trick I too was so amazed that I forgot to applaud! *(Pause and they will clap, then when they stop say)* Was that a round of applause or has somebody just put the chips in?

(Usually one or two people will clap this comment at which point I say) Thank you, your very kind but please don't clap on your own or else somebody will throw you a fish!

After the show I went backstage and asked him how he did the trick with 1,2,3,4,5 cards, where he threw away 1,2, gave them a flick because its the flick that does the trick and then counted them again to show 1,2,3,4,5, cards and the whole audience go *(gesture for them to join in)* "Good God Man!"

But he said he couldn't tell me because he's a member of the Secret Five, in fact its so secret he didn't know who the other four members were! But he did give me some very good advice, he said that when I did manage to find out how to do the trick I should practise it somewhere nobody would see me, so I did **(pause)** I went on Digital TV!

Then I discovered a magic shop in a local town so I knocked on the door, the man answered the door in his pyjamas, I thought what a stupid place to keep a door in your pyjamas?

The guy had wooden legs but real feet, he told me that his shop burnt down once and the fire brigade had saved the shop but he was burnt to the floor. Apparently he tried to claim on his insurance but they said he didn't have a leg to stand on.

I asked him if he had the trick with 1,2,3,4,5, cards where you throw away 1,2, give them a flick cause it's the flick that does the trick and then count them again showing 1,2,3,4,5, cards and the whole audience goes *(gesture to them)* "Good God Man!".

He said he'd sold out but he did have a really good trick using 1,2,3,4,5, cards where you throw away 1,2,3,4,5, cards and are left with 1,2, as opposed to throwing away 1,2, cards giving them a flick cause it's the flick that does the trick and then counting them again to show 1,2,3,4,5 cards and the whole audience going *(gesture again)* "Good God Man!".

So you see Ladies and Gentlemen I've searched far and wide, high and low and I was going to show you the trick using 1,2,3,4,5, cards where you throw away 1,2, give them a flick cause it's the flick that does the trick and then count them again showing 1,2,3,4,5 cards and the whole audience goes *(gesture)* "Good God Man!" *(Pause)* But I just couldn't find out how it was done! *(Pause)* THANK YOU!

(Here as I say thank you I throw the last five cards up into the air and take a call, which acts as a cue for the audience to applaud loudly which invariably they do anyway and when the applause has died down I continue as follows!)

Well Ladies & Gentlemen, to be serious for a few moments, it was shortly after this time in my life that I started to discover my Psychic Talents which as you can imagine was very strange and in many ways quite scary!

Apparently it all has something to do with Astrology and the fact that I was a Test Tube Baby, **(pause)** I was born under the Sign of Pyrex.

Actually when I think back Strange Psychic things have happened to me and around me ever since the day I was born.

When I was younger I once played Poker with a deck of Tarot Cards **(pause)** I got a Full House and Three People Died!

Then I discovered that I've got Crystal Balls **(pause)** it's a disability **(pause)** but I do my best.

By the way Is this your first time as an audience? **(Pause)** I just wondered because I thought we could all join hands and try to contact the living!

Seriously Though, before we start our experiments tonight, here's a quick Joke for all the Psychics in the audience *(pause and put hand to head as if telepathically sending the joke, then after a few seconds when no-one laughs say)* Oh so you've heard it before then?

Well in that case Lets try our first experiment............

(This is the point when you go into your Psychic Routines which can either be 100% Serious, or as I used to present them when regularly appearing in the British Media with a touch of Humour, a Cheeky Chappy Style and some very funny one liner jokes thrown in. Now I know many of you will think Magic & Comedy should not be mixed with Serious Psychic Work and that's up to you, but I've always got away with it, indeed after witnessing one of my Clairvoyant Shows in 1990 which I opened with this 5 card Repeat Comedy Routine, International Publication " Psychic News" dubbed me "The New Uri Geller and Doris Stokes Rolled into One!" – So I think that proves you can still convince people you have genuine Psychic Powers even if you combine some magic and Comedy into the proceedings.)

OTHER GAGS FOR THE ROUTINE?

You will have noticed that near the start of this Patter Routine, I pointed out the time which would be ideal for adding in any other gags which you may choose to include to make the routine longer as and when required.

Good comedy writers advertise each week in The Stage & TV Newspaper or you could commission me to write more gags for you by contacting me on *hypno@hypnotorious.com*

And please don't overlook the Internet as a good source of Comedy material, especially that of a topical nature. My personal experience has shown me that within minutes of a news story breaking many Internet sites will be posting topical jokes about the events.

Simply use the words "Comedy" – "Jokes" – "Topical Comedy" – "Topical Jokes" – and other similar phrases in your search engine and you'll soon find sites listing many thousands of gags which are of potential use to us as comedy performers and best of all they won't cost you a penny!

This is the section of the routine where any topical gags about what has been going on in the news that week should also be included, which is something I do at every show.

I have not given you these gags in the routine, as it is impossible to do so, due to the topical nature of such gags and the fact that one-week they are funny and the next they are not.

I shall however give you some examples now of the types of one liner jokes I would include at this section of the routine as and when the particular venue and audience made it appropriate.

1. I've noticed that a few children have managed to sneak into the show tonight **(pause)** so if they could all move to that corner of the room please **(pause)** it's just that I've only got one hand grenade!

2. Now don't get the wrong idea I love Kids **(pause)** but obviously I couldn't eat a whole one.

3. Seriously though if any kids have sneaked in that was just a little joke **(pause)** Jolly good Father Christmas is Dead!

4. As some younger ones have managed to sneak in, lets play a little game of Simple Simon! Simple Simon Says Hands on your legs. Simple Simon says Hands on your Head. Simple Simon says Fingers in Your Ears *(pause and then into next gag which is mucky and as such makes this gag funny)*

5. There was a Lesbian, A Pakistani, Two Homosexuals, 3 Asians and an Irish Bloke in a pub **(Pause)** what a fine example of an integrated community!

6. Anyone in from Halifax? **(Pause)** I went there once (pause) it was shut!

7. Anyone in from Ireland? **(Pause)** this will all be new to you then won't it? **(Pause)** You know Gas, Water, Electric!

8. Anyone in from Scotland? **(Pause)** some of those Scottish towns are really small aren't they? **(Pause)** I went to one once, it was so small that all the road signs were back to back!

9. Nice venue this **(Pause)** although to be honest I've never worked in a Skip before!

10. Were did they get the furniture from? **(Pause)** MFI?

11. You know what MFI stands for don't you? **(pause)** Made For Idiots.

12. I met one of the barmaids earlier, she's got a glass eye **(Pause)** she didn't tell me intentionally **(Pause)** it just dropped out in conversation.

13. She's got an embarrassing mole on her neck as well! **(Pause)** Very embarrassing **(Pause)** It kept jumping up and swinging on her earring!

14. They say that Laughter is the best medicine **(Pause)** unless your Diabetic and then Insulin seems to work much better!

15. Seriously though **(pause)** Where would we be without a laugh? **(pause)** Here! *(as you say the tag line of Here! Also nod your head to emphasise the gag.)*

16. I was in the restaurant down the road earlier and there was this woman next to me **(pause)** she had Frogs Legs and Chickens Breasts **(Pause)** but she had a smashing personality.

17. Whilst in the restaurant I heard that your Local Football team has just been offered a new sponsorship deal with Tampax **(Pause)** apparently they'll have to accept it as they've been going through a bad period at the moment.

18. I've just noticed that it's heaving in here tonight! **(Pause)** personally I blame the Scampi!

19. Incidentally for all you T-Totaller's who don't drink Alcohol, they have just started selling Virgin Cola behind the bar! Which reminds me that Virgin

Cola has a lot in common with a Virgin Bride **(Pause)** in both cases you have to get the ring on your finger before you can open her up!! **(pause)** Actually I've heard rumours of 7-Up!!

20. The bar manager in here's a bit strange **(pause)** he was telling me earlier that yesterday he served a White Talking Horse which wondered in off the street. **(Pause)** Apparently this White Horse came in, walked over to the bar and said, "I'll have a double Whiskey Please!" **(Pause)** to which our friendly bar manager said "Well that's a coincidence, we sell a Whiskey named after you!" **(Pause)** to which the White Horse said, "In that case I'll have a double George please!"

21. They sell some funny coloured drinks these days don't they? **(Pause)** which reminds me, what's Green and gets you pissed? **(Pause)** a giro!

22. On a serious note, you girl's need to be careful these days, its all to easy for a bloke to take advantage when you've had one too many. Or indeed to make a real idiot of yourself just because it seems a good idea whilst your drunk. I mean I was walking home the other night and I saw this young woman stood in a doorway with her skirt lifted up around her waist **(pause)** nickers around her ankles **(pause)** leaning up against a wall **(pause)** eating a bag of chips! I said to her "Do you realise your knickers are around your ankles and your skirt is around your waist **(pause)** your giving everyone a right show you know love!" **(Pause)** to which she said, "You mean the Bastards buggered off?" **(pause)** Well it takes all sorts!

23. I was very close to winning the National Lottery last week **(pause)** oh yes very close! **(pause)** The guy next door won it!

24. Seriously though, if I ever won the Lottery the first thing I'd do is give my girlfriend some plastic surgery **(pause)** I'd cut up all her credit cards.

25. To be honest I'm not really mean **(pause)** in fact I'm always buying my girlfriend presents **(pause)** the other week I bought her a Tupperware bra **(pause)** it doesn't do much for your figure **(pause)** but it keeps what you've got very fresh!

26. Then there was the time when I was going to buy her a new car! I asked her what she thought of The Renault Five **(pause)** she said, "I think their all innocent!"

27. I picked her up in a nightclub using one of my corny chat up lines. I told her I was a racing driver, to which she replied "I bet your Hard-on tyres!" *(Sounds like hard-on tires)* – *(pause)* to which I said, "I bet it doesn't!"

28. Then I went for the kill and used my best line **(pause)** I said "Actually I'm an insect surgeon **(pause)** so if you'll come back to my house with me

(pause) I'll gladly show you the inside of a Fly! *(at this point visually unzip your trousers to emphasise the gag)*

29. Surprisingly she did come home with me, so we both attempted to make love on my waterbed! **(pause)** But her half froze **(pause)** and she called my half the Dead Sea.

30. I wouldn't say my girlfriend was old when I got with her **(pause)** but one day I told her to act her age **(pause)** and she died!

HECKLER STOPPERS & INSULTS

Especially when working the Alternative Comedy circuit and at times in Working Men's Club's you will be glad of a few comedy insults and heckler stoppers in your repertoire.

Many Working Men's Club's have at least one audience member who thinks he is the centre of attention and feels it is clever to shout out insults during your act.

When this happens if you can respond immediately with an insult or witty comment which makes the rest of the audience laugh at him then not only will this shut him up but also it makes you look like an even better performer to the rest of the crowd for having dealt with things so well.

On the alternative Comedy circuit you will find, especially if doing a support slot that the audience will make it their sole aim to fire insults at you one after the other.

Its not that they don't appreciate you or your act, but rather as I have learnt through hard experience is because they have been conditioned as an Alternative Comedy audience to believe that unless you are the top of the bill act, they have free reign to join in and believe me they will!

Rather than fear this you should, as I learnt the hard way embrace this, as when they interrupt it gives you the ideal opportunity to apparently reply with your witty adlibbed insults which makes the alternative comedy audience warm to you even more.

If your booked for an alternative comedy venue as a support slot and say for example have been told to do 20 minutes, then often you will find that 5 to 10 minutes of this can be killed shutting up the audience in this comical manner (or as they say in comedy interacting with the crowd).

Therefore it would be wise for me to provide you with some of the best comedy insults & heckler stoppers that have proved invaluable to me over the years both at mainstream venues and on the alternative comedy circuit.

I have also included here a few gags which are ideal when a joke doesn't get as many laughs as you'd expect or the applause for something you do is poorer than what it should be!

1.   He didn't get a Birth Certificate **(pause)** his parents got an apology from Durex!

2.   In fact he was circumcised as a baby **(pause)** unfortunately they threw the wrong piece away **(pause)** mind you its no skin off my nose!

3.   He's just had a personality bypass operation **(pause)** unfortunately it failed!

4.   He's like a broken tape recorder **(pause)** brain on rewind and mouth on fast forward.

5.   They ruined a nice arse when they put teeth in your face!

6.   Look what happens when Cousin's marry.

7.   Go and sit against the wall **(pause)** that's plastered as well.

8.   Don't move **(pause)** I want to forget you just the way you are now!

9.   That was quite funny Sir **(pause)** only quite funny **(pause)** that's why I'm stood up here and you're sat down there.

10. I think they've let him out for the night **(pause)** isn't care in the community a wonderful thing?

11. I've heard he makes love like a Video recorder **(pause)** Insert **(pause)** Pause and Eject!

12. Why shouldn't you make a joke? **(Pause)** after all your parents did.

13. Does your mouth bleed once every 28 days?? **(Pause)** well if it doesn't **(pause)** it should, because you're a cunt!

14. Did you hear that? **(Pause)** that was the voice of a Lark! **(pause)** A Pil-Lark!

15. I tell you what Sir, lets do a double act? I'll sing Swanee River **(pause)** and you can jump in it!

16. Join hands with your friend's mate and show us what a dope ring looks like!

17. Your about as much use as a one legged man at an arse kicking contest!

18. You're about as much use as a one armed weight lifter with cramp.

19. I bet you're about as popular as a RattleSnake in a lucky dip!

20. Is that a Moustache? **(Pause)** or has your eyebrow popped down for a drink? **(pause)** I tell you what Sir with a nose like that I wouldn't have underlined it! **(Pause)** Incidentally did you pick that nose yourself **(pause)** or does it run in the family?

21. Nice Jacket your wearing Sir! **(pause)** I bet there's a Ford Cortina outside with no seat covers.

22. Where do you live Sir? *(Wait for answer)* well that's a coincidence my Uncle's working in that area tonight **(pause)** he's a burglar!

23. *(Point at an empty table and say)* Please put your hands together for the Japanese Kamikaze Pilots reunion party!

24. *(no laughs)* And some fell on stony ground!

25. *(no laughs)* No laughs for that one (pause) well you must have heard it **(pause)** you were all facing this way.

26. *(no laughs)* Look Guys **(pause)** it might be a night out for you **(pause)** but for me it's a career!

27. *(no laughs)* Is this an audience or a bloody judge and jury?

SOME OTHER JOKES FOR YOUR REPERTOIRE

For the sake of completeness I'll now include a few more one liner jokes, which over the years have always gained a good audience response for me, when used in the right circumstances!

1. Heard about the Gay magician? **(pause)** He disappeared with a puff!

2. Two brooms in a cupboard **(pause)** they can't get married **(pause)** they've not swept together!

3. Two pigs go to a party **(pause)** they come home after half an hour **(pause)** they got bored! *(bored sounds like the term meaning pigs have had sex)*

4. A quick joke for all the Paranoid people in the audience **(pause)** he's behind you!

5. I'm going to say something now that's really going to shock you all **(pause)** Boo!

6. A quick joke for all the Psychics in the audience *(pause and put hand to head as if telepathically sending the joke, then after a few seconds when no-one laughs say)* Oh so you've heard it before then?

7. Quick impression now of an Irish magician! *(at this point hold out both hands with fists clenched and whilst keeping one still, move the other hand up and down then say)* Which hand is the Frog in?

8. I can do a trick that Paul Daniel's can't! **(pause)** I've got hair! *(As you say, "I've got hair" pull on your hair to visually emphasise the gag).*

9. American Illusionist David Copperfield once walked through the Great Wall of China **(pause)** which is a big coincidence really, because the other night I got pissed and walked into the wall at my local Chinese!

10. If the early bird catches the worm **(pause)** then why doesn't the worm have a lie in?

11. If 8 out of 10 cats prefer Whiskas **(pause)** does that mean the other two prefer shaving?

12. Why is there only one Monopoly's commission?

13. Where do you complain about the complaints department?

14. I played Poker once with a deck of Tarot Cards **(pause)** I got a full house and three people died!

15. I don't do a lot of live shows **(pause)** I do a lot of auditions **(pause)** in fact I've done so many auditions I thought my name was next!

16. I did a show once and the audience consisted of ten thousand midgets **(pause)** I got a standing ovation and I didn't know a damn thing about it!

17. Did you know that all midgets are excellent cooks? **(pause)** Oh yes they are **(pause)** that's why there are so many Little Chefs around!

18. I backed a horse once at 10 to 1 **(pause)** it came in at 20 to 4! **(Pause)** in fact it was so late back it had to sneak into the stables!

19. I was in Ireland once visiting family and I saw my Uncle Paddy walking down the road with the front door under his arm! **(pause)** I said to him "what you doing with the front door under your arm?" **(Pause)** to which he said "I'm going to get a key cut" **(pause)** "But don't worry you'll still be able to get in the house because I've left the window open for you!"

20. Why do Gay men have Moustaches? **(pause)** To hide the stretch marks!

21. Why do Italian Men have Moustaches? **(pause)** So that they can look like their mothers!

22. What's the difference between an Oooo! And an Aarrgh? **(pause)** About an inch and a half!

23. How do you fit a 100 Asylum Seeker's **(or Refugees)** into a telephone box? **(pause)** Tell them they own it!

24. Why did God put men on this earth? **(pause)** Because Vibrators can't mow the lawn! **(Women love this one!)**

25. I'm not religious **(pause)** Thank God I'm an Atheist!

26. In the bible it says Jesus had a bum made of elastic! **(Pause)** its true **(pause)** it says he tied his Ass to a tree and walked ten miles.

27. In the bible it also says that Moses was in fact constipated! **(Pause)** its true **(pause)** it says he took ten tablets **(pause)** went high into the mountains **(pause)** and so it came to pass!

28. I went on a Cannibalistic Holiday once! **(pause)** It was self-catering **(pause)** it cost me an arm and a leg!

29. Coco the clown stopped to give me a lift the other day **(pause)** he said he was on his way to the garage **(pause)** when I asked him why, he said he couldn't get his doors to fall off!

30. Did you hear about the Clairvoyant Contortionist? **(pause)** She saw her own end!

SOME TIPS ON BEING A FUNNIER COMEDIAN

As you may have noticed already, throughout this manual I have when listing jokes to use in the routine made it clear on every occasion when a (pause) is important to make the gag funnier.

A mistake often made by aspiring Comedians is that they often forget the comedic power of a pause or to put it the another way the power of silence.

This brief pause when made at the right time gives the audience just long enough to compute what you have said so far, meaning that after the short pause when you hit them with the punchline (the funny bit) that they are instantly able to register in their minds why it is indeed funny and as such are more likely to laugh.

This technique is often called "Comedy Timing" and is the something that makes the difference between a joke getting no laugh or getting a laugh!

Indeed it is also this technique which makes the difference between a joke getting a small laugh or a belly laugh, and in short is the most important thing about becoming a Comedian that I could ever teach you.

And its because of this techniques importance that I have at all times throughout this manual indicated where short pauses are necessary to make the reaction to each of the gags bigger than they may be otherwise!

To this end I would also advise you to watch as many videos featuring stand-up comedians performing their act as possible, and as you do pay close attention to the times when they pause briefly before delivering the punchline to their audiences.

Although experience is by far the best teacher in life, observation comes a very close second and you will learn much by emulating (not copying) the style and manner of established successful comedians.

Another technique of much value is "Pointing" a gag as it is called in the trade. The easiest way to do this is to deliver the lead in of the joke in a conversational manner, then pause briefly as explained earlier before delivering the punchline in a slightly more forceful/enthusiastic tone of voice.

For example take the one liner joke of: "Did you hear about the gay magician? He disappeared with a puff!"

Whilst it may get a laugh if read out parrot fashion from the page it becomes funnier when a slight pause is inserted at the correct time as follows:

"Did you hear about the gay magician?" **(Pause)** "He disappeared with a puff!"

The joke becomes even funnier to an audience hearing it if you "point" the gag, in otherwords make it obvious that what they are now hearing is the punchline and the time they are expected to laugh, for example:

"Did you hear about the gay magician?" **(Pause)** "HE DISSAPEARED WITH A PUFF!"

In the above example the opening line is delivered in a conversational tone of voice as if asking a genuine question, then you pause briefly to give the punchline more impact when you deliver it and finally the punchline (section in block capitals) is delivered in a slightly higher/more excited & enthusiastic tone of voice which in itself signals to the audience that this is the punchline and time for them to laugh!

Due to the fact that you will be following this formula for each gag you tell, the audience will become conditioned to this style of delivery and as such it becomes automatic for them to laugh when your voice tone changes and the punchline is delivered.

It is this technique which accounts for the fact that even very successful comedians can get away with some fairly poor material during the middle of their act, as by this time the audience has become conditioned to laughing as the performers voice tone changes.

It is also important to note that when an audience laughs you should give them time to laugh. This may sound obvious but the number of times I've seen a comedian deliver lines one after the other without giving the audience time to laugh is amazing.

Just as the slight **(Pause)** prior to delivering the punchline signals the audience to get ready to laugh and enables them to fully appreciate what you've just said, so a very slight pause at the end of a gag once the punchline has been delivered gives the audience time to laugh.

It's also worth mentioning that the more concise and direct your gags are the bigger laughs they are likely to get! By this I mean always tell a joke in such a manner that the least possible number of words are used to get the joke across. The reason being that the more direct/concise the wording of your gags is, the easier it is for your audiences to compute what you are saying quickly and as a consequence the easier it is for them to find it funny and as a result laugh!

An example of a joke being told using more words than necessary would be as follows:

"I've got a very strange star sign me, not normal like you lot, oh no I was not born in the normal way **(pause)** I was a test tube baby! **(Pause)** I was born under the sign of Pyrex!"

OK so the gags still funny, but it becomes funnier to an audience when you get straight to the point and keep things as concise or short and sweet as possible, for example:

"I was a Test Tube Baby" **(Pause)** "I was born under the sign of Pyrex!"

This is exactly the same gag, but delivered in a far more concise manner and as such far more likely to get a bigger response from your audience.

So at all times when writing routines of your own remember the principle of KISS = Keep It Short & Simple!

Another valuable comedy technique to make some of your gags seem funnier than they actually are is to use what we call in the comedy trade a "Foil".

Now quite simply a "Foil" is an audience member sat somewhere near the front that appears to have a good sense of humour who as comedians we keep referring to at various points during our acts.

Read the patter routine explained in this manual and you will see examples of several gags which are made funnier because I am apparently talking (directing the gag) at a particular person in the audience.

Usually this is done in the manner that they are the only person in the room that has misunderstood what you are saying, then later in the routine when they apparently misunderstand something again and you point this out to the audience it becomes even funnier that you keep referring to them.

Effectively they become your unpaid comedy partner and the more you refer to them the more it turns into a running gag, and as with all running gags they become funnier the more they are repeated at intervals during your routine.

You can also use a "foil" in the manner that you keep referring to them because they are the person enjoying themselves most, for example if they laugh and no-one else does you can point them out and say "Move around Love and tell people what's Funny!" or if she is the one who claps loudest you could say "Can you move around and make it sound like I'm doing well please?".

Backtracking is another useful comedy technique which you will see lots of Comedians using. By backtracking I mean that early on in a routine you tell a joke and then throughout your routine at unexpected times the punchline to other jokes refers back to the joke you made much earlier in your act which both makes you look very clever as a comedian to your audience and as I've found guarantees a much bigger laugh for jokes which may not even be very funny, just because they cleverly relate back to a joke/punchline made earlier in your routine.

Watch the videos/acts of several professional stand up comedians and what I have just explained will become much clearer to you, but to try and illustrate more clearly in writing what I mean here is an example of some gags which all interrelate to each other and as such when spread at intervals throughout your routine would be exploiting the "backtracking" technique as each gag or punchline refers back to ones made earlier in the act. So here is an example of what I mean:

"Golden Eagles are funny creatures **(pause)** they nearly die every time they make love **(pause)** seriously **(pause)** when they make love the male mounts the female Golden Eagle and starts the funny business **(pause)** but the moment he enters her both of them stop flying and start plummeting towards the ground at high speed! **(Pause)** And then if they are lucky they finish having sex in time to split apart and fly off just seconds before crashing to their death on the ground! **(Pause)** Now be honest girls if you were a female Golden Eagle **(pause)** Before it was to late You'd fake an orgasm wouldn't you?"

THAT'S THE INITIAL GAG WHICH WE WILL NOW KEEP REFERRING BACK TO!

"I've recently turned almost Vegetarian **(pause)** now by almost Vegetarian I mean I won't eat any meat that's been killed on purpose, but I will eat meat that's died of natural causes, which is quite handy really because a Butcher has just opened near me which only sells meat that has died of natural causes! **(Pause)** The other week I bought a Chicken that had died crossing the road **(pause)** then there was the Cow that fell down the stairs **(pause)** the hedgehog that tried crossing the road to meet his flatmate **(pause)** And he's always got thousands of Lemmings in stock **(pause)** But best of all was the other week when I got a good deal on a pair of Golden Eagles!

THE PUNCHLINE OF GOLDEN EAGLES BRINGS BACK VISIONS OF THEM CRASHING TO EARTH AS THEY MAKE LOVE AND THIS IS WHAT GETS THE BIG LAUGH!!

"Last Christmas I bought my wife two books **(pause)** The Joy of Sex and The Joy of Cooking **(pause)** she keeps getting the two books mixed up **(pause)** now every Christmas she serves us up a Pair of Golden Eagles in one of 69 different alluring positions!"

ONCE AGAIN THIS RELATES BACK TO GOLDEN EAGLES HAVING SEX!

"Last time I was in America I noticed that on their coins it says In God We Trust! **(Pause)** and on the coins is a picture of a Golden Eagle which I think is very apt **(pause)** let's face it if you're a Golden Eagle each time you make Love you are quite literally putting your Trust in God!"

AND YET AGAIN IT REFERS BACK TO GOLDEN EAGLES MAKING LOVE!

In the examples just given we have four very different gags, all of which seem to be of a very different nature and yet all of which end with references to Golden Eagles and/or Golden Eagles making Love.

During an actual Comedy Routine these examples jokes which relate to each other would of course be interspersed with other jokes which are about entirely different subjects and as such means that each time one of these jokes referring to Golden Eagles suddenly pops up it will instantly draw a far greater reaction from the audience than if you just told all 4 of the relating gags in a row.

Now that I've drawn your attention to this technique, watch as many comedians at work as you can and it will become blindingly obvious to you just how often they use this ploy and also how effective it really is.

These days, especially in Alternative Comedy Venues many audiences will not tolerate Racist, Sexist, Ageist, Sizest or in fact any other form of Ist style comedy which is directed at a particular minority or group of people!

Through personal experience I have found that the best way around this is to either direct these sorts of gags at Celebrities or Politicians, who for some reason are still viewed as fair game or indeed to direct them at yourself!

You will have noticed I'm sure that throughout the routine I detail in this manual I direct all the potentially questionable jokes such as those about Gays, Lesbians & Bisexuals directly at myself.

By so doing I have found with particular reference to the Alternative Comedy venues that I can still get away with telling these jokes as the audience don't take offence at me taking the piss out of myself and as such don't view it as an attack on any minority or particular group of people.

This is a very important point to keep in mind when writing your own routines, as it means that with a little thought and common-sense you can quite easily adapt or alter an existing gag of a questionable nature so that it becomes either directed at yourself or at a famous celebrity or politician who is seen as fair game by the audience.

And incidentally however old the joke may be, if you adapt it so that it is directed at someone currently in the news, then by your audience it will also be viewed as a topical gag.

An example of such a gag that can be altered on a daily basis to appear relevant to whoever is the person held up to hate that day by the media is:

"What's the difference between **(whoever)** and a bucket of shit?" **(Pause)** "The Bucket!"

With a gag such as this it is still funny with whatever name you use and as such using the name of someone held up to hate in the media means that you instantly look like a Comedian who is up to date and using topical material in their act.

From the point of view of delivering your material, my personal advice is to make your style as conversational as possible, word your routine so that each of your jokes flows logically into the next one as then not only is this good continuity, but also it sounds as though you are just telling a group of friends a story which happens to have lots of humorous bits along the way!

This means that the audience will start to feel involved and warm to you as if you are a friend of theirs telling them a story.

No longer is it a psychological situation of us and them **(Comedian against audience)** but rather it is now a case of us all together, one friend telling all his other friends a funny story.

Using this approach it does not matter if a few of your gags don't get any laughs (die) as your friends (the audience) will be eagerly awaiting your next funny line as you continue to tell them this logical sounding story.

Read the routine I have detailed in this manual and you will see that I do indeed practise what I preach, incidentally as you read through the routine again, notice how easy it is to remember the correct order of the gags and the way they logically link together.

This is made easy due to the fact that they have all been linked together as a story and as such it makes it easier for us as human beings to remember and then relate back in the correct manner to our friends (audiences) at a later time.

Another useful comedy technique is the double punchline, here you tell a joke and deliver its punchline and then as the laughter dies down you immediately hit the audience with another funny punchline, relating to exactly the same joke as you told a few seconds earlier and as they don't expect this double whammy it becomes twice as funny to them! A couple of examples are:

"At School I didn't get any A levels, I didn't get any O levels **(Pause)** But I did get three Spirit Levels **(Pause whilst laughs die down and then into)** Well the teachers Always said I was Well Balanced!"

With the above example the phrase "Well Balanced" relates to "Spirit Levels" and so it's a double punchline for the same joke!

Another example of a double punchline is:

"Whilst In Ireland I bumped into my Uncle Paddy walking down the road with the front door under his arm! **(Pause)** He told me he was going to get a key cut **(Pause whilst laughs subside)** but he told me not to worry as I could still get into the house as he'd left the window open!"

Once you've read the previous two examples a few times I'm sure you'll see what I mean about a double punchline for the same joke being such a useful comedy technique!

Situation comedy can also be put to good use in the stand up comedians act, and here by situation comedy I mean something that unexpectedly (from audiences point of view) happens there and then in the situation you are in, which in itself is obviously funny!

A couple examples of what I mean being:

"Could we just lower the lights Please" *(Here you pause and nothing happens)* "You just can't get the staff these days!"

OR:

"Could we just lower the lights Please" *(Here as you pause a prop spotlight made of foam drops from the Flys above the stage onto your head knocking you to the floor, then as you get up apparently dazed you casually say)* "Well Maybe not that Low!"

In both these examples you have apparently from an audience point of view made the best comedy possible out of an unexpected situation whereas in truth we know that we have planned these things to happen on cue every time we perform.

Combine everything that I have taught you so far with the apparent ability to be able to ad-lib and respond to hecklers or audience comments as they happen and you are well on the way to becoming a successful professional stand up comedian.

And as I explained earlier ad-libs, most of the time only appear to be ad-lib whereas in truth you are just relying on one of the heckler stoppers or other one liners stored in your memory banks for use in such occasions.

At this point it would be wise for me to explain that the reason I have decided to teach you how to become a stand up comedian by using my five card repeat routine is because that is how I first got the confidence to become one myself.

Initially I figured that with some playing cards in my hand and a trick to perform around which the gags fitted that it was just like doing my comedy magic act and as such it instantly gave me enough confidence to go out on stage and do it.

However as time went on and my five card repeat routine stretched from 5 minutes to half an hour and I realised that I was now mainly just telling gags, I had effectively become a good confident comedian without even realising it.

In all honesty I can now go onto a stage and easily do 30 minutes or more of stand up comedy without any props and indeed on many occasions have done exactly this, but most of the time I still structure my stand up routine around the five card repeat making the final point of my act throwing the five cards into the air as I say "I just couldn't find out how it was done!"

The main reason for this being that this in itself is a very good applause cue for the audience and has proven to be over many years a very strong and memorable way to end my stand up comedy act.

Practising the delivery of your gags before live audiences is by far the most valuable thing you can do and to this end there are countless Comedy Clubs springing up all over the place that will happily let you do an "Open Spot" at their venue before a paying comedy audience.

Do as many of these as you can until you feel confident within yourself that you can be and are funny and then its time to unleash your act on paying clients, which ironically may be obtained along the way as you do the "Open Spots" at the comedy clubs as if you get a good reaction it often leads to paid bookings!

Whilst it may at first glance appear that I have told you very little in this manual, please take my word for it that using the techniques that I have revealed to you *WILL MAKE YOU A FAR BETTER COMEDIAN WITH EASE!*

ROYLE'S METHOD FOR FIVE CARD REPEAT!

Before I finish for this manual, I'd like to explain my personal method for the five card repeat.

As I am a great believer that the simpler the method, the more you can concentrate on the presentation I used to use the "Pocket Cards" method when performing this effect at shows.

However I soon got fed up with collecting all the cards after the show or making up a new set and that's when I set about thinking of an easier to make way of doing the effect.

The result came to me when messing around with some cellotape and some paperclips, and perhaps by now the astute performer will be way ahead of me?

Quite simply you prepare your five fake "pocket" cards by sticking two paper clips to the left-hand edge of the card and one to the bottom edge of the card.

The two paperclips on the left hand edge are stuck so that one is about a quarter of the way down from the top of the card and the other so that it is about a quarter of the way up from the bottom.

To attach them in place you simply take a small length of cellotape, push the cellotape between the sections of the paperclip and then stick it into position so that the closed end of the paperclip is against the edge of the card and the open end is pointing towards the right hand side of the card.

A final paperclip is then fixed in the centre of the bottom edge of the card so that the open end points upwards and your "Pocket" card is now prepared.

After a few attempts you will find that you can easily prepare five of these pocket style paperclip cards in just a minute or two.

You will then also need another 17 playing cards, which are placed into the pocket cards as follows:

Three of the pocket cards get three cards each in them and two of the pocket cards have four cards placed into them making a total of 17 extra cards plus the five pocket cards making a grand total of 22 cards!

From top to bottom (back designs facing you and faces towards the audience) the cards are stacked so that the two pocket cards containing four extra cards are on top, followed by the pocket cards containing three cards each!

In performance the cards are held in your left hand so that the paperclips are on the left-hand side, this means that as you count
The cards from your left hand to the right in a gentle manner the cards will stay in their pockets.

However apply a little pressure and you can remove cards from their pockets as you need to in order to be able to count the cards and still show them as five every time.

Make up a set of cards in the manner I have just described and the next bit will be far easier to follow as I am now about to explain the position of the cards at each stage of the routine as it relates to the comedy patter routine that I have detailed within this manual.

1. Firstly count five Cards leaving all cards in their pocket and as you do each and every time you count the cards ensuring that they remain in the same order as they are counted from your left to right hands as they started out in. This means that the cards are always in the correct position for what follows each time they are replaced into the left hand after counting.

2. Throw away two cards by taking pulling two cards out of the pocket card and throwing them away.

3. You can now show five cards again just as before.

4. Throw away the next two cards by removing them from the pocket card.

5. You can now again show five cards as before.

6. Throw away the pocket card in front of you and one of the cards from the next pocket card.

7. To show five cards you now pull one card from the pocket card and then show the other four as before.

8. Throw away two cards out of the pocket card.

9. Remove the final card from the pocket card in front of you and then count the final four as before.

10. Throw away the single normal card, then the pocket card, and then all three cards from the next pocket card so that you are seen throwing five cards away.

11. Remove the pocket card in front of you in the right hand leaving the two pocket cards together as one in the left hand as you state this leaves two cards and then replace in original position.

12. Throw away the empty pocket card and one card from the next pocket.

13. Count the two normal cards out of the pocket card and then their pocket card making three cards, remove one card from the next pocket and then count the pocket card as the final of the five.

14. Throw away the two normal cards.

15. Finally at this point it should be self explanatory you count them to show five cards at the end by removing any cards left in their pockets as you count them.

This may sound complicated on paper, but rest assured when you make up a set of the cards and try it out once following my instructions in front of you all will become clear and you will grasp the working in less than 20 minutes!

The advantages of this method are that at the end I just leave all the cards on the floor at the venue, it only takes a couple of minutes to make up a new set and the sight of the paperclips facing me makes it obvious under working conditions which are the pocket card as opposed to the normal cards.

With the pocket cards, which had, actual pockets made from half of another playing card in dimly lit venues I found it would often be difficult to tell which were normal cards and which were pockets.

Admittedly you could tell by feeling but when you have your mind on presenting something, keeping the audience happy and getting laughs the less you have to worry about the better.

It is also for this reason that I never use the Biddle Count Sleight of hand method for this trick unless I have to suddenly perform impromptu at a party or something, as I found that on very hot stages my fingers would often sweat a little, but enough that I started to concentrate to much on doing the fake count as opposed to presenting the trick in a comical manner.

As I always say if there is a simple & easy way to fake something and it looks the same, then you may as well use it as your audiences will be none the wiser and you certainly won't get paid anything extra just because you know that you did it the sleight of hand way!

Remember at all times **ENTERTAINMENT VALUE** should be the key thing in all that you do and present to your audiences and to this end I have always found that **SIMPLICITY** and 100% **RELIABILITY** of method are by far the best choice and easiest ways to concentrate on your presentation.

TRUST ME I'M A PROFESSIONAL!

CHAPTER SIXTEEN

SHORTCUTS TO ALTERNATIVE MEDICINE

This section of the book is purposely presented in a hap-hazard way, so that you have to re read what I say and think about it, so you discover the truths within. As always you can only fully understand and discover all the truths when you put what you have learnt into action.

Although the information below is meant to be used in conjunction with your standard therapy in order to speed up the process, some people, I'm sure, could see how the knowledge could be used on the phone to convince a potential client to come and see you instead of a different style of Complementary or Alternative Therapist.

Of course, you show them the way to treat themselves for free with the other methods, but suggest to them it will be even better for them if they had a session or two with you.

Treating peoples problems is a Lucrative Sideline to Psychic Readings & Entertainment and as such you are advised to obtain my 513 paged training course on the subject "Confessions of a Hypnotist" which is subtitled "Everything You Ever Wanted to Know About Hypnosis But Were Afraid to Ask" and at time of writing is available for £19.99 from *www.diggorypress.com*

EXPERIENCE IS THE BEST TEACHER IN LIFE

OBSERVATION AND EXPANSION OF KNOWLEDGE IS THE SECOND BEST

ALWAYS LEARN FROM OTHER'S MISTAKES SO YOU DON'T MAKE THEM

SPIRITUAL DEVELOPMENT IS PURE INTELLIGENCE

WE TREAT FROM THE EYES UP AND DOCTORS TREAT FROM THE EYES DOWN

OVER 90% OF ALL REPORTED ILLNESS IS PSYCHOSOMATIC

OF THE 10% THAT ISN'T, MOST CAN BE HELPED WITH HYPNOSIS

PROBABLY ALL UNREPORTED ILLNESSES ARE PSYCHOSOMATIC

THE HUMAN MIND IS BY FAR THE MOST POWERFUL COMPUTER EVER CREATED

JUST LIKE A COMPUTER, THE PROGRAMMES IN IT CAN BE CHANGED

AROMATHERAPY

The shortcut to aromatherapy is to surround yourself with fresh flowers of the season, the smell (aroma) will naturally get into the air of your house and their bright visible colours will cheer you up. Also surround yourself with plants, by doing this you are returning your body to nature and as such, it will feel better. Also as plants take in the carbon dioxide which we breathe out and in turn give out fresh oxygen, in turn the air in your home will be cleaner and this too will protect your health and make you feel better. Should you wish to actually use the essential oils of the plants, it couldn't be easier, just go to the Body Shop and get the Tisserand leaflet on the oils, this tells you how to use them and what each oil does. The leaflet costs nothing, I recommend the use of the flowers and plants in conjunction with a vaporiser ring and an oil suited to the specific complaint, this is the easiest and I've found, most effective way to use aromatherapy.

REFLEXOLOGY

The shortcut to reflexology is to simply walk around at home barefoot. It is unnatural for our feet to be covered with shoes, which store up a huge electrical charge and as such, knock the body out of balance. If we were to return to nature then we would walk barefoot. Well today it is only safe to do this at home, so do it whenever you are at home and naturally all the points will be stimulated automatically and without effort. The other way, is to massage the whole area of your own or your partners foot and in that way you have got to feel better as a result, as the whole correct point will be massaged.

HERBALISM

As with all the examples I am going to give, return to nature, buy lots of different herbs from the Herbalist and on them it will tell you what food each herb can be added to. If you are adding the herbs to your cooking on a daily basis then it will become unnecessary to use any other form of herbal treatment, as it's natural and automatic. Should you wish to proceed further and make up actual remedies, get a copy of Potters new encyclopaedia of botanical drugs and preparations, with this you can check up which herbs should be used for what problem. Then the general rules of thumb to follow are as follows: If the herb is on sale to be added to food then it should be safe for use. You give the patient a one month course of treatment for each year they have had the problem. You use one ounce of herb to one pint of boiling hot natural spring water. The contents are placed in a teapot and stirred up and left for about 10 minutes to stand. The liquid is then poured into a strainer and into a bottle for dosage so it's then clear liquid but has the goodness of the herbs within it.

This pint of liquid is to be consumed over the period of one day, so half a pint is drunk the same morning and half a pint that night. It must be used the same day, as no preservative has been added to the mixture, this is called an infusion. If you can't find a strainer, a silk stocking, which has not been dyed, will do the same job if the liquid is poured through it.

Some people add brandy to the mixture so it lasts longer as it acts as a preservative, but I'd advise as above. The other way of preparation is a decoction, this is used with root herbs, such as garlic etc., it's put into a pan with the water and boiled for about the same time as above and then strained, this is the way to get the goodness out of root herbs. By the way, half a pint is basically the amount an average household coffee mug holds, so if you have no jug you could use that as a measure. Lastly, if you use a mixture of 8 herbs, of course one eighth of an ounce of each is used so the total herb total is 1 ounce to 1 pint, then you can't go wrong.

HYPNOTISM

In a suggestion form, any suggestion you wish to make to yourself out loud three times a day, will, if you have faith and belief in it, become genuine and happen. In other words, it's positive thinking or self hypnosis.

MASSAGE

Regular sex is the best form of massage and relaxation there is, if you do it correctly. Also, by telling your partner what you like and don't it can be fun and beneficial to experiment with your own amateur massage. The art of massage goes back thousands of years and providing you keep to the more gentle strokes, no harm will be done. The golden rule is, JUST FOLLOW YOUR INSTINCTS, but please don't use essential oils in any "sensitive areas".

NATUROPATHY

The basis of this therapy is to return to nature and eliminate any unnatural habits from the patient's life. They may just need more light or more of a kind of food, they may not have a good posture.

By studying your patient and questioning them, common sense will lead you to a correct solution and as in analysis, if you remove the cause of the problem all the symptoms will vanish. For example a friend kept getting corns on her toes, so I knew extra weight must be putting onto her toes. I asked her what she did, any sport? No. Did she have to reach up to high shelves at work? No. Then I asked if she danced. She said she did up until a year or two ago. This explained it. She didn't wear high heels, so I knew that wasn't the cause of the problem. As it turned out, I got her to walk around a bit and without realising it, she was putting more weight onto her toes. I asked what kind of dancing. She said ballroom and then the problem was solved, she had loved ballroom dancing and as it required moving on her toes and her mind had connected this with enjoyment it had become habitual. She then, for a week or two consciously thought of how she was walking and then it became habit not to do this and she has not been troubled with her feet since. So you see it's rather like psycho analysis find the cause of the problem, remove it and the symptoms vanish.

Someone with a bad back usually does office work and no gardening. Nature designed the body to plant things, so if they did some gardening the joints in their body would loosen up. Arthritis is more likely to be usual in people who have used the joints of their body in a repetitive way. (Tai Chi exercises will help stop arthritis.)

HOW TO HELP WITH MEMORY LOSS DISEASES

If you have any aluminium pans or cooking utensils, throw them away, as, if you keep using them, later in life you are likely to get a mind disease. Aluminium, is highly toxic, but has a coating on it to stop such effects, but once a metal spoon has accidentally scratched this surface off and made the pan or utensil shiny, then the toxic part can get into the food as it's cooked and you then eat the food and as you can see, it's a vicious circle. If you are going to have metal pans and utensils then please have stainless steel. By throwing out items of an aluminium nature of someone with a mind disease already it could help stop the problem getting much worse.

HOW TO HELP WITH LONG AND SHORT SIGHTEDNESS

Both long and short sightedness are, in some cases a conditioned problem and as such, a cure of conditioning can be used to help them. If short sighted, these people have probably been used to sitting near the TV and always looked at things close up, or without the correct light etc. If long sighted, then they have probably looked at things from a distance for much of the time. In both cases it has become a conditioned response and by reversing things and conditioning themselves to do the opposite they will very quickly have no need for glasses. Another way to help as well as reversing their habits and acting in a more natural way, is for them to stand outside at night and look at their thumb, (which is near) for a minute and then to look at the sunset (which is far) for a minute and to repeat this at least five times, (takes 10 minutes). Done each day in conjunction with the reversal of their wrong habits, their vision will rapidly improve.

HOW MIRACLES ARE WORKED

There are no miracles and yet there seems to be in the bible and in everyday life, well, I think they omit some of the facts. For example, "he caught loads of fish in a short time", well most people don't know that fish get hungry at sunset so your more likely to catch them then. A man stands in a field, he utters a strange command and suddenly about 100 birds land at his feet, coming from nowhere. Well, you are stunned, what you didn't see were the three months of effort that went into making this possible. Each day for the past three months at the same time in the same place, rain or shine, that man has gone with three loaves of bread and fed the birds. This time he takes no food, but they see him, it's the right time of day and so they assume food is on the way and all fly down to his feet leaving you to think it was a miracle. Well as I see it, here the real miracle was the effort put in here to engineer the effect. Some psychics say it would be possible to walk on water, but would take 20 years of study, i say why waste 20 years when the next boat will take you across in 10 minutes time.

Women seem to have periods at different times, this is because artificial lighting has had an unnatural effect on their bodies. If you take these women and put them in prison where they are all subjected to the same conditions and lighting etc., then within a short time they will all commence together, at the same time, as that is how nature intended it.

So I hope you now see the secret behind miracles is TIMING, PREPERATION and the creation of a NATURAL environment.

I hope you realise this section has been included in order to make you think and as a result hopefully open your eyes up to nature more and start to realise what has been under your nose all the time.

As it says in the bible, "His divine power HAS given us everything we NEED for life". Now it's up to us to realise it's there and use it in our every day lives then there would automatically be less illness.

If the body was conditioned to the climate it's in, as nature intended, then like a friend I have, you'd never need the heating on, would have more money and would never get the common cold or other ailments. Heating etc., is unnatural and man made, so it has to be man broken.

For back pain, sleeping on the floor each night will solve the problem quickly.

WE ARE NOTHING ON THIS EARTH

YES, WE ARE NOTHING, NO PHYSICAL THING

WE ARE NOT A PHYSICAL THING, SO WE MUST BE INTELLIGENCE

THIS MEANS THE INTELLIGENCE RULES THE BODY AND NOT VICE VERSA

AND ONCE YOU REALISE THAT, well my dear friend when asked who are you? The best reply would be Pure Intelligence. For that is what you are, so it's wise to expand your intelligence all the time and then your quality of life will improve and once you have faith in knowing who you are, everyday illness will be a thing of the past and will not bother you. Until you have faith in that you are stuck in Hell because we create our own Heaven or Hell.

Spiritual yogis take years in temples to find themselves and then are only allowed to leave when they know and have faith in the fact they are nothing. You are pure intelligence and once you know that and realise that is too valuable to destroy, then you will know you are immortal. You will know you will live again and as such, have lived many times before. Knowing this, all worries will leave you, you have all the time in the world and if you don't complete your tasks in this life don't be surprised if you do next time.

You'll also find the things you're really good at now are probably what you did in a previous life and that would explain how you can have child prodigies etc. The body is just a shell and you will get another shell when you leave this one.

Anyway that's the end of this section, I hope it has given you some food for real deep thought, for within it really are many keys which can be used to unlock the doors which may be blocking your success in life.

So observe and expand your knowledge. Know you will be a success and you will be. Again, as the bible says, "As a man thinketh so a man becomes."

So I hope you now realise you really are in charge of your own life and that luck is engineered by you.

INCREASING YOUR BUSINESS AND INCOME

Below are some keys to increasing your clients and as such, your income. An easy way to get more work is through TV, radio and press publicity and best of all, these can be got for free. To do so, come up with a gimmick, like a novel headline saying The TRANCE of a lifetime, for royle hypnotist or whatever.

The headline must be catchy and preferably humorous, this increases your chances of the story getting into print. The press release should be typed in double space format on to single sheets of white A4 paper.

You stand a better chance of getting the story in print if you supply a few matt finish black and white photos with the story, as papers prefer to print a story if it has a photo with it.

This is what helps to sell papers and make them look more interesting. The release should be short and to the point and of public interest if at all possible. Or you can tie the story in with some event that's in the news etc. and ride on its success.

For example, it hits the news that people are dying of cancer and you offer discount treatment to local people who have cancer and to stop people smoking, as the story is in the news it's topical and up to date and as such, will get in print. This will get you a large, free write up with a photo and on the advert will be the number at which you can be contacted.

This will get you many, many clients. I had a write up on Noesitherapy in a local paper and offered "free sessions" the article got me 107 enquiries within 24 hours of the paper coming out and of them I converted 87 into clients who paid me, YES, they paid me and it was legal.

When they called I explained that they would need about four sessions and half would be free. But so they had to make a commitment they paid for the first two sessions at £50 each and got the second two free.

After that would be at a discounted rate of £35 per session. As I say, 87 of the 107 who called were delighted with the offer and it not only earned me much money, but gave me loads of experience within a short space of time. If I really had given the treatment totally for free and not just partly for free then all of them would have come.

To do that near national no smoking day, say to the local paper if they pay you a fee they can then offer readers free sessions of smoking cessation therapy and this will help their papers and get them much goodwill and new readers. They then pay you say £400 per day for 8 hours of your time (treating 32 clients within that eight hours by doing them in groups of four). The reason for doing it so cheap, is that each person will buy a tape off you at £9.95 to continue the therapy and some may come back again for a paid session.

But most important the paper will run two stories, one prior to the event and one after, both giving details of how to contact you and as such, you get loads of clients, plus the "free" clients become walking adverts.

Any stunt of this kind should be included in the FREE local paper as more homes will get this and more people see it. When you've done a few things for the paper and got on good terms with them, then it will get to the point where they call you and ask for a story as they are running short of news that week.

Each week after such an article you should have a classified wordage advertisement in the paper, giving brief details of your service and contact number. I find I get best results when this goes under the personal column, as more people read this than do the health column.

These adverts should appear each week and that way your name stays on their mind and they will come to you first

To get on radio tell them the TV company have shown an interest and they should get in first. To get on TV, tell them a bigger TV production group has shown an interest and they should get in first. It's a competitive business and this trickery will work many more times than you'd think.

My classified produces at least 20 calls a week. Why? And, oh yes, about 18 of them will become paid clients. The advert below is what I include and you would do the same with your own name and number. When they call I explain as above, that one or two sessions are free, this way you are not breaking any laws and they become clients. Isn't business a lot easier than you thought?

Being qualified in marketing, finance and management and having been in show business 27 years plus, I know all the tricks and pass them on to others.

The advert I used was worded as follows, with the underlined words being printed in bold print. By the way, FREE, is the most powerful and effective word that you can ever use in an advertisement.

FREE HYPNOTHERAPY, Psycho Analysis, Psychotherapy and Past Life Regression, available from professional of many years experience call, Heywood Hypnotherapy Centre, on XXXX XXXXXX and ask for Jonathan.

The above advert cost me about £20 a week to run in the busiest local paper on the busiest day of the week and it worked wonders. I found that I also got extra business and more word of mouth advertising by offering a small discount in fees to students, unemployed and pensioners.

You don't have to advertise of course, but done properly, it is a very good investment and with every one of your clients being a potential source of further business it makes good sense.

There are many other ways of getting yourself known than the ones I have explained so far and a good pointer is to look at your "opposition". Do regard other therapists in your area as opposition.

Each client that your opposition treats is a blow to your business.

Look in your copy of Yellow Pages under Hypnotherapists and assess how your own advertisement would look against the others. Yellow pages can be a little expensive compared to other publications, but it does come up with the results.

People tend to look here first when seeking therapy of any kind. An advertisement in Yellow Pages also gives you a professional perception. People see it as carrying bonafide advertisers (although this is not strictly true).

If you decide to choose Yellow Pages, you will notice that they cover many different sizes. If you can stretch to it, you will do much better with a quarter column including your own photograph, or at least some type of picture. People warm and respond much better to a human face in an advertisement, especially so with therapy.

In this publication, you also get over the principal of having to be visible time after time, before someone responds.

If you are in a rural area, the local church or village magazine can give good results for very little outlay.

As an extension to actual therapy, with what you have learned in this course, you have more than enough information to give talks, lectures and seminars to countless numbers of groups and organisations. Start with the local women's institute and prepare yourself for lots of bookings and enquiries.

Small cards in local shops are inexpensive and although do not give high numbers, they do help to get your name established.

Strangely enough, dependant on his or her views, your own and surrounding Doctors centres may see you as an asset. Especially if you write a professional letter explaining that you can provide private counselling and psychotherapy.

The last piece of advice in this section will leave your mind racing and your body reaching for a pen to write down all the other potentials which will be stimulated.

Design a poster or write out a card carrying your speciality subject as CURING FLYING PHOBIA'S. Pop down to your local travel agent and they will almost pay you to display it!!!!!

So get a "Local" or "Regional" Newspaper to do a feature on your Bizarre Psychic talents first by simply calling them up and/or sending them a press release both by snail mail and email which informs them of your bizarre talents and offers them an interview.

When the "local" article has appeared you should copy this and then fax or send it urgently through to all the National Newspapers and Magazines and also the TV & radio Shows which feature such Bizarre Style items and this will often lead to National Exposure.

You then Copy the National Articles which appear and send them along with copies of the "Local" articles also to International Publications around the world, both Newspapers and Magazines and often this will lead to International Coverage.

Regards TV & radio shows initially send the "Local" articles to get on your first TV & radio Shows, but thereafter record all radio and TV Shows you appear on and put together a demo audio CD of radio Interviews and a DVD of TV work which Can then be sent out to the TV & radio Stations locally, nationally & internationally to keep the Publicity bandwagon rolling along nicely.

It's also good in this day and age to email Press Releases to all relevant "Special Interest" Newsgroups and information sites as this could also lead to other Media Exposure both on and off the Internet.

In all cases you should have an Internet Domain name to promote which can be given out in all Interviews so that people can contact you easily and also so that you have a chance of merchandising your Bizarre Psychic Products and also your personal 1 to 1 readings.

Its Merchandising that will make you the money in the long-term and make you rich, also of course your fees for Live Psychic Shows will increase more and more based on the more media Exposure and the more famous you become.

When you have a certain amount of fame its time to get a regular radio or TV slot and perhaps start writing a weekly column for various Newspapers and Magazines.

Its also time to start hiring theatres and selling tickets to your own live Psychic Shows as your fame helps fill the theatre and means as you're the organiser all the profits are yours.

Local Spiritualist Churches & new Age groups are ideal mediums through which to advertise such events at next to no cost whilst guaranteeing maximum bums on seats.

Motivational & Self Help Seminars presented with a Psychic theme would also be profitable ventures once you have established a Media presence.

Its very useful to befriend a Journalist who can then submit Stories and feature items on your behalf, they of course get paid directly from the publication for sourcing and writing the story which is their incentive and quite often they can also negotiate a fee for you to be paid, but at the very least they often get you more media exposure than you would perhaps get yourself.

In England do an Internet Search for "The National Union of Journalists" and then you will be able to find the direct contact details of many freelance journalists who you can contact directly with your story.

Also sites such as www.mediauk.com contain directories of the direct contact details of all Local, Regional, Nationals and even some International TV, Radio, Newspaper and magazine Contacts to whom you can easily email your Press Release, explaining your Bizarre Psychic Talent and offering them a feature interview.

If you can involve a Celebrity Angle such as reading The Navels of famous people for example or reading the Paws of Dogs belonging to famous people then this will be even easier to get into print.

Remember that the Photo is the Story so if a Photo contains a loveable looking animal and/or looks eye catching and bizarre, or contains a famous person then whatever the story is there is far more chance thanks to the Photo of getting it into print.

Indeed Psychic Fairs at which you may attend doing Psychic Readings are excellent places to gain clients for your Hypnotherapy Treatments, so you get paid for doing the Psychic reading during which you find out what health issues, Habits or Phobias they have and then you sell them the "cure" of Hypnosis and book them in for another session at another fee!

Oddly enough you will also find that Studying my book *"Confessions of a Hypnotist"* will also help make you a far better Psychic Reader as it contains much real world information on Body Language and Secrets of other Psychological Ploys, Techniques and approaches which will prove invaluable to any Psychic Reader who truly desires to Master The Art of Cold Reading.

Well you now have all the keys you need for success, so now go and use them to open up the doors of opportunity.

CHAPTER SEVENTEEN

OTHER IDEAS TO GET YOU THINKING?

Well this book has almost come to a close and our time together is fast approaching an end, but before I sign off I would like to remind you of this Internet Site: *www.serenapowers.com*

Visit The Site and click on "Unusual" and many other bizarre methods of Fortune Telling & Psychic Divination will both be suggested and explained in enough detail to get you started on your own "unique" Psychic Publicity Path!

Examples of some of the Bizarre approaches Explained, all of which I feel with a little thought could make you famous are:

PODOMANCY – Reading People's Feet.

PHALLOMANCY – Yes You've Guessed it reading Men's Privates.

GASTROMANCY – Interpretation of the noises made by your stomach and the marks on the stomach area.

MAMMOMANCY – Reading Women's Breasts & Nipples to divine their fate & fortune, would be great for late night TV shows!

ONYCHOMANCY – Similar to Crystal Ball Reading but done by staring into the clients shiny fingernails.

PHYLLORHODOMANCY – Fortune telling with Roses which for Romantic issues also involved bashing the Roses on your head several times.

TYROMANCY – A form of divination using different types of Cheeses and little messages which are left on the cheese for your "Psychic Mouse" to pick the answers from.

And they are just a few examples of the many Bizarre Fortune telling Methods which are explained and/or taught on the site.

In fact the truth is that you are only Limited by the Power of your own imagination as when all said and done whatever approach you decide to use the Secret every time is either Cold Reading or the use of a Psychic Carbon Impression Clipboard both of which are detailed within this book.

CONTACTING THE DEAD

Observe, Obtain & Study all of the items mentioned in the recommended reading list section at the start of this book and your job of apparently contacting the "Dead" and appearing to be a Genuine Clairvoyant – (See Spirits), Clairaudient – (Hear Spirits) and/or Clairsentient – (Feel Spirits) will be easy!

For several years I passed myself off successfully as a genuine Psychic Consultant and also as a Stage Clairvoyant and during this time I appeared at The Park Hall Hotel Conference Venue, The Lancastrian Hall in Swinton, Middleton Civic Theatre, The Britannia Hotel in Manchester and other Large Venues all over England playing to Large Capacity audiences convincing them of my abilities to contact their loved ones in Spirit.

I was regularly endorsed and featured in International Media Publication "Psychic News" as being genuine and yet I can tell you now the basis of my Secret is as explained in the "Navel Cold Reading" Chapter of this book.

However I did once describe every nuance and technique used by me whilst a Fraudulent Stage Clairvoyant in a series of articles for British Magical Magazine **"Club 71"** which was published by Repro Magic in London – England.

As I recall the series of several detailed articles ran from late 1996 into around Mid/Late 1997, I only have article three to hand of the series and that appeared in The Easter Edition during April 1997, to try and obtain the back copies containing these articles you could visit the site of *www.repromagic.co.uk* as they truly do make invaluable reading for anyone who desires to work in this field.

However before I sign off and say goodbye, I'd like you to know that in my opinion one of the best ways to learn to become a Professional Psychic Consultant is to go along and have actual Psychic readings yourself at various different readers

In each case have a hidden pocket tape recorder so you can record the session and listen to it again afterwards as this will help remind you of the patter lines & verbal tactics used by the person claiming to be a real Psychic and will make it easier for you to use them in your own work!

Same applies to becoming a Stage Clairvoyant see as many of them working live as you possibly can and secretly record them for reference afterwards and very quickly you'll spot exactly what's really going on and be able to do it just as well yourself.

You can also see Stage Clairvoyants working on Television and for next to no cost you can join a "development circle" at your local Spiritualist Church, which for those taking the route of becoming a "genuine" psychic will not only teach you how to "contact the dead" but also help you build up a reputation as being genuine amongst this group of "shut eye" believers who will then talk about you to other Spiritualist Churches & groups proclaiming that you are genuine which ultimately will help you get bums on seats and make far more money when you stage your first Spiritualist Evening!

Read this book several times, then obtain the books and DVDS I recommend and study them,

THEN BECOME A RICH & FAMOUS PSYCHIC SUPERSTAR!

Good Luck

Dr. Jonathan Royle
www.hypnotorious.com